WOODCARVING

WOODCARVING

STEP-BY-STEP TECHNIQUES

Jeremy Williams

The Crowood Press

First published in 1992 by
The Crowood Press Ltd
Ramsbury, Marlborough
Wiltshire SN8 2HR

British Library Cataloguing in Publication Data

A catalogue record for this book is available from the British Library.

ISBN 1 85223 583 7

Line-drawings by Noel Trimmer

Typeset by Avonset, Midsomer Norton, Bath
Printed and bound in Great Britain by BPCC Hazells Ltd
Member of BPCC Ltd

CONTENTS

ACKNOWLEDGEMENTS

Thanks are due to the following manufacturers and distributors: Black and Decker for permission to reproduce photographs of their Workmate (page 37), the orbital sander and the Powerfile (page 117); Robert Bosch for assistance and photographs of the jigsaw, the router (page 116) and the Multi-sander (page 117); John Boddy's Fine Wood and Tool Store Ltd for the photographs on pages 8 and 21; Brimarc Associates for the photograph of the Sjoberg workbench (page 38); De Walt Power Tools for permission to reproduce the photograph of their bandsaw (page 116); Hermes Coated Abrasives for the photograph on page 104; Ashley Iles (Edge Tools) Ltd for permission to reproduce the photograph of their gouges and the London Pattern Chart (page 25); Liberon Waxes for the photographs on pages 108 and 115; Lervad (UK) Ltd for the photographs of their workbench (pages 38 and 39); Microflame Ltd for the photograph of the Dremel Moto-Tool (page 117); Sandvik Saws & Tools Ltd for photographs of their tools (page 35); Record Marples (Woodworking Tools) Ltd for the photographs of the G-cramp and the Holdfast (page 37); Stanley Tools for the photograph of their Surform (page 35); Henry Taylor (Tools) Ltd for the photograph on page 29; Alec Tiranti Ltd for the photograph of their woodworker's vice (page 39); F. Zaulauf of Switzerland for permission to reproduce the chart of Pfeil gouges (page 32).

Thanks also to Tilgear Ltd for the photograph on page 28, Craft Supplies Ltd, and to others in the woodworking trade who assisted me.

The carving on page 80 is based on a design taken from *Traditional Japanese Crest Designs*, edited by Clarence Hornung (Dover Publications Inc., New York, 1986).

I should also like to express my appreciation to Ashley Iles for the historical information on woodcarving tools; to David Scholes, who took the photographs of my work; and, finally, to my wife for her assistance and encouragement.

Woodcarving is an absorbing hobby. There is something about fashioning and handling wood that is very satisfying. You only have to watch people anywhere carvings are on display to realize that wood is very tactile. Everybody wants to touch a carving, to run their hands over the smooth or textured surfaces; to trace the lines of grain with their fingers. Wood has a feel and warmth possessed by no other medium.

The desire to carve wood is centuries old – I believe one of the earliest examples of woodcarving is dated around 2000BC. So, in setting off down the path of learning to carve, one is following a very old tradition.

Woodcarving makes an ideal hobby at any age. I have taught students whose ages have ranged from thirteen to eighty. It is time consuming and the hours rush by.

Each carving is a voyage of adventure. Usually you reach your planned destination, but occasionally Nature takes a hand, and as you carve through the wood, elements of grain or colour are discovered that can be used to advantage. The results are often very satisfying, but do not be put off too easily by a failure. Regard it as a learning experience and try to analyse where you went wrong. No true craftsman is ever fully satisfied with his work, and this is the spur to greater achievement.

However, the possibility of failure and frustration will be greatly minimized if the basic principles of woodcarving have been clearly understood. There is no mystique about the technique; it is really quite a simple process. Think of it as a foreign language; you must learn something of its grammar and you have to start building up some vocabulary before you can make yourself understood. You would start with some basic learning exercises and would not expect to pick up a newspaper and understand every word. In this book I have endeavoured to cover the early learning stage and with practice, the reader should advance quite quickly.

To work in sympathy with wood, it is necessary to have an understanding of how trees grow, which ones produce good carving timber and how it is seasoned. A lack of this knowledge can cause no end of frustration and disappointment. Similarly, with the tools, some basic points must be understood. The array of tools used by an experienced carver can look quite bewildering, but it is actually all very simple. Sharpening woodcarving tools is a daunting task if you do not know how to go about it, but again, it is quite a simple operation and, like learning to ride a bicycle, once you can do it you wonder what all the fuss is about.

Over the last ten years, many people have come to me for tuition. Some have had the urge to carve but have never tried, others have tried but become frustrated. I have regularly found that after a few days of instruction their doubts and frustrations have disappeared and they begin to enjoy their work. In this book I have used the same methods of instruction covering the broad guidelines of the technique of this fascinating craft. If you, the reader, will supply the other ingredients of enthusiasm and patience the recipe should work.

There are two basic forms of woodcarving, relief carving and three-dimensional sculpture.

Panels, plaques and furniture are carved in relief. It is the detailed and decorative cutting of wood. Personally I always think of this as **woodcarving**, whereas the creation of a three-dimensional object, be it an animal study or an abstract, is more in the realm of **wood sculpture** since often the line of form is vital. Three-dimensional work is also known as 'working in the round'. The two methods can overlap, especially when a three-dimensional carving is highly decorated. A typical example of this is a church lectern eagle with every feather carved. While this is a sure sign that the work was carried out by a skilled craftsman, too much embellishment can detract from the line of form, to the point that one is left with a well-decorated but static piece of wood. 'Life' and 'movement' are very necessary aspects of good three-dimensional work and these points are fully covered in the section on design. These are the important and fundamental differences between wood sculpture and woodcarving; though in general they are both frequently referred to as woodcarving, and this term is used where appropriate.

Some metric measurements have been given to the nearest practical equivalent of the corresponding Imperial sizes.

Learn the basic technique, work in sympathy with the wood and progress slowly, and you will find woodcarving great fun. I very much hope it will give you as much pleasure as it has given me over the last forty years.

WOOD

Wood is the basic material of the carver. While in theory it is possible to carve any and all types, obviously there are some woods that are more suitable than others. It is important to be selective if early attempts are not to be frustrated by an unsuitable choice of wood. To understand the make-up of timber is to work in sympathy with it, with a better chance of both finishing a carving and enjoying the work.

Although there are exceptions, in general there are only a limited number of woods used which mainly come from the slower-growing trees.

One tends to think of oak as 'the carver's wood'. It certainly has its uses, but by no means is it the best wood for all occasions. Perhaps this misconception about oak is because there are so many oak carvings, especially in churches. To work with oak alone would be very limiting. The same would apply to mahogany, which used to be used for much decorative carving, mainly because mahogany was a popular timber for furniture making, not because it was especially suitable, for carving.

To avoid the frustration of trying to work an unsuitable piece of timber, some basic understanding of how trees grow will be helpful. The woodcarver needs to be able to relate the chosen subject to the most suitable timber. This section deals with the make-up of trees, the difference between a tropical tree and one from a temperate climate; the conversion and seasoning of wood to form the material for carving; and a list of recommended species.

The woodcarver needs to know about the grain and the texture of various timbers, and the best starting point from which to learn about these is to understand how trees grow.

The basic material of the carver – ash logs at the start of the process to turn them into usable timber.

All trees respond to sunlight. In temperate climates they grow from spring through to autumn. There are two actual periods of growth, the main one being in the spring to early summer. Secondary growth occurs during the late summer. The pattern of growth can be seen easily when a tree is felled.

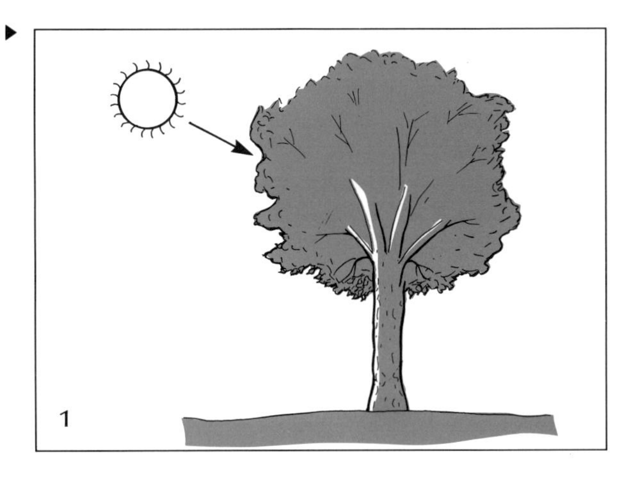

Some trees drop their leaves in winter. They are the deciduous species and they generally have broad leaves (a). In the timber trade, they are known as hardwoods. This description, though, is only a general one and does not fully relate to the density (hardness) of the wood.

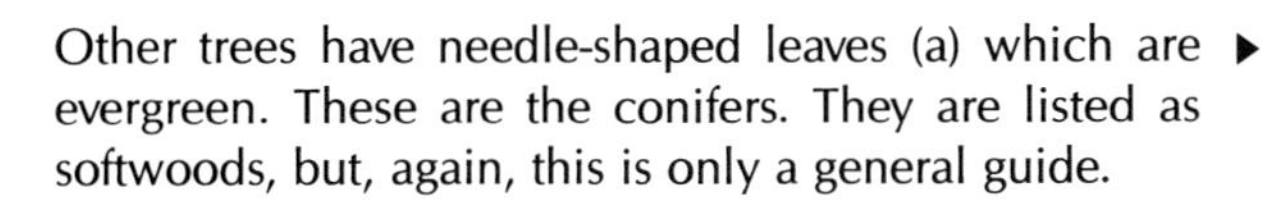

Other trees have needle-shaped leaves (a) which are evergreen. These are the conifers. They are listed as softwoods, but, again, this is only a general guide.

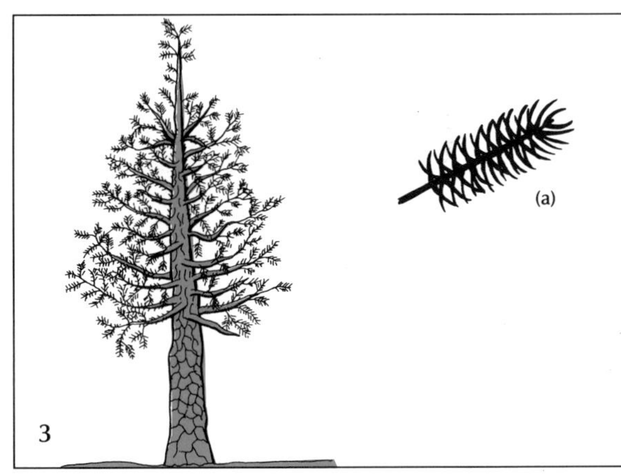

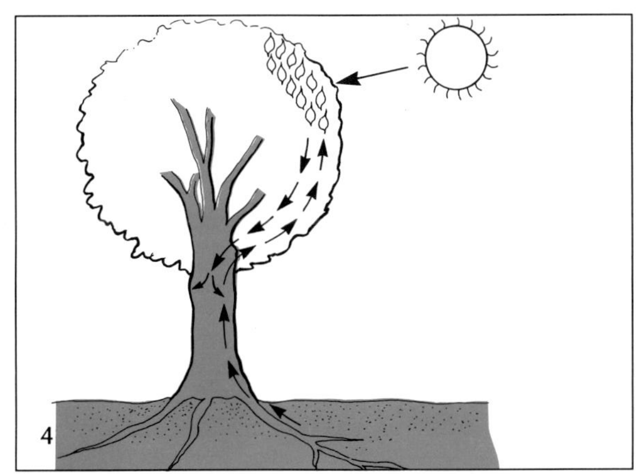

Trees grow by taking up nutriment and minerals in solution through their roots. These rise up to the leaves through the sapwood where the action of sunlight converts them into sugars and starches (this process is called photosynthesis). This chemical change also requires carbon dioxide from the air and chlorophyll (the green part of the leaves).

The sugars and starches travel as sap via the inner bark (phloem) to all parts of the tree where they are either used immediately or stored in the cells.

HOW TREES GROW

Each year a tree increases in diameter. The growth is in rings. The wide bands are spring to early-summer growth; the narrow bands are formed in late summer or early autumn. New growth takes place in the layer of cells just below the bark (a). This is known as the cambium layer (b). The cells divide to form either more sapwood (c) or more bark. Later the first-formed cells of the sapwood become heartwood (d).

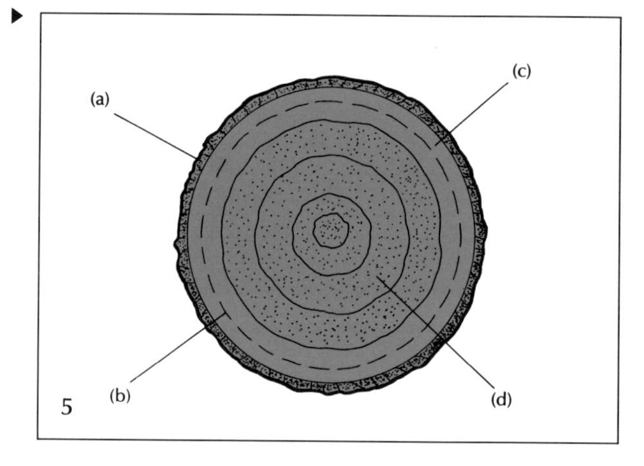

5

6

Growth rings – annual rings – can be seen when a tree is felled and cut into sections. These rings can provide a history of weather conditions during the life of the tree.

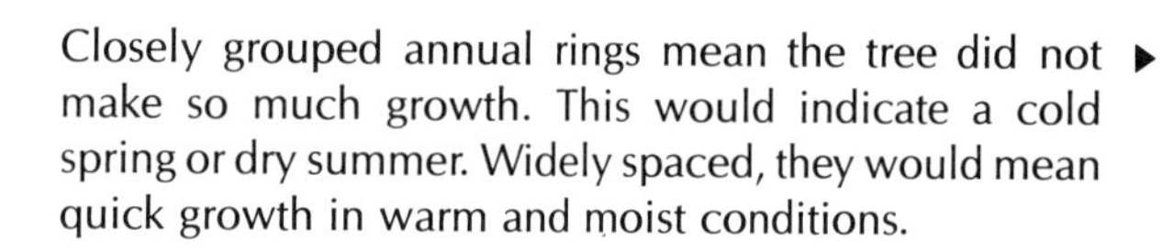

Closely grouped annual rings mean the tree did not make so much growth. This would indicate a cold spring or dry summer. Widely spaced, they would mean quick growth in warm and moist conditions.

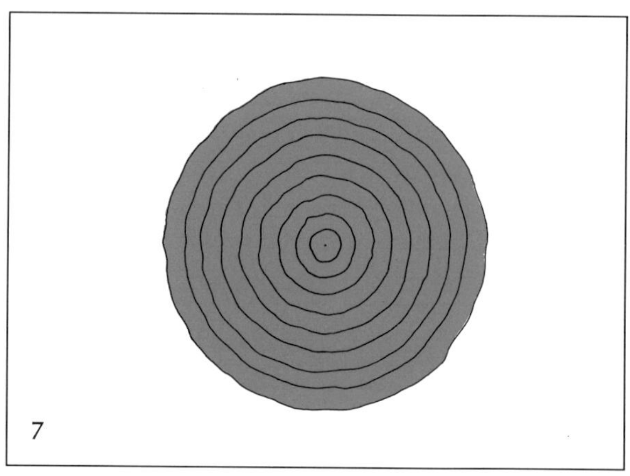

7

The rate of growth is also dependent on altitude. The higher the altitude, the lower the temperature and the shorter the growing season. A tree growing in low-lying, warm, moist ground will grow quickly and will have wide annual rings, whereas one of the same species half-way up a mountain would grow more slowly and have narrower rings.

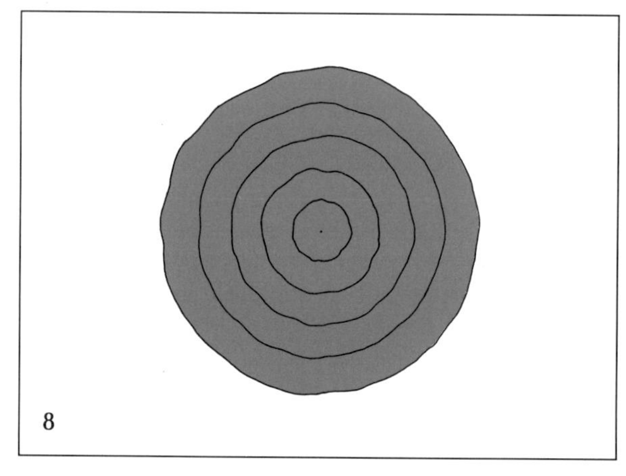

8

Pith (a) Pith in the centre of the tree provides rapid flow of nutriment when the tree is very young. The wood in this area is unsuitable for carving. It may be pithy. In some trees the centre will have a distinct channel.

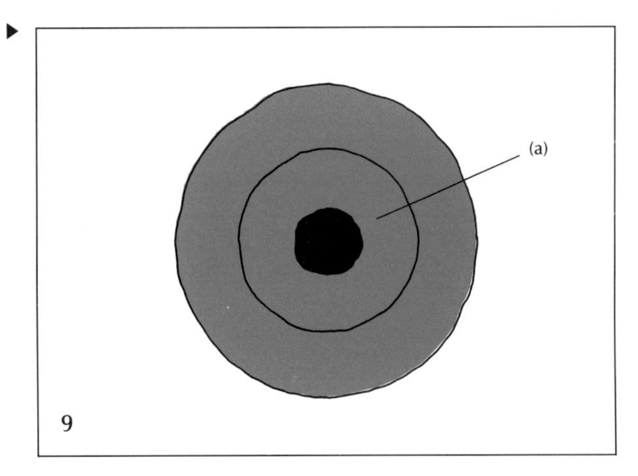

9

Heartwood (a) This is inert wood and is created by a change in the cell structure from sapwood (b) to heartwood through the cambium layer (c). Heartwood is the best part of the tree for carving.

(c) (b) (a)

10

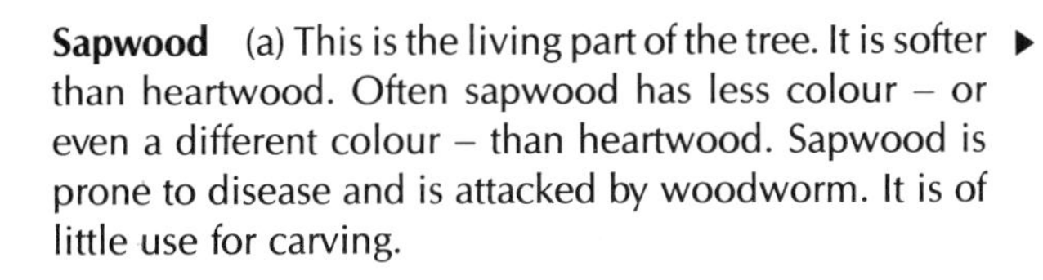

Sapwood (a) This is the living part of the tree. It is softer than heartwood. Often sapwood has less colour – or even a different colour – than heartwood. Sapwood is prone to disease and is attacked by woodworm. It is of little use for carving.

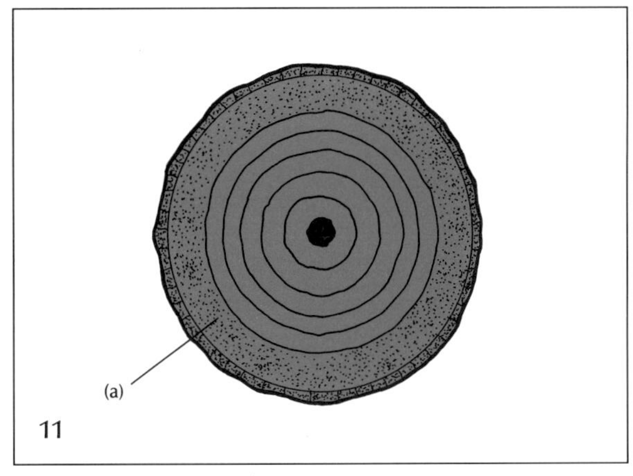

11

Bark (a) Bark is the protective clothing of the tree. It has no value for carving and, if left on, usually separates and falls off. Much beetle and grub infestation may lie either in or just below the bark, so this is best removed out of doors.

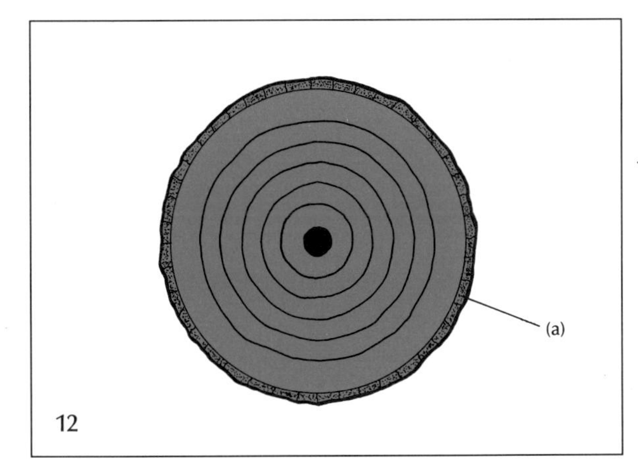

12

Wood is made up of cells shaped like a cluster of drinking straws. Softwood trees have more open cells than hardwoods. Each cell is bonded to its neighbour. This gives strength to the wood. The degree of strength depends on the species of the tree. Some, such as oak, produce long cells, whilst others, such as lime, have a small cell structure.

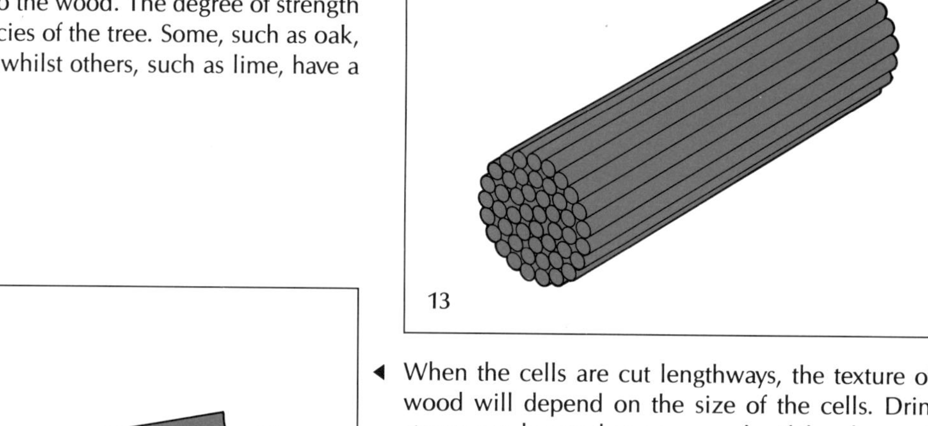

13

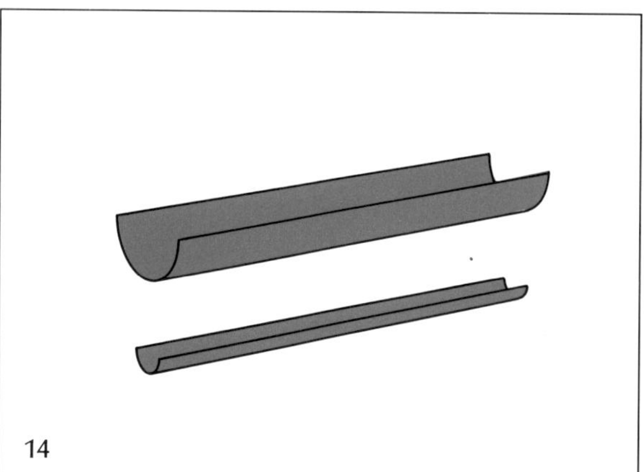

14

When the cells are cut lengthways, the texture of the wood will depend on the size of the cells. Drinking straws can be used as an example: if they have a large diameter and are cut lengthways the channels would be wide; if the straws are of a small diameter, the channels would be narrow.

Some trees produce a more resinous cell structure in their late-summer growth period. Pine is typical, having soft spring growth and hard, dark, late-summer growth. This is easily seen in the annual rings. Hard, resinous growth is shown (a) and the soft fibrous cells (b).

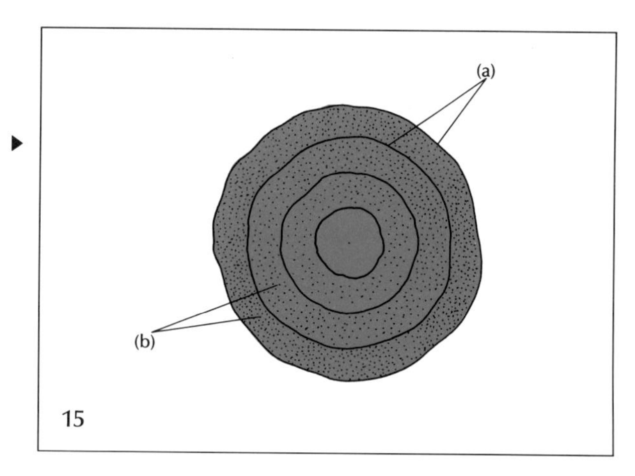

15

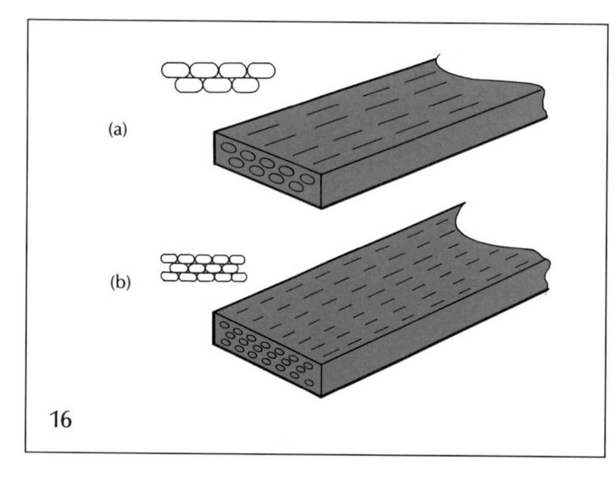

16

Cell size and rate of growth determine how fibrous the wood will be when cut. The more slowly the tree grows, the more dense the wood will be. Timber having large cells is 'open grain'; timber having small tightly packed cells is 'close grain'. With the exception of certain pines, generally only hardwoods are used for carving. The end cell structure for a softwood is shown (a) and for a hardwood (b).

Within a tree there are rays of cells, 'medullary rays'. In some woods they are very pronounced, as in oak. When the wood is cut at an angle (tangentially) to the annual ring, figured grain is produced. This feature is important in cabinet making, but not especially so in wood-carving. Too dominant a grain can detract from the design. Wood may split on the line of the medullary ray (a).

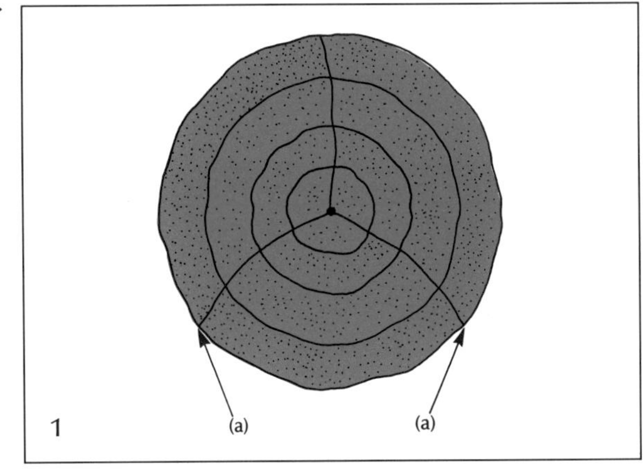

1

2

Some cells lie at angles to the vertical structure of the tree and show up as flecks when the wood is cut in line with the grain. This is very noticeable in beech but nearly all trees have this characteristic.

Branches do not just grow on the surface of a tree. They form when the tree is young and can be traced well back into the heartwood. Branches have the same arrangement of cells as the main trunk of the tree.

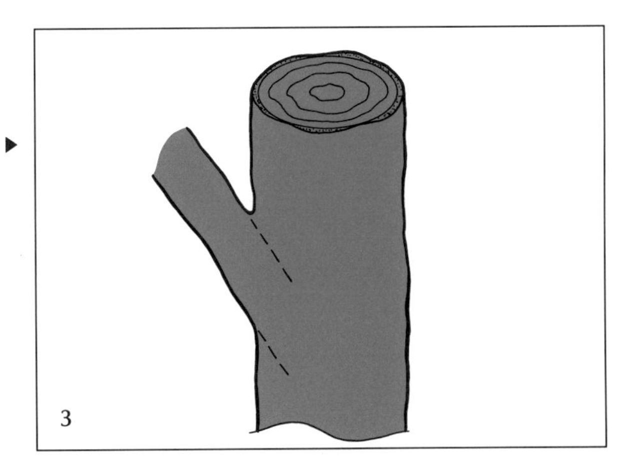
3

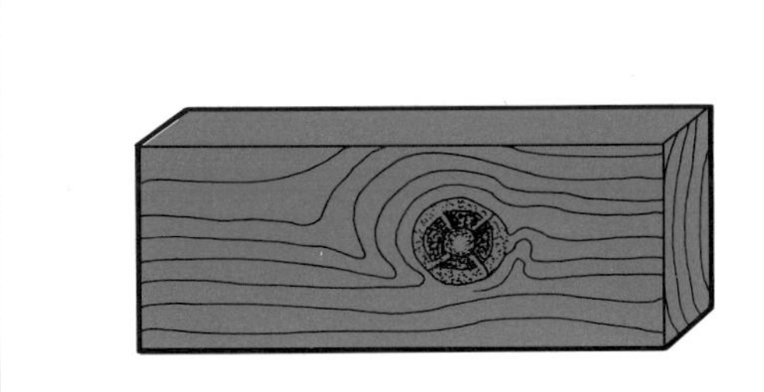
4

When a tree is cut into planks, the branches appear as knots. Because the annual rings of a branch are small, a knot will be harder to work than the surrounding timber. Due to an imbalance of moisture between a knot and the wood surrounding it, a knot will develop star splits.

PATTERNS OF GROWTH

All trees grow towards the sun. In temperate climates, the sun is at a lower angle than in the tropics or on the equator. Also, there is a climatic variation between winter and summer which affects the growth cycle. Altitude and the amount of rainfall play an important part in determining how fast the cycle is.

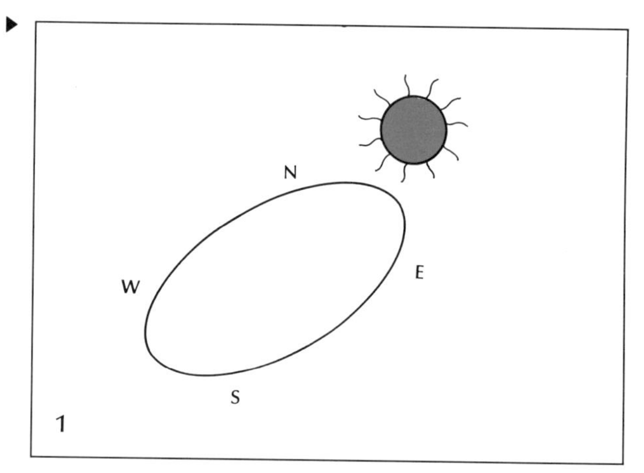

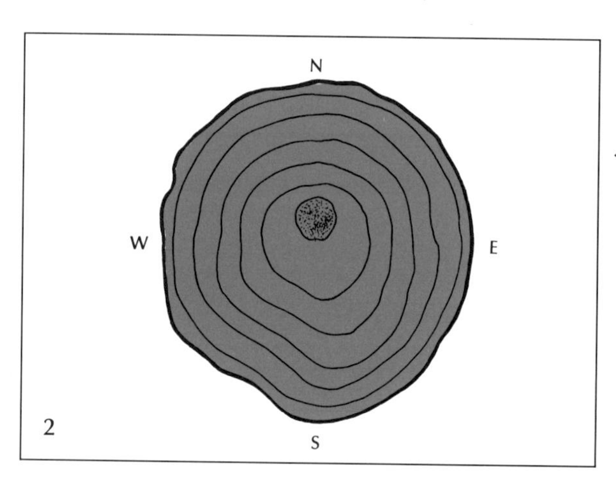

Temperate trees will grow more on the south side – towards the sun – and this can be seen on the end-section of a tree when it is felled. The annual rings do not grow uniformly to the middle of the diameter.

Commercially produced timber is usually grown in plantations or in blocks, 'stands', to create straight-growing trees. Those which grow in isolation form very twisted branches and irregularly shaped stems.

In the tropics the sun is more overhead. Some trees have a tendency to twist. Known as spiral growth, it is caused by axial cells forming at various times in the life of the tree. This may be related to the gyration of the sun being more directly overhead.

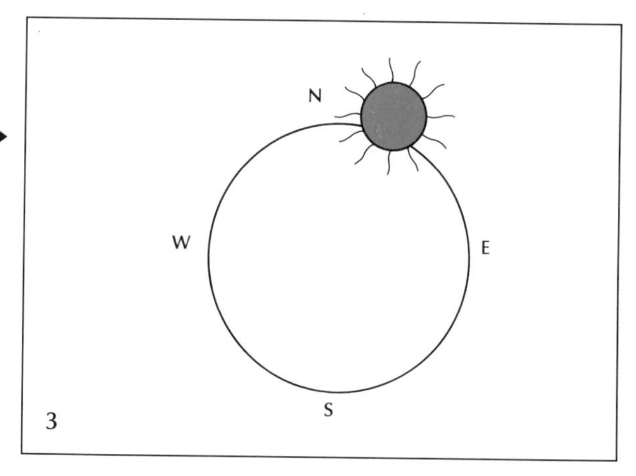

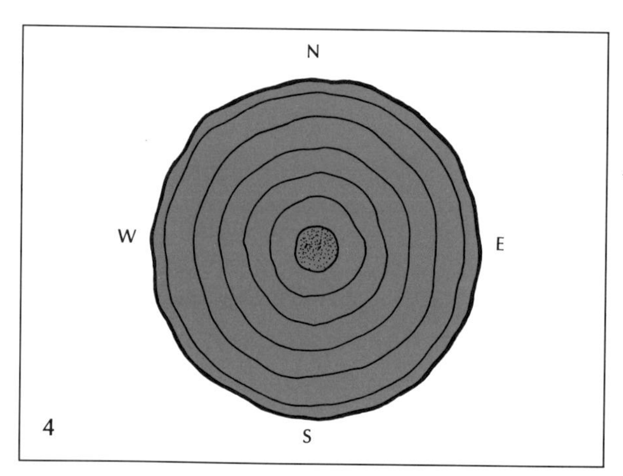

With less seasonal climatic variation, most tropical trees sustain near-continuous growth. Annual rings form more equally, but are less marked in certain types of tree, such as mahogany, whilst in others, such as teak, there is a strong grain.

Spiral growth produces interlocked grain (a). This is seen when the wood is cut into planks. In some areas, the grain will run along the length of the timber but there will also be bands of flecked grain set at an angle (b). This makes the wood difficult to work as the direction of cut has to be constantly changed.

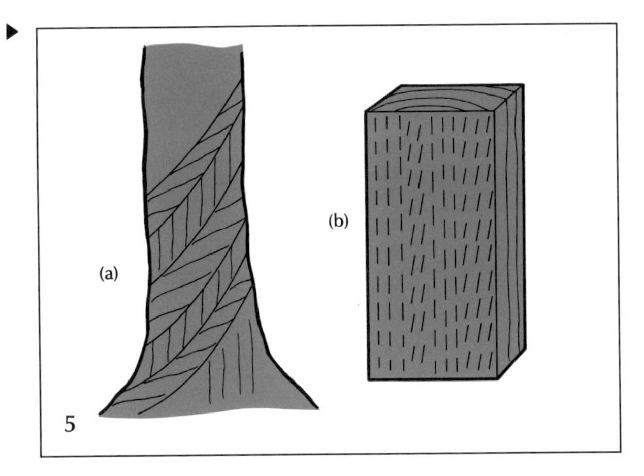

5

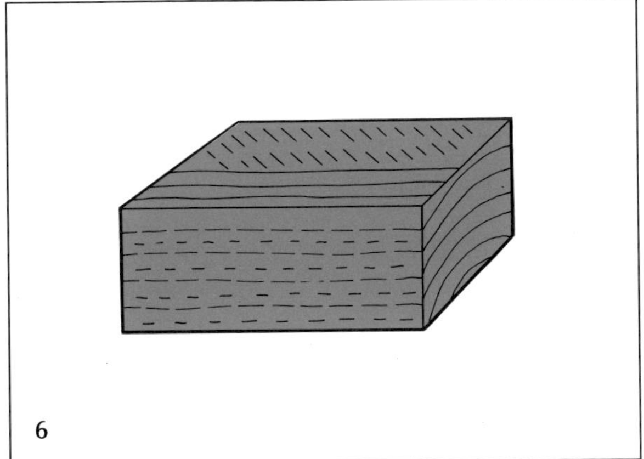

6

The cells of tropical trees are not bonded together as they are in temperate ones and are prone to split apart when worked, which makes delicate carving much more difficult. The drawing shows this weakness between layers of cells.

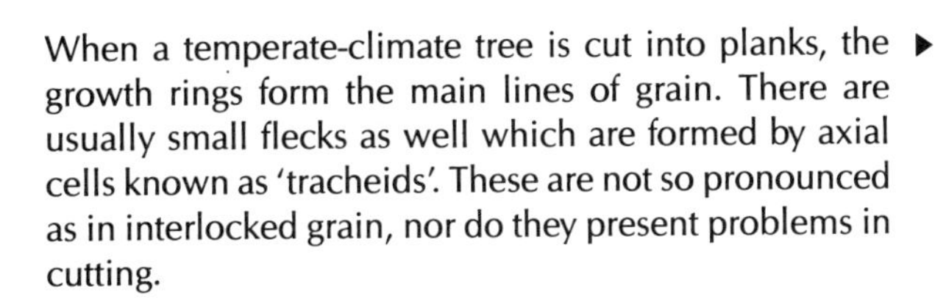

When a temperate-climate tree is cut into planks, the growth rings form the main lines of grain. There are usually small flecks as well which are formed by axial cells known as 'tracheids'. These are not so pronounced as in interlocked grain, nor do they present problems in cutting.

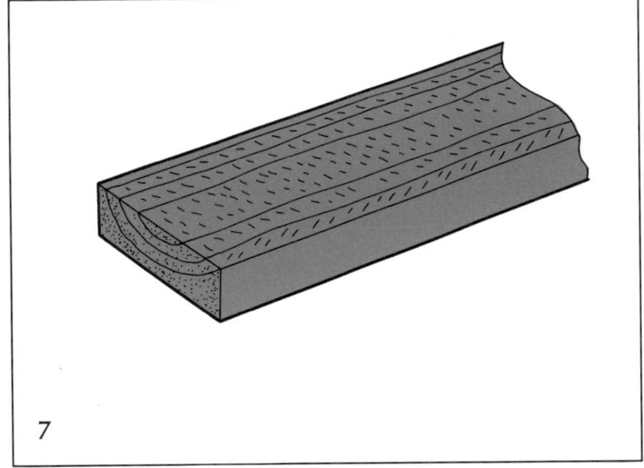

7

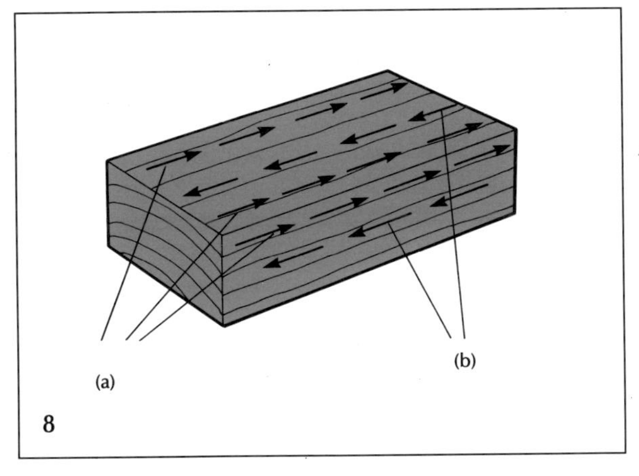

8

Timber cut into planks from temperate trees that have grown in isolation will have a wavy grain rather than a straight grain. When cut with the 'lie' of the grain, the finish will be smooth. If cut in the wrong direction, the finish will appear rough (a), but when cut with the 'lie' of the grain, the finish will be smooth (b).

After a tree has been felled, the moisture in it starts to dry out. Depending on the time of year, the moisture content can be very high. Normally trees are cut in the winter when the sap is at its lowest. The cut surfaces dry first and in doing so moisture is drawn to them from the cells further back by capillary action.

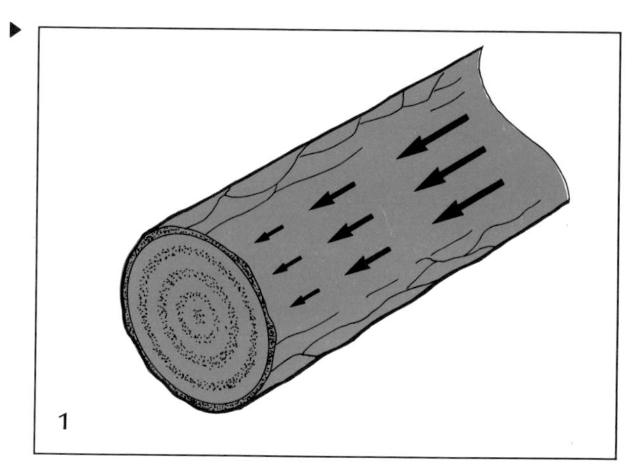

2

As the tree trunk starts to dry out, the cells nearest to the cut surfaces begin to shrink. The circumference tries to contract but this is not possible to any degree, because of the solid mass of the wood. Drying out causes the wood to be under stress.

Pressure builds up inside the trunk as moisture forces its way to the cut surfaces through the drying wood. Further contraction cannot take place without the wood splitting.

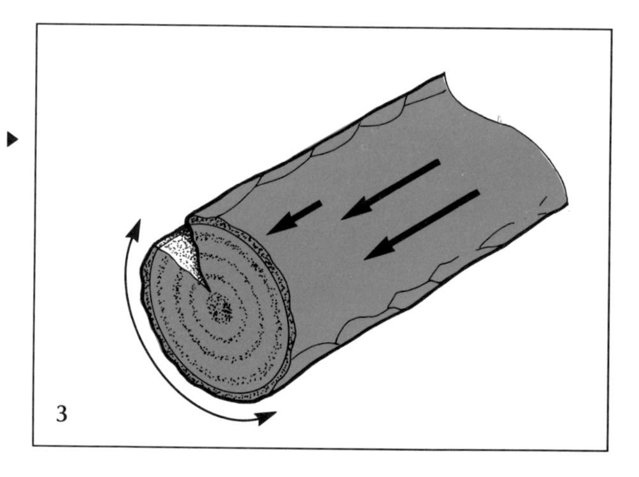

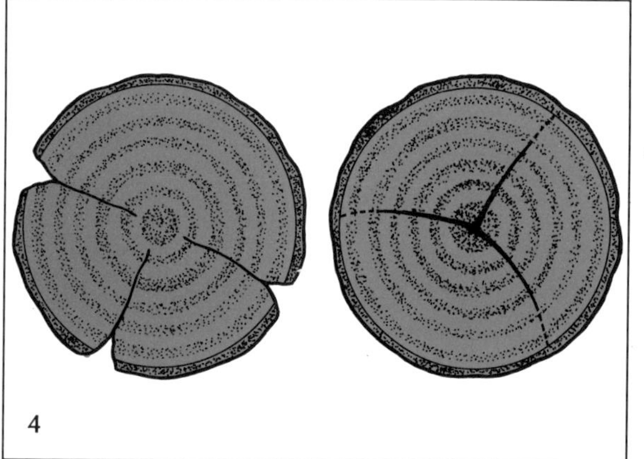

In end-section, the line of split will usually follow the line of the medullary rays. Splitting may also occur from the centre outwards. Even wood which has appeared to be stable for a number of years can suddenly split. This can happen at any time when left in log form.

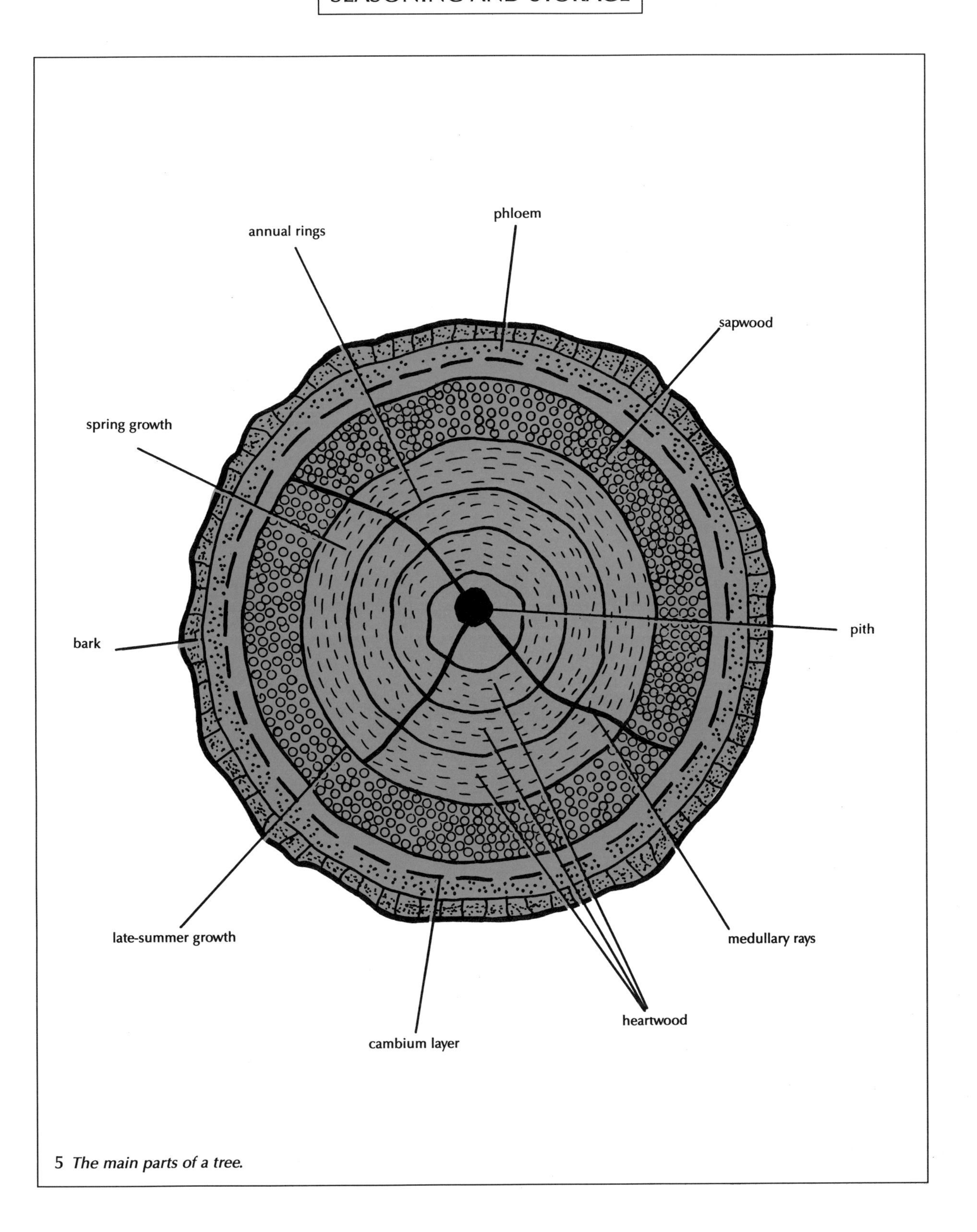

5 *The main parts of a tree.*

The conversion of a tree into planks prevents major splitting as the increased surface area speeds up the drying out process. Plank ends should be sealed with paint or wax to arrest splitting of the end-grain caused by too rapid drying.

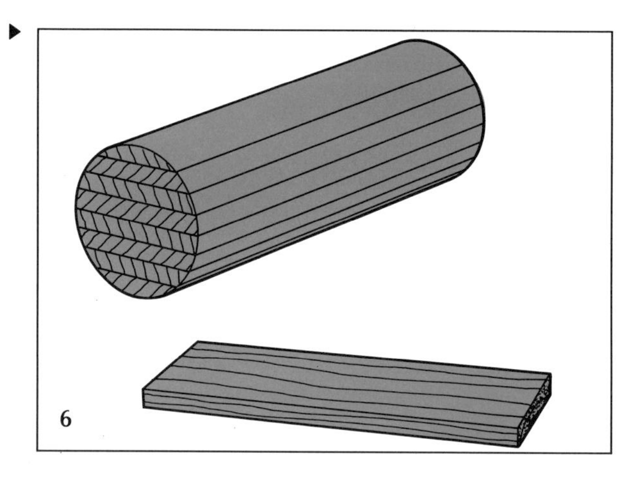
6

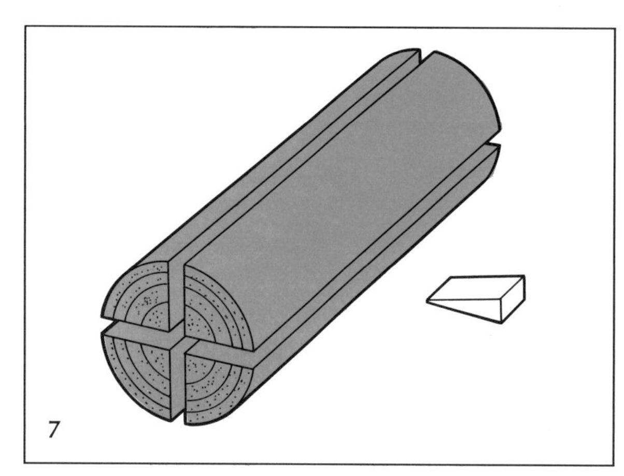
7

A log may be split into halves or quarters by using an axe or wedges. For this, the length of the log should be about 3ft (1 m). Cleaving into sections will minimize shrinkage of the circumference. The end-grain should be sealed.

It is vital to realize that if a whole log is used for carving, splitting will occur, either while the work is in progress, or afterwards (a). It is virtually unavoidable. The only exception is when the centre is hollowed out. Therefore, carving is usually done with blocks cut from thick planks.

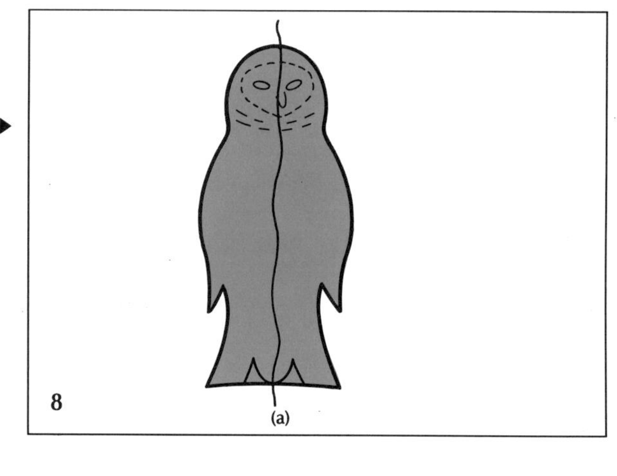

8

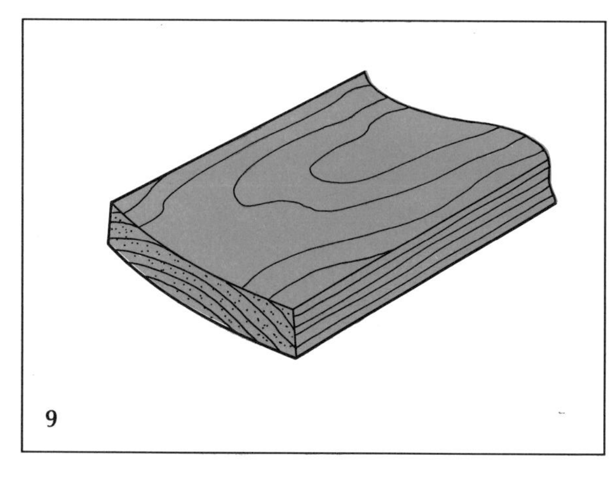
9

Wood has to be seasoned to remove the moisture (sap) and to reduce inherent tension. A tree takes many years to grow and during its life it has to withstand the stresses of high winds, so it has a built-in tension to support the weight of the branches. Once cut, tension has to be released or it will cause warping. Unseasoned timber will distort. Seasoning can be a problem with very thick blocks.

There are various ways in which a tree is sawn into usable timber. Usually, trees are cut longitudinally into planks. This is known as 'through and through' cutting, usually listed as T/T, the sapwood appearing on each side. Wide planks, prone to warping if the centre of the heartwood is left in, are cut down the middle – at point A – and are referred to as having one square edge (IS/E), or squares if both edges have been trimmed after the board is divided. ▶

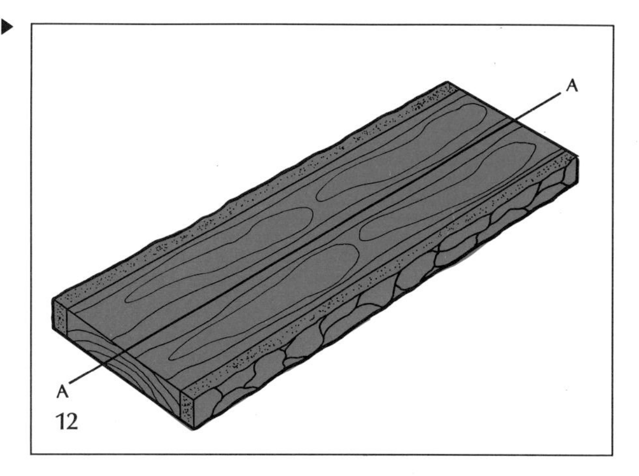

12

◀ Air-dried timber is stacked out of doors – the sawn planks spaced with small strips of wood to provide airspace – and left to stand for one year for each 1in (25mm) of thickness. This will reduce the moisture content to the ambient humidity. Note that this is higher than the humidity indoors. It is, therefore, advisable to buy air-dried carving wood well in advance of use, and to store it in an airy shed.

Air-dried wood provides the best timber for carving.

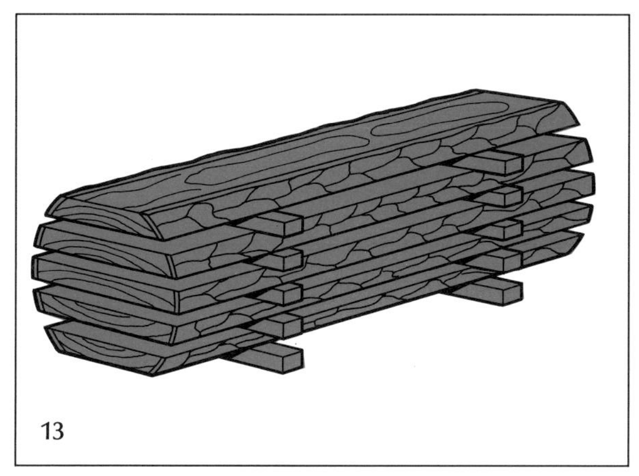
13

Kiln-dried (K/D) planks are artificially seasoned to reduce the moisture content to between 9 and 15 per cent. Kiln drying is only effective with thicknesses up to about 2½in (60mm). Beyond that, internal splitting (shakes) can take place. It tends to make the wood slightly harder, with some colour change, and rather open grained as the cells tend to expand. Kiln-dried timber can be used for relief carving. ▶

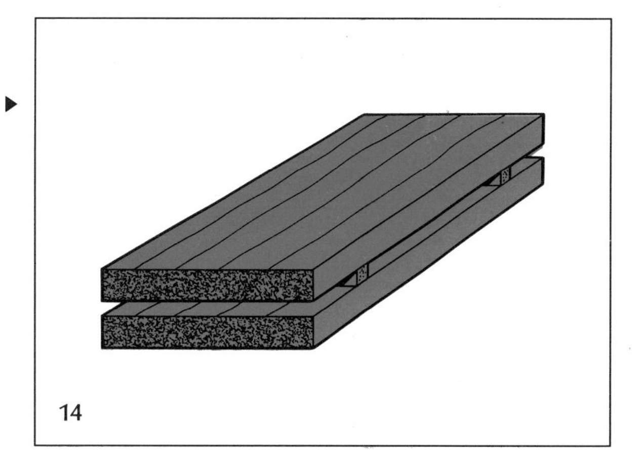
14

◀ Timber is usually sold by cubic measurement, but some exotic woods are sold by weight. To calculate a cube in metric measurement, multiply the length by the width by the thickness. The calculation for imperial measurement is: length (feet) by width (inches) by thickness (inches) divided by 144.

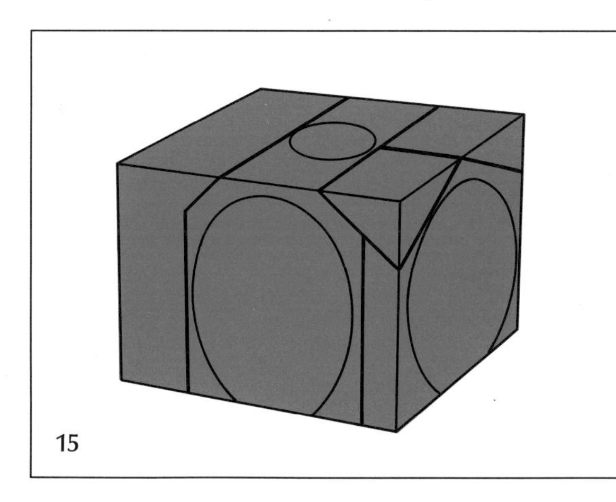
15

Timber can reabsorb moisture. Once seasoned it must be kept dry. Carving wood can be bought from specialist merchants; of which many advertise in the popular woodworking magazines. Merchants usually offer seasoned wood. They will cut to size and plane for a small extra charge. Timber mills offer freshly cut wood. This will need seasoning, but the price will be lower. Other sources of timber are tree surgeons, foresters and firewood suppliers.

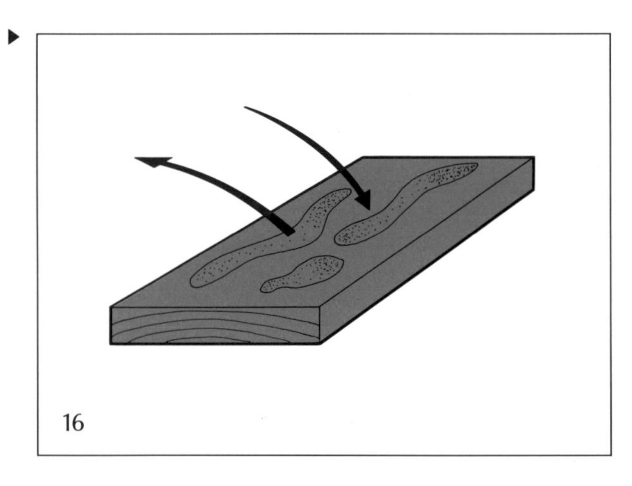

16

Planks or blocks should be kept under cover, but with plenty of ventilation. Separate each piece with spacers. These should be made from the same timber to avoid the wood being discoloured. Cut strips ½in (1cm) square and position them across each plank or block every 12in (300mm) or less if the blocks are small. End-grain should be sealed with wax or undercoat. If the wood develops a white mould, it is a sign of dampness and insufficient ventilation.

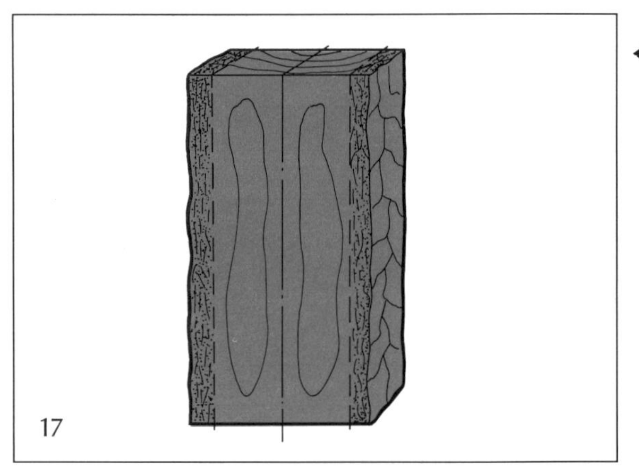

17

If the planks have been cut 'through and through' the bark and sapwood should be removed, as only the heartwood is required. The area of wood 2in (50mm) in from the sapwood, and the same distance in from the centre core, will provide the prime carving timber. Saw the timber into carving blocks of varying sizes as soon as possible.

Some woods are available up to 4in (100mm) in thickness with a few species up to 6in (150mm). Beyond this, seasoning will take many years; large pieces never fully dry out and become stable. With very large pieces it may be necessary to rough out the shape of the carving to remove the surplus timber, wax it lightly and then allow the seasoning to continue.

SEASONING – KEY POINTS

- Avoid too much heat or direct sunlight.
- Spray with water if the weather is very hot and dry.
- Check regularly for signs of mould.
- If the surface shows signs of becoming speckled with dark patches, it indicates that storage conditions are too damp. Wipe with mild bleach or fungicide and increase ventilation.
- With care, wood can be stored for many years. Some woods become very hard as they age.

Woodworkers are now being encouraged to consider the ecological effects of using many of the tropical hardwoods. A number of reputable timber merchants now specify woods from areas of re-afforestation.

SAVE A TROPICAL TREE

- Good, usable, tropical hardwood can be reclaimed from much old and discarded furniture.
- Even if damaged on the surface, inside it may well be perfect.
- Any old pieces of mahogany are certainly worth having. The wood will be of a far better quality than that which is available today.
- Good hunting grounds are junk yards and salerooms or car boot sales. Also check out any boat-yards there may be in your area.
- Replacement window firms and shopfitters are usually happy to pass on short off-cuts. It may be new wood, but at least you will be putting it to good use.

It pays to be selective with garden trees. Bear in mind the aforementioned points about cutting out the sapwood and heartwood and estimate how much carvable wood will be left. Most ornamental trees are just too small in diameter to produce worthwhile carving blocks. A tree should have a trunk of sufficient size to be worth the effort of conversion, unless very small carvings are to be made. For most purposes anything under 20in (500mm) will probably be unusable. ▶

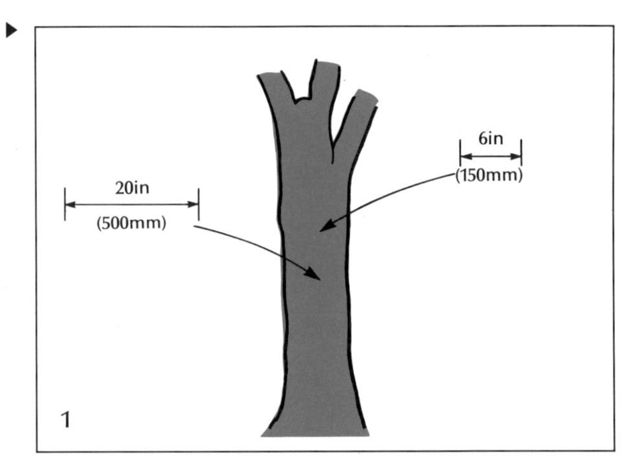

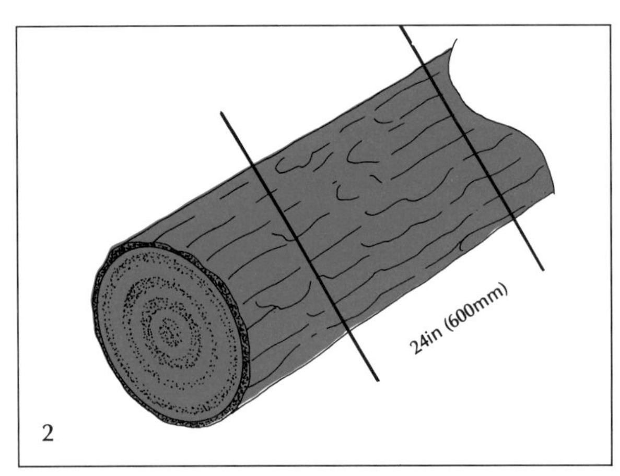

◀ Only the main trunk will be of use and this will have to be cut into lengths of about 24in (600mm). You may wish to retain some of the thicker branches, but bear in mind these will be best used for abstract type work where the centre core can be removed to avoid splitting.

Using an axe or wedges, split each section into two, or preferably, three segments, following, if possible, the medullary rays. There is no real need to de-bark the wood at this stage as usually it will fall off on its own accord when the wood starts to dry. ▶

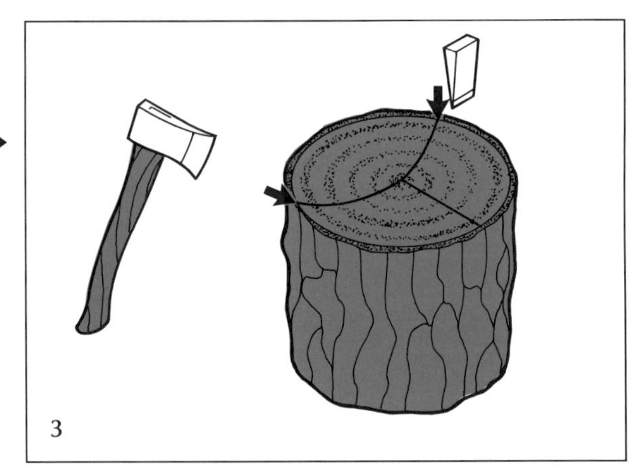

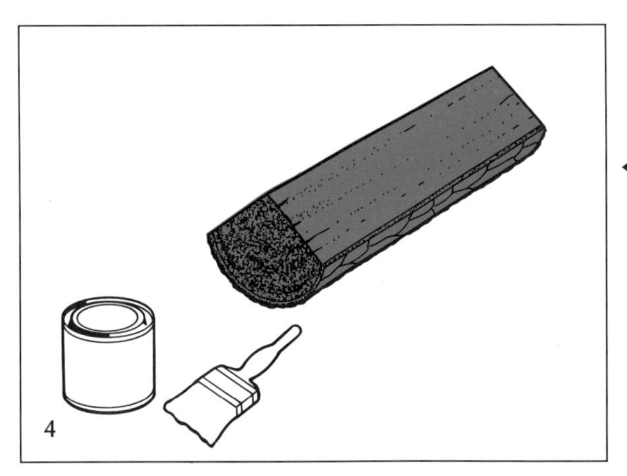

◀ Seal the end-grain with wax or flat oil paint and stack with spacers as previously described. Storage is best out-of-doors on a north aspect. Some protection from rain will be necessary and it is best not to use plastic sheeting as it will create moist air. Seasoning will take one year for every inch (25mm) of thickness. Half-way through the seasoning, the pile should be re-stacked. In very dry weather spray with water to prevent too rapid drying.

Commercially, the water content of timber is measured with a moisture meter. The moisture level produces an electrical resistance which is read off on the meter as a percentage figure. Moisture content is relative to both air temperature and humidity. Regular weighing will show if timber is still losing moisture. Always use seasoned wood. A good timber merchant will tell you the moisture content. The average moisture content after kiln drying is 9–15 per cent. The figure for air-dried wood is variable. It will depend on how the wood has been stored and especially on the ambient humidity.

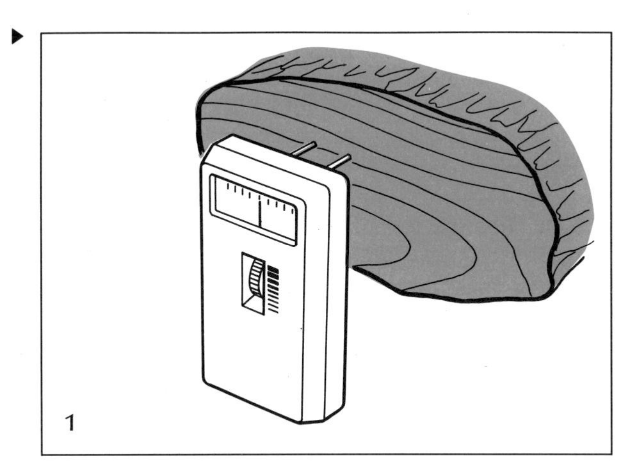
1

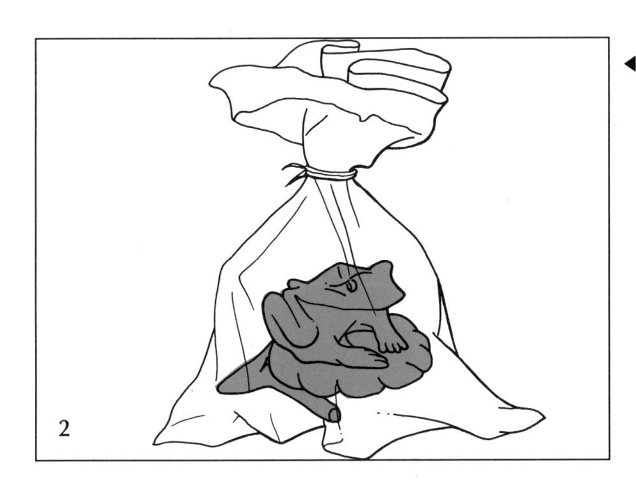
2

If wood is subjected to a sudden rise in temperature or a marked drop in humidity it will split. Be careful not to leave wood in an unventilated shed in high summer, or to have untreated wood indoors for too long. Work in progress should always be stored in a plastic bag to stabilize its humidity. Even 100-year-old timber can still twist, warp and split if it is not cared for. If the wood starts to split whilst being carved, apply a generous coating of wax to the affected area. This should arrest the drying-out process.

Wood does not like being moved from one part of the country to another, or to another part of the world. Changes of temperature and atmospheric pressure will cause it to distort.

Try and have sufficient stock so that any new supply can be left to settle for at least six months. Within reason, the longer you can store it the better. This applies to most woods but note that some do become hard with age. Maple and sycamore are examples. Keep a written record of all timber purchases so that you always know how long it has been stored.

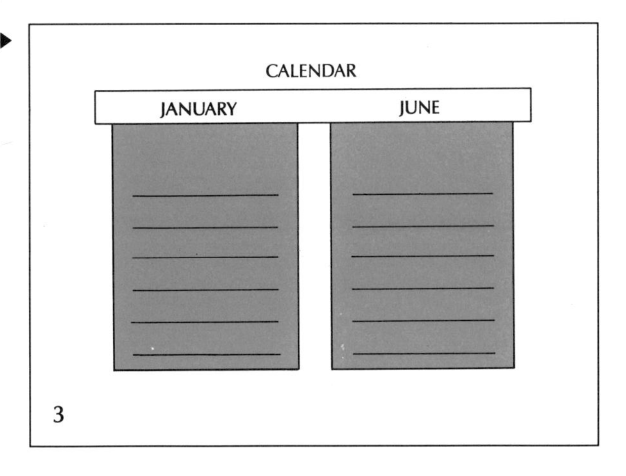

3

The range of a timber merchant's list can be quite staggering. These are some typical carving woods:

Woods easy to carve

Lime (*Tilia* species) The true carver's wood. Soft with close texture and delicate grain. Colour white to honey. Finishes well. Usually available up to 4in (100mm) thick.

Basswood (*Tilia Americana*) Similar properties to lime. Available up to 6in (150mm) thick.

Jelutong (*Dyera costulata*) Often used in schools, by decoy duck carvers and by pattern makers. Open celled and featureless. Very soft. Not an attractive wood.

Pear (*Pyrus communis*) Close grained and moderately hard. Not usually available beyond 3in (80mm) thickness. Light colour except if seasoned by steaming when pink.

Woods moderately easy to carve

Chestnut (*Castanea* species) Resembles oak, but without distinctive rays. Good for relief carving. Cuts well – thin cross-grain sections prone to break. Pale fawn colour.

Sycamore (*Acer pseudoplatanus*) Harder than lime. Has similar characteristics. Good for delicate work. White in colour with attractive ripple grain. Available in large sections.

Field Maple Similar to above but harder.

Cherry (*Prunus* species) Usually has a somewhat wild grain. Very attractive straw colour with darker bands. Finishes well. Can be unstable – requires careful seasoning.

Mahogany (*Swietenia* species) Many varieties from different parts of the world. Interlocked grain. Cells lie in layers making detailed work difficult. See note about endangered trees.

Beech (*Fagus sylvatica*) When steam-dried, it has a pleasing pink tinge. Useful and easily obtained. Fairly hard to work.

Woods more difficult to work

Pine (*Pinus* species) Pines have attractive colour and grain. The resinous bands make it difficult to work. Columbian or Oregan pine make good carving woods. Pitch pine, somewhat harder, is attractive but can contain too much resin. Trees from high altitudes are best. Cutting end-grain can be difficult.

Yew (*Taxus baccata*) There is a marked colour difference between sapwood (cream) and heartwood (reddish). With careful design this can be used to advantage. Colours mellow with time. Difficult to obtain without internal splits (shakes) or presence of buried bark. Good for small carvings.

Apple (*Malus sylvestris*) Hard and a little brittle. Twisted grain. Colour light to dark brown. Prone to split when seasoning.

Plum (*Prunus domestica*) Easier to work than apple. Reddish-brown colour, very attractive.

Ash (*Fraxinus excelsior*) Quick growing, wide soft/hard growth rings, and fibrous. Pale, almost white, colour. Obtainable as olive ash with dark centre. Large sections.

Oak (*Quercus* species) Generally hard with coarse texture better suited to large carvings. Pale fawn. Evergreen or ilex oak has a finer texture. Also brown oak.

Elm (*Ulmus* species) Coarse, attractive, brown grain. Owing to Dutch elm disease, there is not much good wood now available.

Walnut (*Juglans* species) European/American. Most attractive. Cost might well dictate the need for some experience. Light sapwood, dark heart. Australian walnut is more interlocked.

Hawthorn (*Crataegus monogyna*) Hard to cut with gouges, but an attractive grain, and unusual shapes of some branches make it very suitable for free-form carving.

Laurel (*Laurus nobilis*) Has an attractive colour. The wood is naturally oily but can be very prone to splitting if left in the round. An ideal wood for abstract work of a tactile quality.

THE FULL RANGE OF SWEEPS AND SIZES

London Pattern Straight Gouges	London Pattern Curved Gouges	London Pattern Spoon Bit Gouges (Front Bent)	London Pattern Spoon Bit Gouges (Back Bent)	Fish Tail Pattern Straight Gouges	LONDON PATTERN CARVING TOOLS: 1/16" 3/32" 1/8" 3/16" 1/4" 5/16" 3/8" 7/16" 1/2" 5/8" 3/4" 7/8" 1 in; 1.5 2.25 3 4.5 6 7.5 9 10.5 12 15 19 22 25 mm
3	12	24	33	54 x 3	
4	13	25	34	54 x 4	
5	14	26	35	54 x 5	
6	15	27	36	54 x 6	
7	16	28	37	54 x 7	
8	17	29	38	54 x 8	
9	18	30	–	54 x 9	
10	19	31	–	54 x 10	
11	20	32	–	54 x 11	

London Pattern carving tool chart.

Ashley Iles gouges.

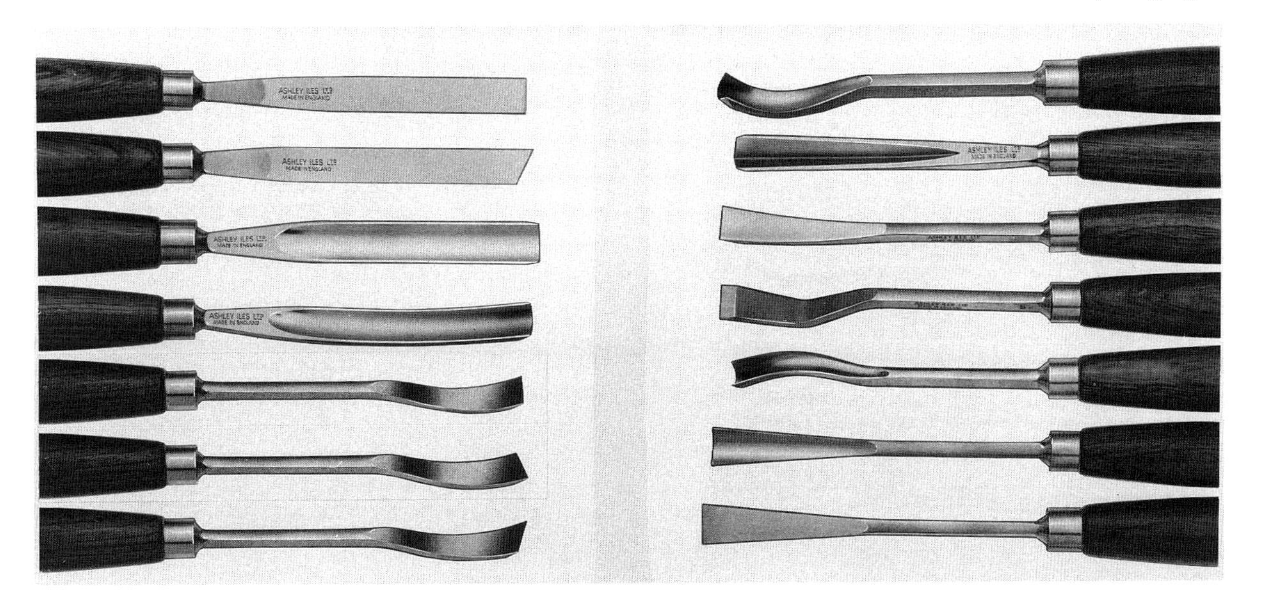

The woodcarving tools with curved cutting edges are known as gouges (a), the ones with flat edges are chisels (b). Their shapes have evolved over centuries of use. By the latter part of the nineteenth century, carving tools were standardized, each maker producing a similar range. This standard became known as the London Pattern of Carving Tools, although most were produced in Sheffield.

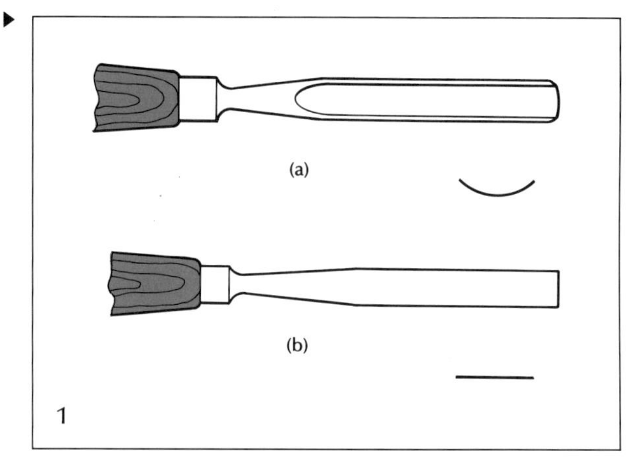

1

Gouges are graded by the degree that the cutting edge is curved. This is known as the sweep (a). They come in widths varying from 1/16in (1.5mm) up to 1in (25mm). Larger sizes are made for really big sculpture work. These are from 1¼in (31mm) to 2in (50mm) in width and are often made to the alongee pattern (b) with sides of the gouge tapering. Normal gouges have straight sides and are made to the London pattern.

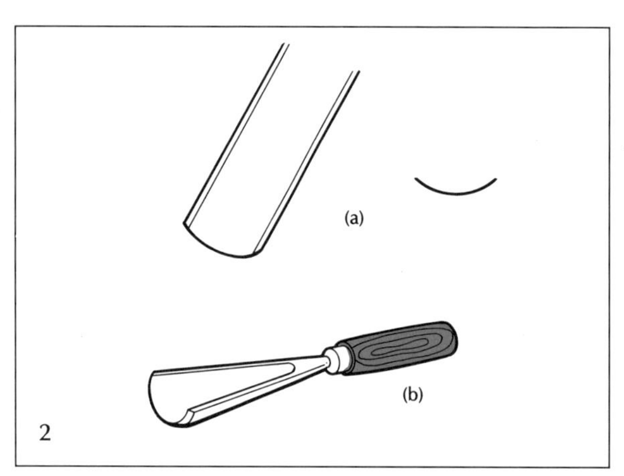

2

The sweep progresses from a nearly flat cutting edge to a steep-sided 'U' shape and are numbered from 3 to 11 when the gouge has a straight blade (Nos 1 and 2 being flat chisels). The London pattern is shown (a). All are ground with the cutting edge at right angles to the blade with the exception of the No. 2 chisel (b) which has an angle of 20 degrees to permit working into a corner.

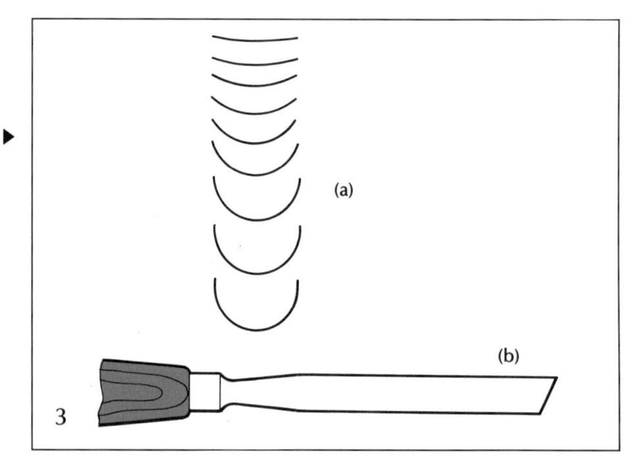

3

Generally the same range of sweeps is repeated with blades which are curved or which have a steep reverse taper. Each type has a different numbering sequence. The numbering system of Continental gouges varies slightly from the London pattern. The curved blade (a) is useful for hollowing. The spoon bit (b) can be used in restricted areas. The fishtail (c) is ideal for cleaning up.

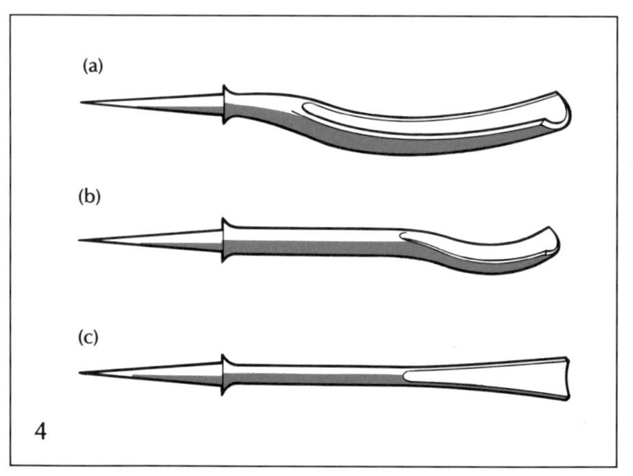

4

A woodcarving gouge consists of the following:

Blade This should be forged from high-grade steel, tempered to retain a good cutting edge. While it has to be strong, the blade should not be too thick and cumbersome. The best blades are forged by hand following very traditional methods.

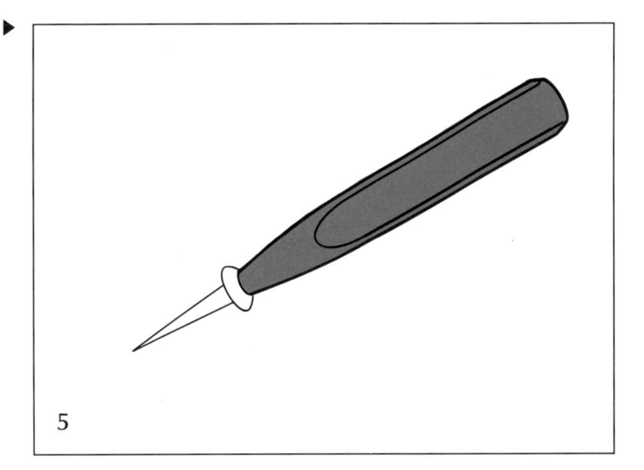

5

Bolster (or shoulder) This is necessary to prevent the blade being pushed too far into the handle. It should not be too small as strength is needed where the handle fits.

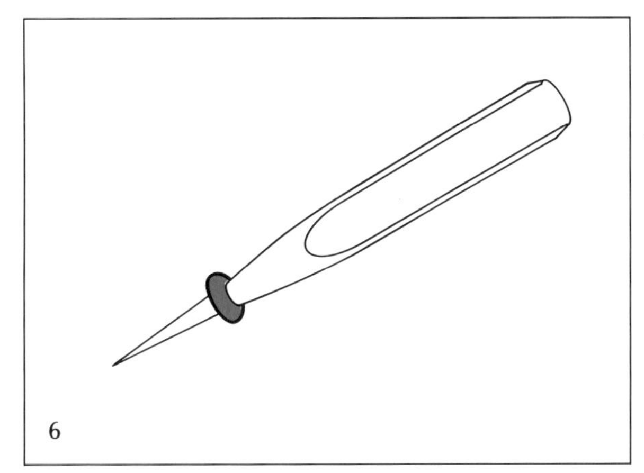

6

Tang This fits into the handle. It is essential that the tang is forged in line with the blade. If not, the blade will be crooked, making accurate cuts difficult.

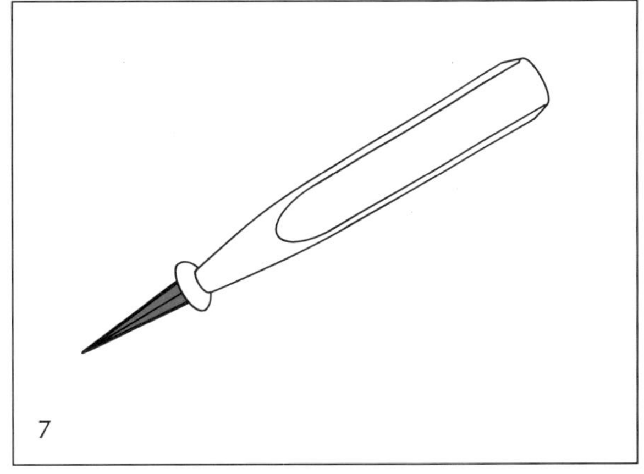

7

Handle This is either round, fitted with brass ferrules, usually made of beech and 4½in (115mm) long, or octagonal, usually made of ash, 5¼in (135mm) long with internal ferrules. English gouges traditionally have round handles and Continental gouges octagonal ones. The overall length of an English gouge is about 9in (230mm) – a Continental tool about 10in (250mm). One theory for this difference is that the English worked originally in oak and used mallets, whereas the Swiss and Austrians worked with hand pressure in softer woods and the longer gouge gave more leverage.

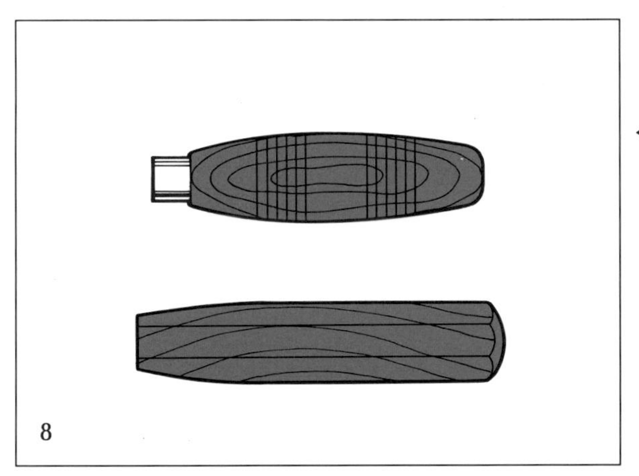

8

The manufacture of good woodcarving gouges requires careful production techniques, frequently employing traditional methods. Two of the leading English manufacturers are Henry Taylor Tools Ltd of Sheffield and Ashley Iles (Edge Tools) Ltd of Spilsby, Lincolnshire. Both produce gouges to the London pattern designs. Very good gouges are also produced by the Swiss maker, Pfeil. All of these are widely used by professional woodcarvers.

As mentioned earlier, the Swiss numbering system differs slightly to the London pattern numbers. This mainly applies to the flatter sweeps. For example, an English No. 3 gouge is more similar to the Swiss 'cut 2' and the Swiss 'cut 3' is more like the English No. 4. As long as these differences are understood and reference is made to the maker's charts, little confusion should exist.

There are cheap gouges on the market, usually of Far Eastern origin, which should be avoided. They are normally of very small size.

Most makers offer boxed sets of tools. Some discretion is needed, as one may find that a set includes one gouge which is never used, which is a waste of money.

Of the makes mentioned, both Ashley Iles and Pfeil sell their gouges already sharpened, whereas Henry Taylor tools come ground but not sharpened. The beginner will undoubtedly be attracted to a gouge which is already sharp, but it should be borne in mind that this sharpness will not last for ever, and some skill must be acquired to restore the cutting edge. The section covering bevel angles and the procedure for achieving a sharp edge covers the main points.

The actual choice of make may well come down to personal preference and local availability. Cost should not be of prime importance as, with care, a gouge will last a lifetime. It is possible to buy second-hand gouges. Make sure, though, that any gouge offered is a woodcarving gouge and not a carpenter's tool which has been reground. It is easy to identify a carpenter's gouge by the waisting of the blade just before the handle.

As to which gouges to buy, the best advice is to start with a few straight-bladed ones and add to the range as experience grows.

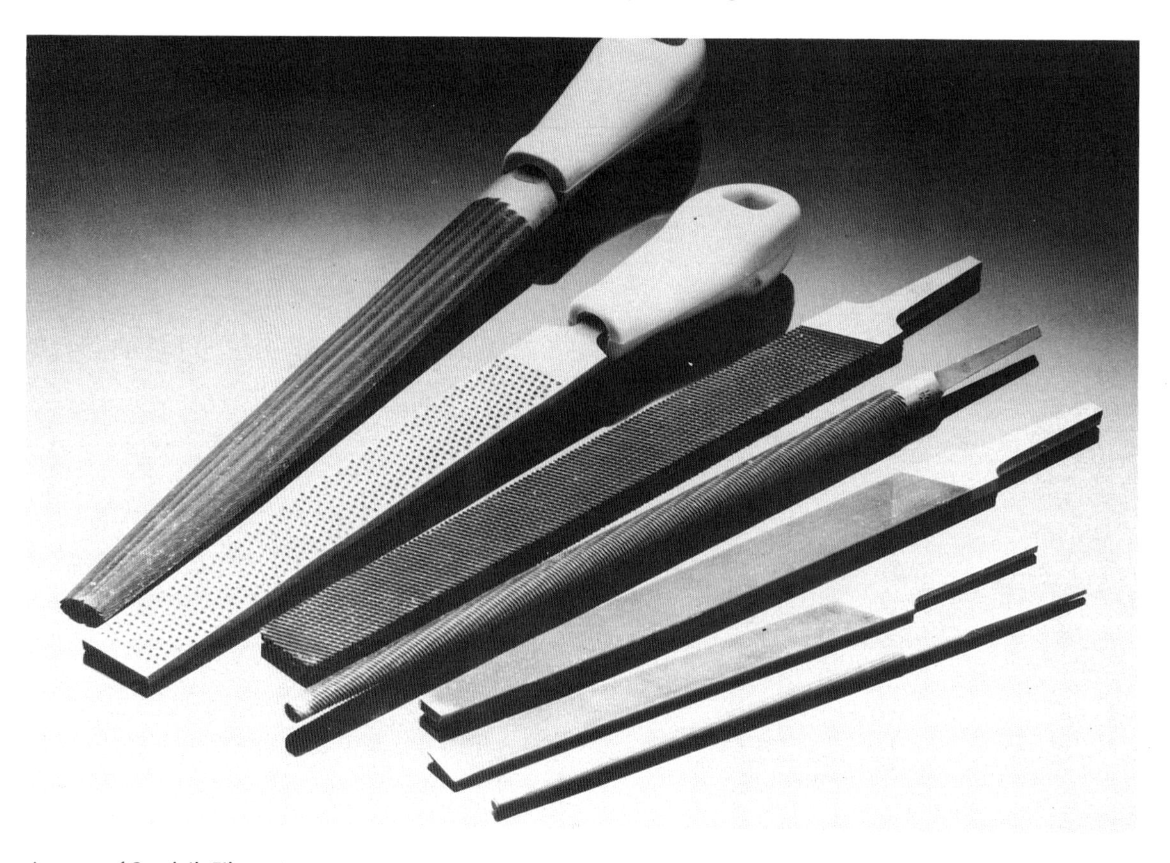

A range of Sandvik Filemaster rasps.

The following history has been kindly supplied by Mr Ashley Iles, founder of Ashley Iles (Edge Tools) Ltd, East Kirkby, Spilsby, Lincolnshire.

A Brief History of Woodcarving Tools

Up to the nineteenth century, the history of woodcarving tools is shrouded in mystery. The most outstanding fact is that the great pieces of carving through the centuries, from cottage homes to cathedrals, were done with what, by our standards, can only be described as primitive tools, made by the village blacksmith.

Woodcarving came into national prominence during the nineteenth century and set patterns and shapes of tools were firmly established. The shapes were more or less fixed for all time by the Sheffield Illustrated List of 1913, the 'Family Bible' of the tool trade.

The major types and patterns are as follows: London pattern; alongee pattern; fishtail, spade, curved, spoon bit (front bent), spoon bit (back bent), V-tools in angles of 45, 60 and 90 degrees. All were black backed with a straw-coloured temper on the inside.

Prominent in the nineteenth century were the firms of S.J. Addis and also Herring. These two made the bulk of the tools up to the Second World War. Either of these makes are collectors' pieces.

In post-war years, Addis continued under J.B. Addis; Herring ceased. Aeron Hildick of the Herring Company then worked with Henry Taylor Tools Ltd (founded in 1834).

In 1949 Ashley Iles produced an entirely new range of London pattern carving tools, having an all-bright polished finish. In 1967 the firm moved to East Kirkby in the heart of rural Lincolnshire.

Various foreign tools are on the market, some of good quality, but none competing with the wide range of the British manufacturers.

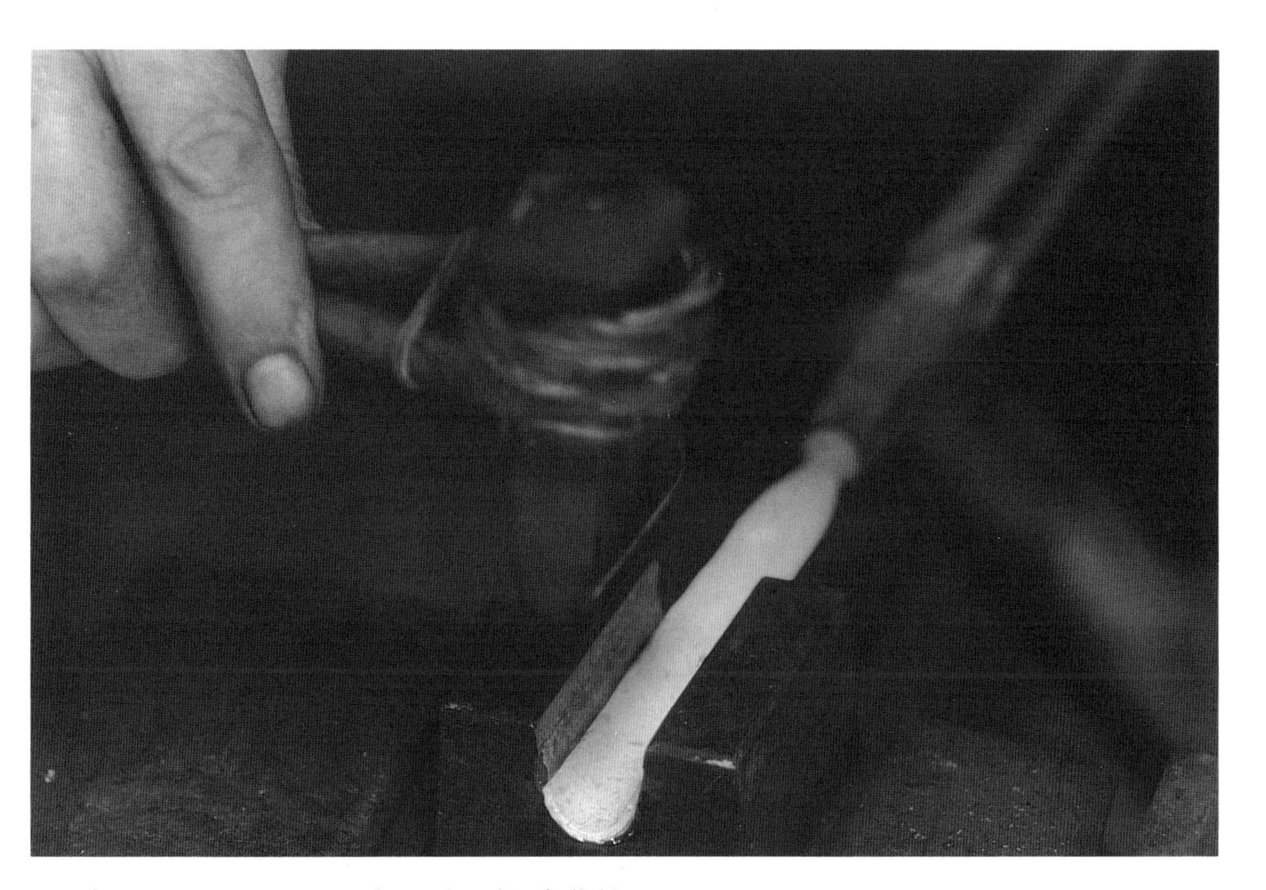

Manufacturing a gouge at Henry Taylor (Tools) Ltd in Sheffield.

The No. 9 gouge (a) has one of the most useful sweeps in the range. It is used for the initial removal of waste wood – roughing out – and for cutting concave areas. Ideally two sizes are needed – ¼in (6mm) and ½in (12mm). Note that the sweep of this gouge is half-round. It can be used to define a circle which is useful when carving such features as eyes.

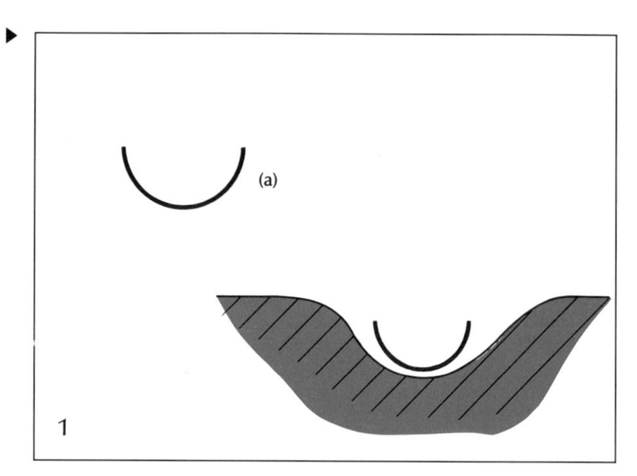

1

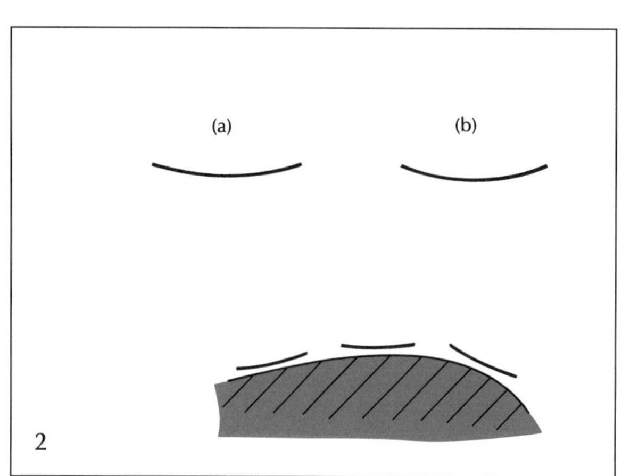

2

The No. 3 (a) and No. 4 (b) gouges, being flatter, are used for making convex curves, which would become grooved if a gouge having a steeper sweep was used. These numbers are also used for shallow paring cuts. It is useful if these are in differing widths, for example No. 3 – ⅜in (9mm), No. 4 – ¾in (19mm).

The No. 5 gouge (a) falls into the intermediate range. It will remove more wood than the Nos 3 and 4 but less than the No. 9. A width of about ⅝in (15mm) is ideal.

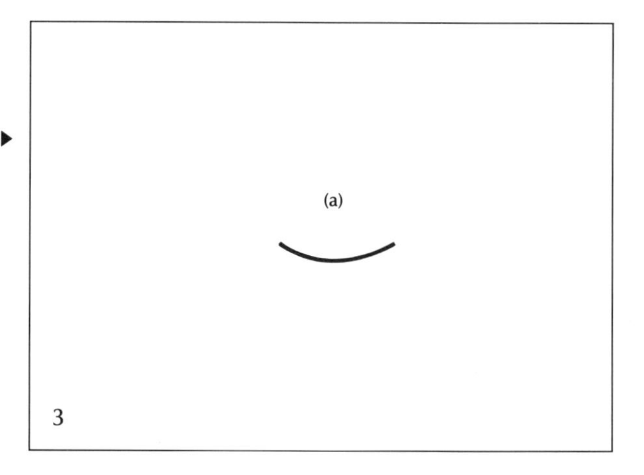

3

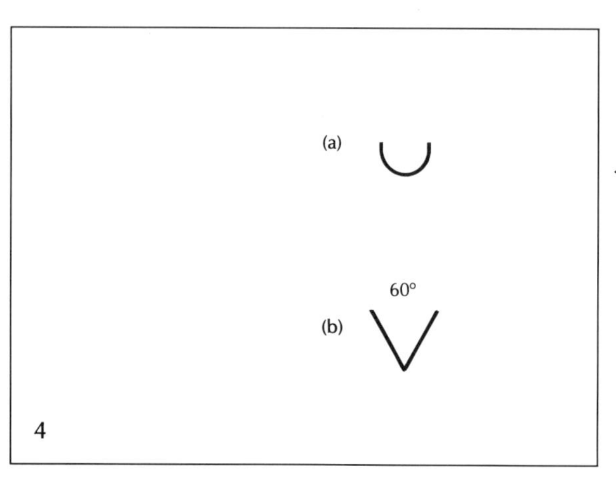

4

For marking out a design prior to carving, or for creating textured effects, either a No. 11 (a) or a No. 39 V-tool (b) is used. The old name for a No. 11 gouge was 'veiner' as it was used for cutting veins of leaves. This term is still used. The sweep is U-shaped and a small size such as a 1⁄16 (1.5mm) or slightly wider is all that is needed to start with. The term 'V-tool' is self-explanatory; it is sometimes called a parting tool.

An initial set of gouges to execute average-sized carvings would include: No. 1 ⅝in (15mm) flat chisel; No. 3 ⅜in (9mm) gouge; No. 4 ¾in (19mm) gouge; No. 5 ⅝ (15mm) gouge; No. 9 ¼in (6mm) gouge; No. 9 ½in (12mm) gouge; No. 11 $\frac{1}{16}$in (1.5mm) veiner; No. 39 ¼in (6mm) 60 degrees V-tool.

Note: The numbers and sizes apply to the London Pattern chart. Swiss gouges use a slightly different scale, for example: No. 3 London pattern is nearer to Swiss cut 2, No. 4 London pattern is nearer to Swiss cut 3 and No. 5 is nearer to Swiss cut 7. Widths will vary – choose the next highest millimetre size. If you plan to produce large-scale work you may need to buy wider varieties.

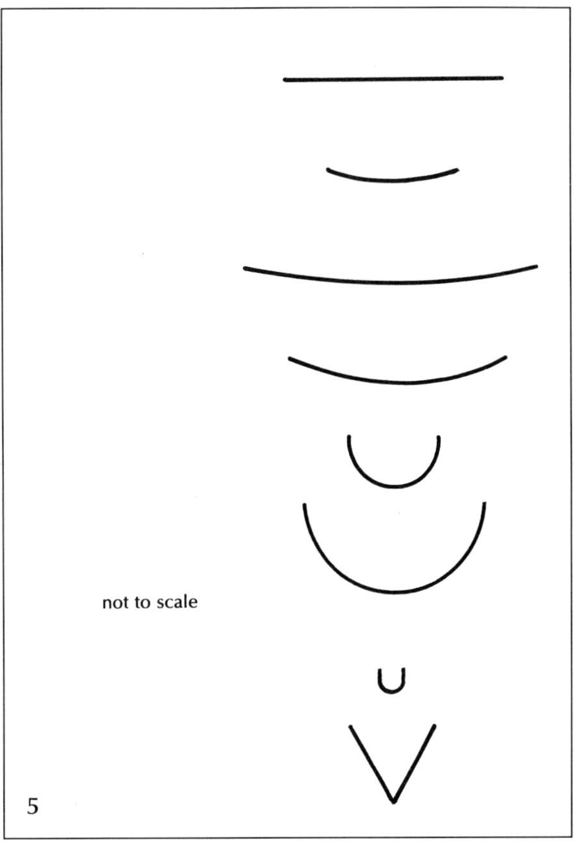

5

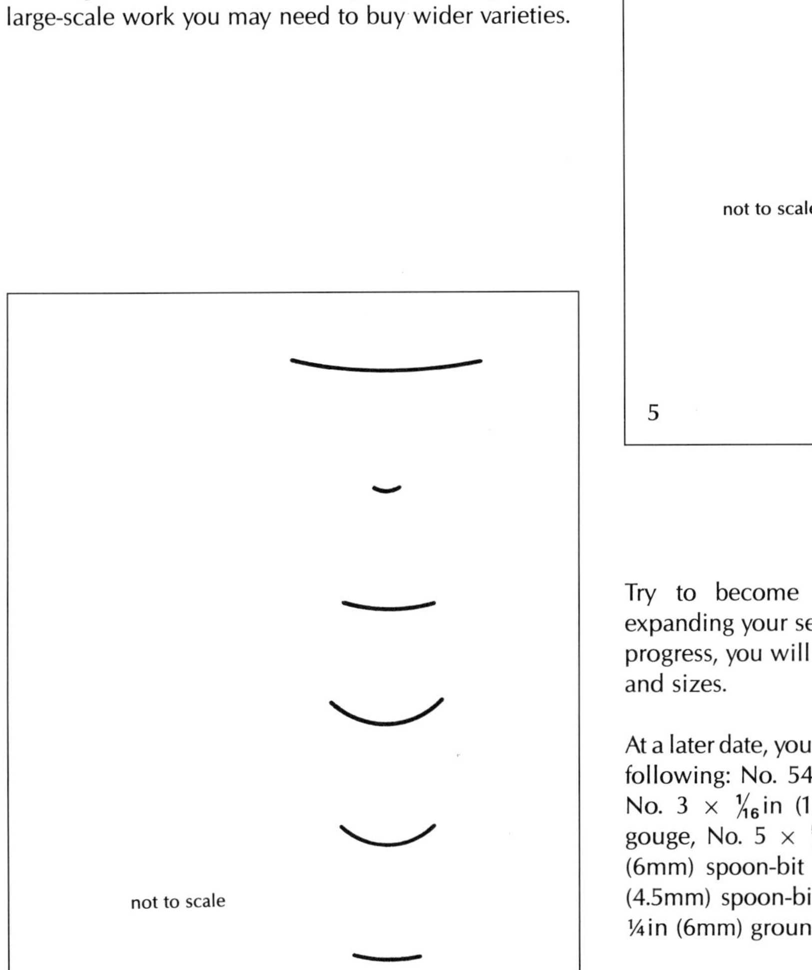

6

Try to become 'fluent' with the first set before expanding your selection too quickly. However, as you progress, you will find that you need additional shapes and sizes.

At a later date, you can add to your set of gouges with the following: No. 54 × 3 × ½in (12mm) fishtail pattern, No. 3 × $\frac{1}{16}$in (1.5mm) gouge, No. 4 × ¼in (6mm) gouge, No. 5 × $\frac{5}{16}$in (7.5mm) gouge, No. 28 × ¼in (6mm) spoon-bit gouge (front bent), No. 33 × $\frac{3}{16}$in (4.5mm) spoon-bit gouge (back bent), No. 47 × 3 × ¼in (6mm) grounding tool.

Buy a suitable tool roll at the same time as the gouges. One with twelve compartments will allow for later additions. You will find that it is money well spent, as each gouge is kept separate and will not blunt against another.

pfeil

Gerade Form
Gouge droite
Straight shape

Stichtabelle

Ouvertures des outils

Table of cutting edges

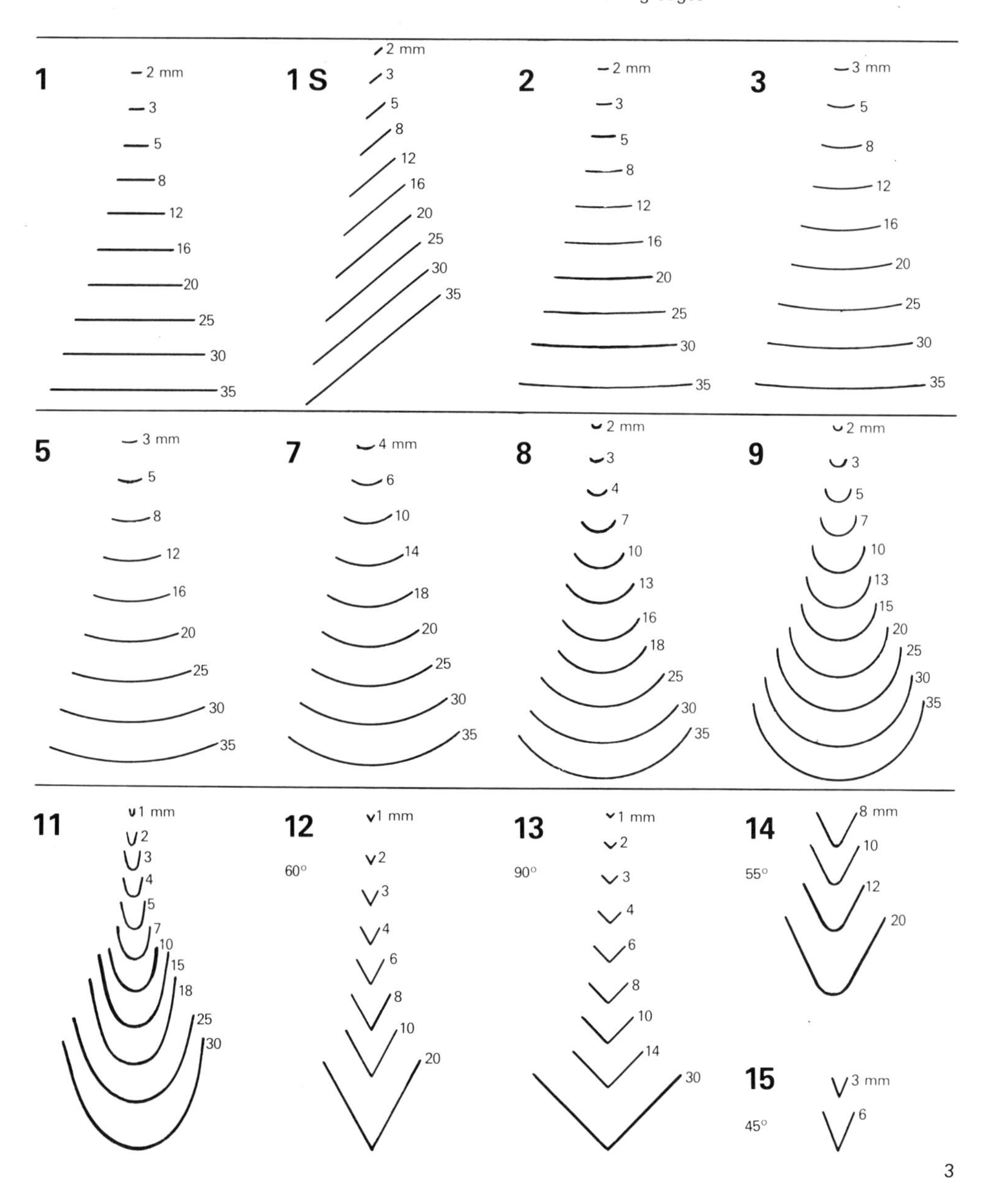

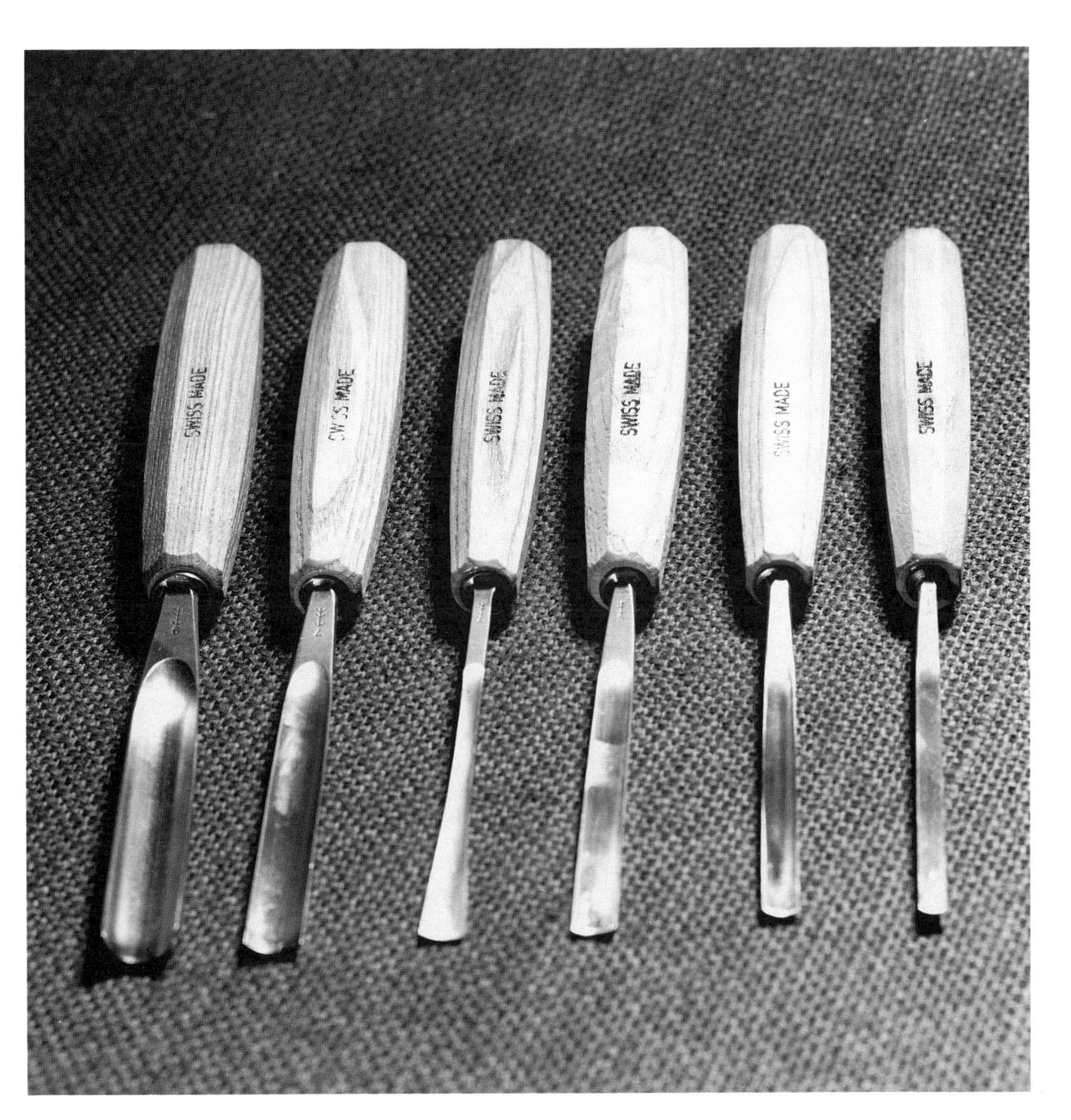

Pfeil gouges.

Opposite – Pfeil gouge chart

The woodcarver's mallet (a) has a distinctive shape, which goes back centuries. The handle is short and the head round. This shape of head prevents the gouge being hit off course (c). Carving mallets are usually made from a dense wood, beech or lignum vitae being preferred. The latter is heavier for a given diameter. The handle should be made of ash which absorbs impact well. For general use a mallet having a head diameter of 3½in (90mm) is about right. The carpenter's mallet (b) in comparison has a square head. An off-centre impact causes the gouge to be deflected (d).

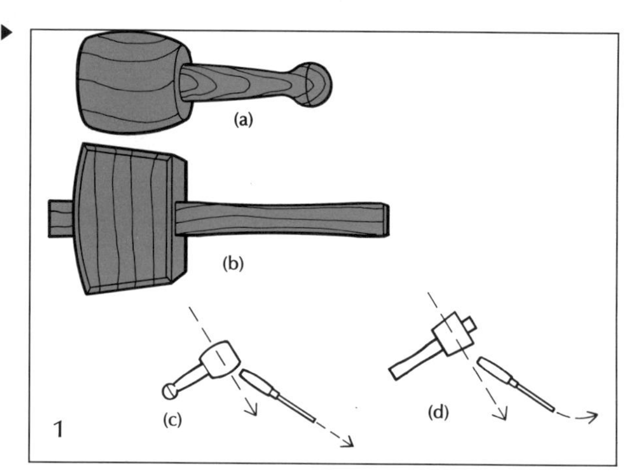

Because the mallet has a short handle, the action when using it comes from the forearm with the wrist stiff, the fulcrum being the elbow. It is wrong to use wrist action, as one would with a hammer or carpenter's mallet.

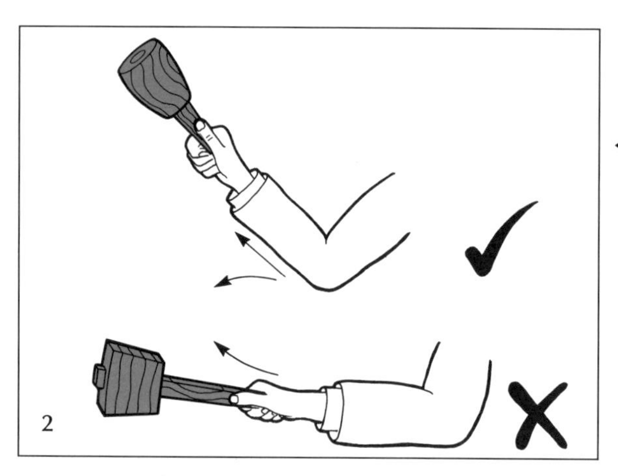

A general purpose DIY type handsaw (a) is needed for rough cutting. A coping saw (b) is very useful for shaping small areas. A great deal of time and effort can be saved if the initial cutting out is done with a bandsaw. This is an expensive item for the beginner to buy, but local enquiry may well lead you to one which can be used occasionally.

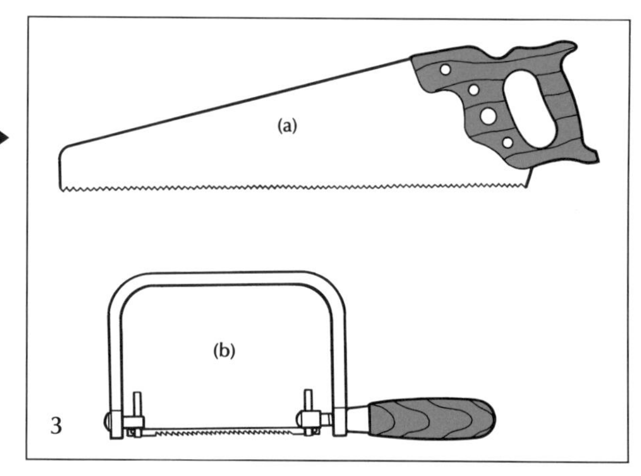

Small rasps are known as rifflers (a) and come in many shapes with both coarse and fine cut. The normal wood rasp (b) is usually coarse and will damage the wood fibres below the surface, but the Sandvik Filemaster gives a clean finish. The Sandvik Sandplate (c) is useful, as is the Stanley Surform (d), especially in the round version. Nothing, though, gives as clean a cut as a really sharp gouge.

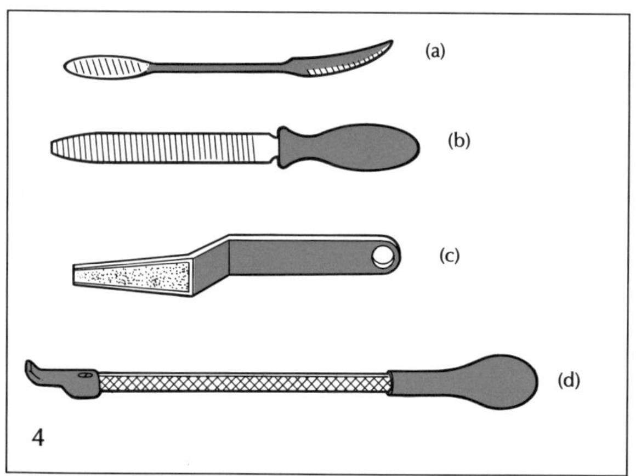

Sandvik saws.

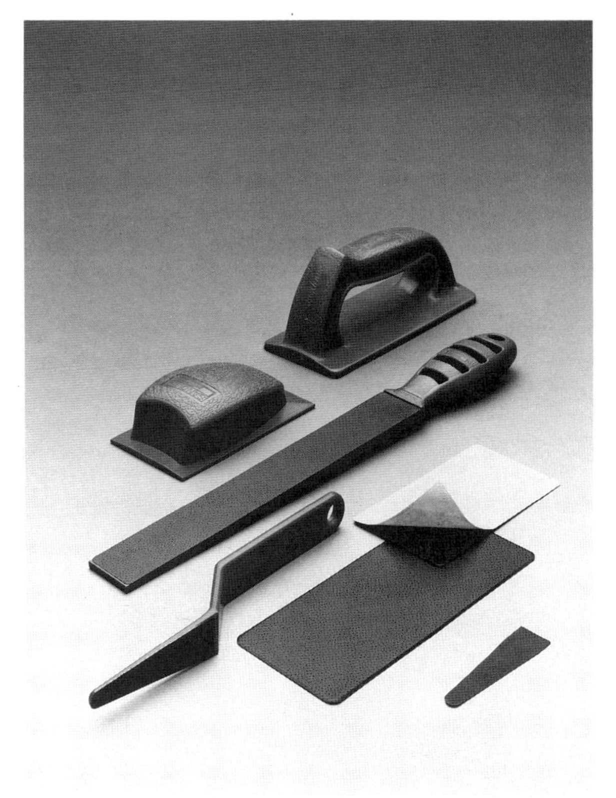

Sandvik files.

Stanley Surform.

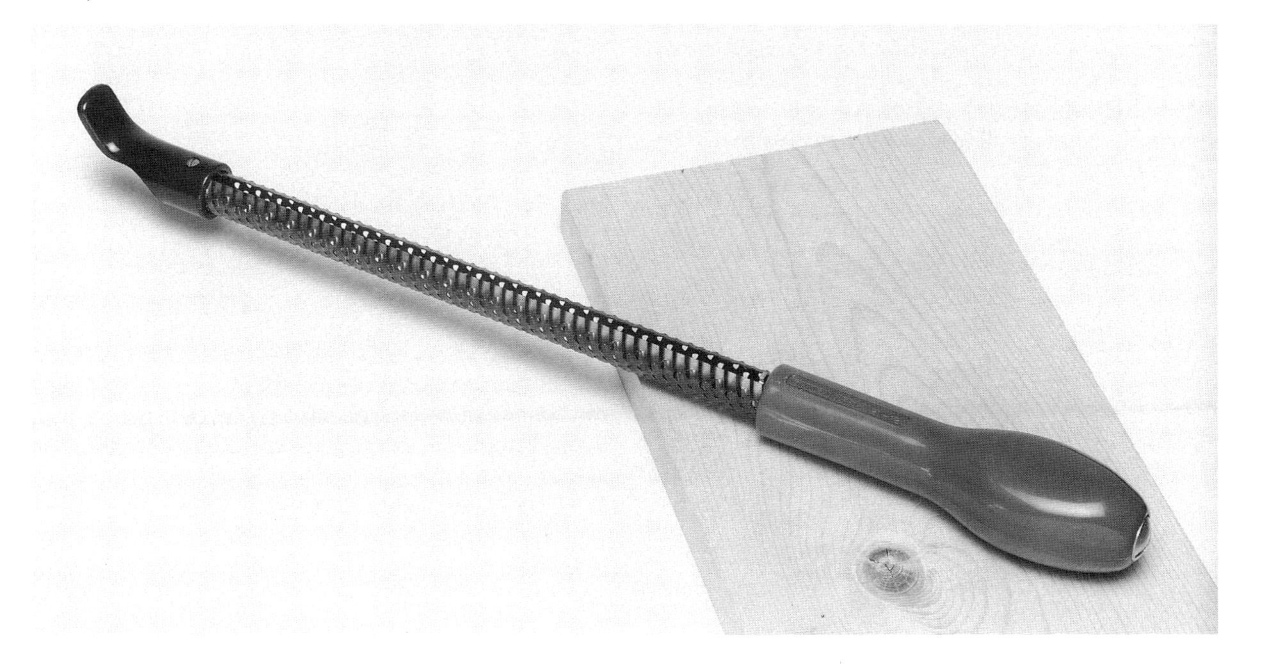

A good workbench is an essential piece of equipment. It needs to be robust enough to withstand the impact stresses of carving. To carve on the kitchen table may be all very well to start with, but a workbench will eventually be necessary. There are various options. The Black and Decker Workmate is very versatile: it is robust enough for light sculpture or relief carving. A woodcarving vice can be mounted, using the pre-drilled holes in the worktop. Its disadvantage is its height, since, like most carpentry benches, it is designed for sawing wood, and one needs to bend over the bench to do this. However, the Workmate is a good starting point.

1

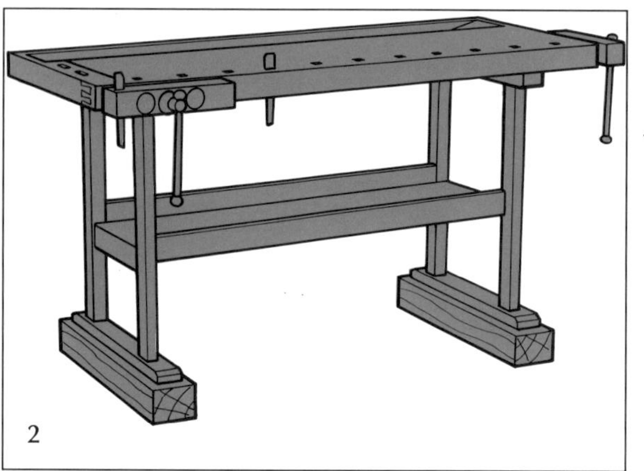

2

Specialist carpentry workbenches are quite expensive to buy. Most commercially made ones have a working height of 32in (820mm) which will mean some bending over the work for an average-sized person, although benches can be raised on blocks as shown. Slightly taller benches are available from the leading makers. This type of workbench is good for relief carving, but does have its limitations for sculpture.

It is vital to be comfortable when working for fairly long periods of time. If the bench top is even a fraction too low you will soon develop backache. Experiment with various heights to obtain the optimum work positions. If the bench is to be used for more than one purpose, fix the bench legs to blocks with coach screws.

3

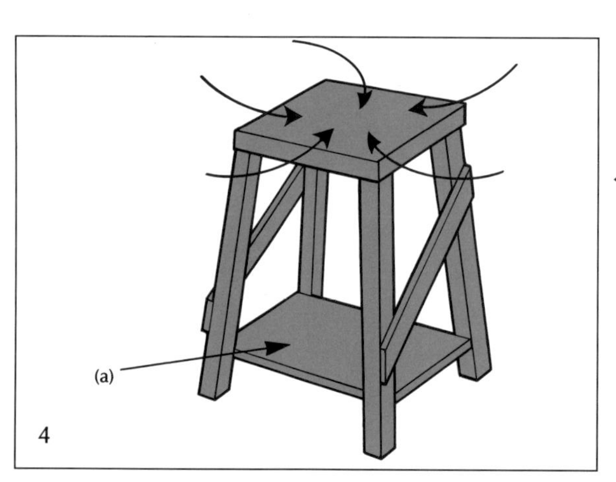

4

Sculpture necessitates working round the carving block. This requires a fairly small worktop to the bench for all-round access as shown, usually about 20in (500mm) square. The carving needs to be at chest height, when standing with the back straight. Normally the bench top will have a height of 34–36in (860–920mm) if the vice used is mounted on top of it. The whole construction must be strong, the legs splayed and well braced. Weight (concrete blocks) should be added to the base to lower the centre of gravity (a).

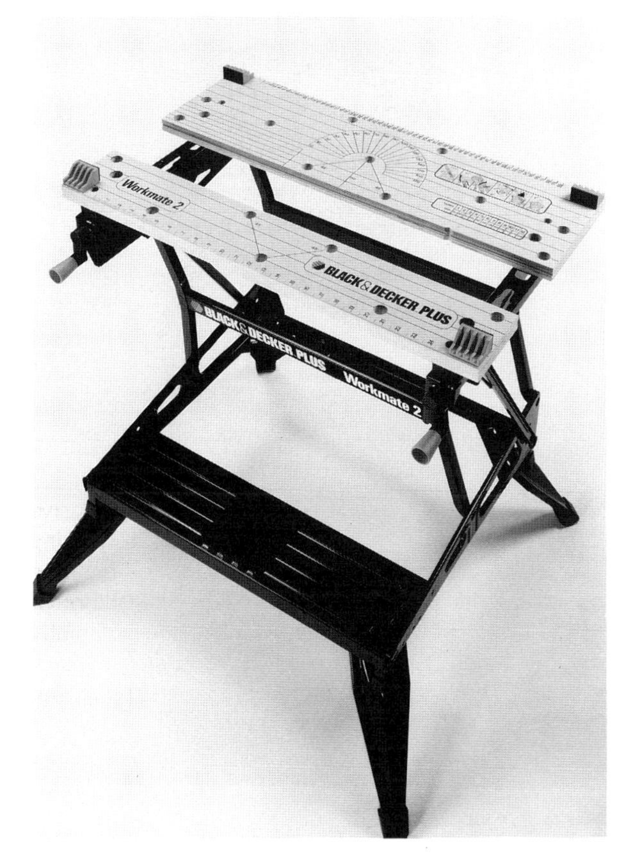

Black and Decker Workmate.

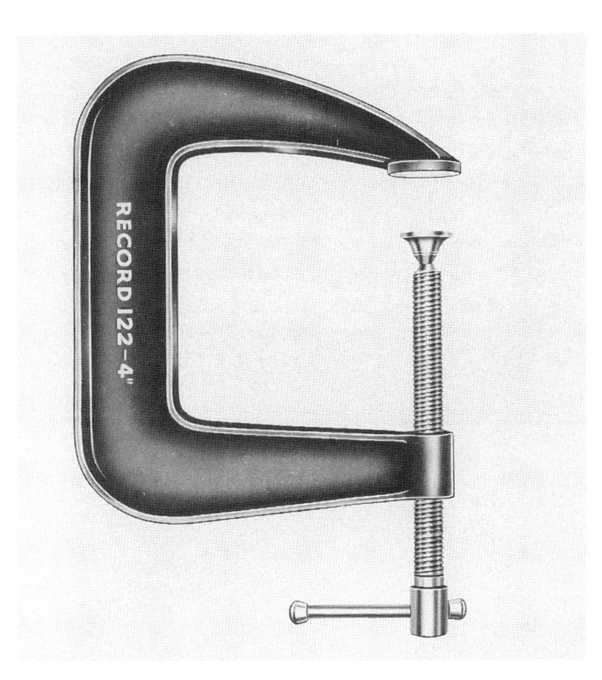

Record G-cramp.

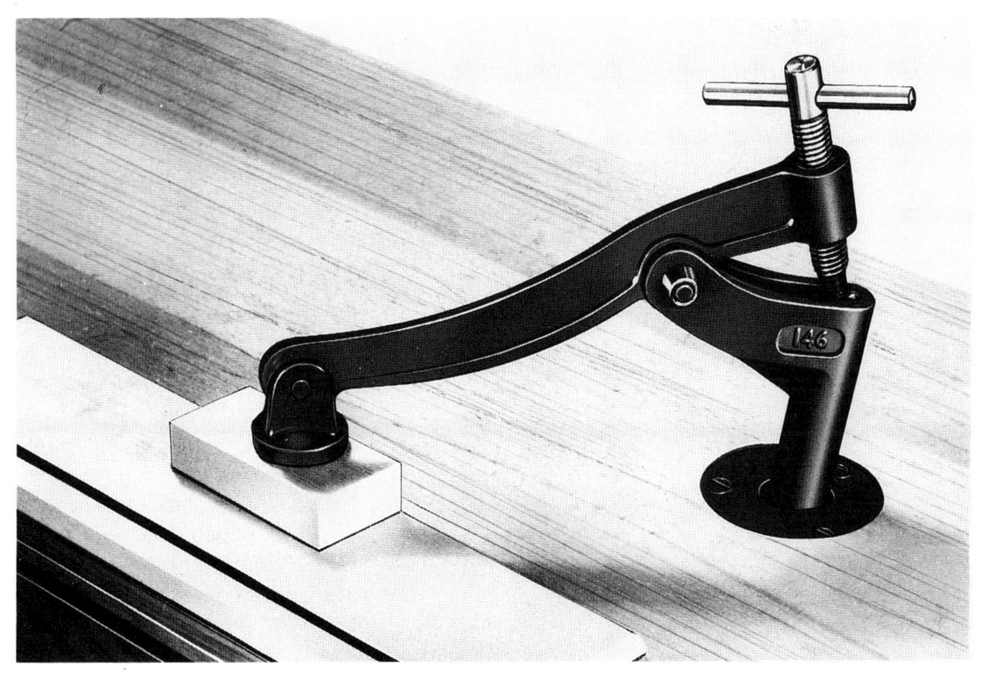

Record Holdfast.

Lervad workbench.

WORKBENCHES – CHECKLIST

- Regard the purchase of a workbench as a long-term investment.
- Before buying make certain your chosen model is strongly made.
- With reasonable care, the workbench should give years of service.
- Avoid using the workbench for any dirty, oily or paint jobs.
- Cut plywood or chipboard to cover and protect the surface.

Sjborg workbench.

Carving bench with Tiranti Scopas Chops.

WORKBENCHES – TIPS

- One of the most common causes of back pain is incorrect bench height.
- You may spend many hours carving, so it makes sense to spend time in assessing the height you need for optimum comfort.
- You may need different working heights for sculpture and for relief carving.

The use of bench dogs.

There are many ways of holding a block of wood for carving. The most basic method is to reduce the base of a carving block to a size which will fit into the clamping space of a Black and Decker Workmate (a), or a standard woodwork vice fitted outboard to a carpentry bench. If the carving block is reduced to a depth of ¾in (20mm) sufficient hold will be provided for average-sized work. If the reduced area is cut to have six sides (b) it will be possible to turn the work round. The reduced area is removed when carving is completed. A false base can be added to a carving block. If it is sandwiched with a piece of thick paper, removal will be easy. The problem with this method is that screws are usually needed to hold the two pieces of wood firmly together, and this leaves unsightly holes in the base of the finished carving. Cork or baize is usually used to cover up the holes, but it does not give a very professional look.

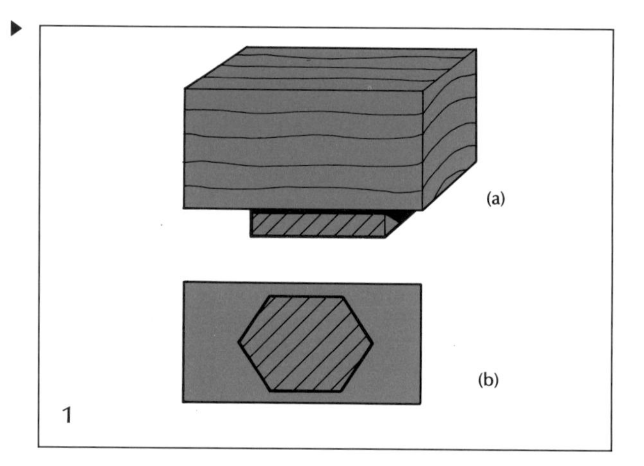

1

A device which has been on the market for many years is the carver's screw. The tip is cut with a wood thread to permit screwing into a pre-drilled hole in the base of the carving block. The carver's screw is mounted through a hole in the bench and secured from underneath. The disadvantages of this device are firstly the unsightly hole left in the base of the carving; secondly, the screw can work loose whilst carving is taking place; thirdly it is possible to cut through the surrounding wood and hit the screw with the cutting edge of the gouge.

2

Woodcarver's chops as shown have been widely used for more than eighty years. They are very versatile, having wide-opening jaws, which are fitted with cork and leather and can be fully recommended. I have used this system for many years.
There are a number of vices made now which rotate through 360 degrees, some both vertically and horizontally, using a universal ball-and-socket joint. They work well, but the good ones are quite expensive.

3

A good system of holding the work is vital to successful carving and the cost involved will pay dividends in the years to come, so regard the purchase as a wise investment.

The simplest way of holding a flat piece of wood for carving in relief is to use G-cramps (a) fixed to either side of the panel (b) with spacers of scrap wood to prevent crushing (c). Care has to be taken not to carve too close to the G-cramp or the gouge may be damaged. If the wood to be carved is reduced in thickness at either end (d) it does help to keep the G-cramps out of the way.

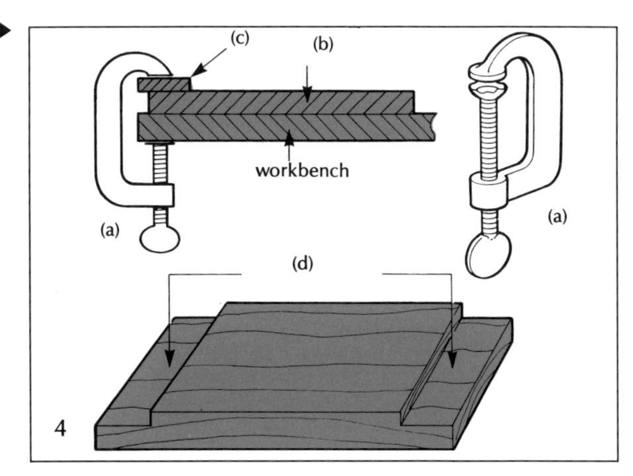

4

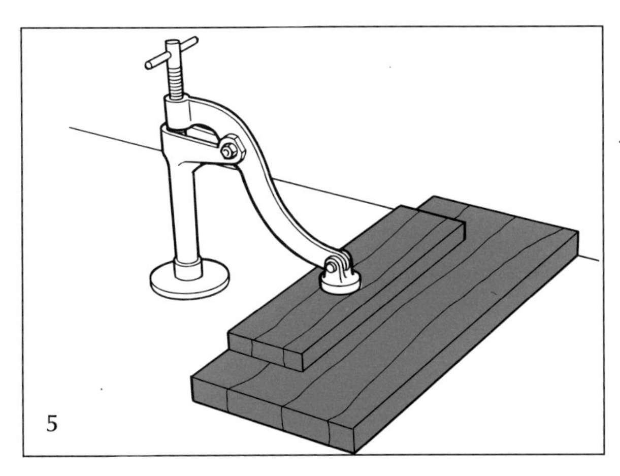
5

The bench holdfast requires a mounting hole to be drilled through the bench. It will hold a flat piece of wood very securely. Any tendency for the wood to swivel can be checked by using double-sided carpet tape on the underside of the panel, or by placing the wood on a thin kitchen sponge. Scrap wood is needed between the holdfast and the carving panel to prevent crushing.

Another popular method, used frequently by woodcarvers in the last century, is to use small cleats of hardwood. These are screwed to the bench on each side of the panel to be carved. The gap in the cleat needs to be less than the thickness of the panel (a). If preferred, the cleats can be fixed to a baseboard (b) which in turn is held onto the workbench by G-cramps.

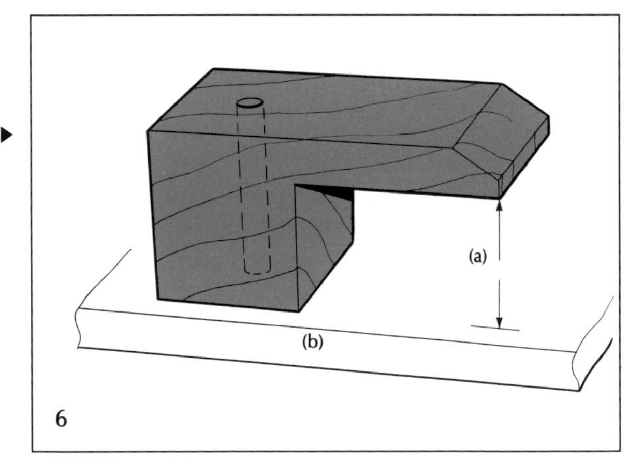

6

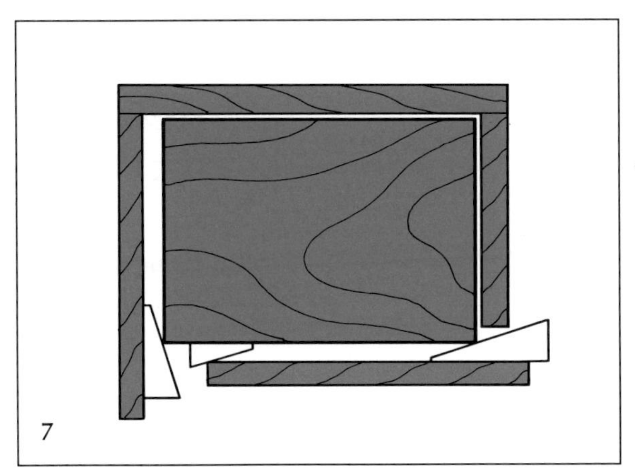
7

Four strips of plywood can be pinned and glued to a baseboard of suitable size and thickness. The panel to be carved is held in place with wedges cushioned with thick card. The strips need to be less thick than the panel and it is essential that a tight fit be achieved. The baseboard can be held in place with G-cramps, or by a block on the underside which can be held in a vice.

A gouge has two bevels on the underside of the blade. The cutting bevel (a) is produced by honing on an oilstone. In most cases, the back bevel (b) is ground at an angle of 40 degrees. Finishing gouges can have lower bevels set at 30 degrees. Two bevels are necessary as the gouge will cut on an arc with only one (c). The back bevel guides the gouge and assists in controlling the depth of cut. There is more about bevels later in this section (*see* page 48).

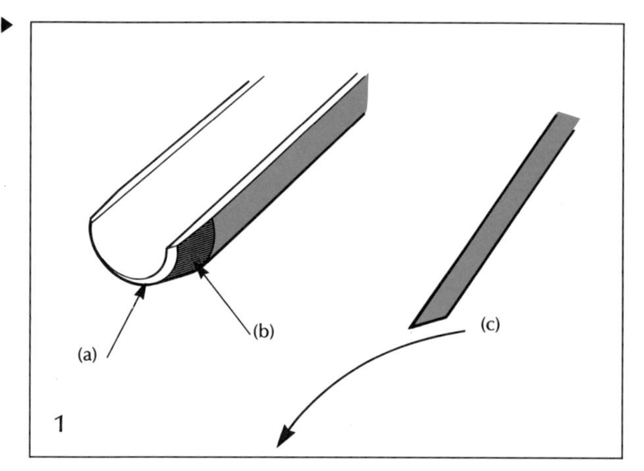

1

2

Oilstones come in various grades. The best are made from natural stone (Arkansas) or they can be man-made (India stones). Combination stones, coarse/medium and medium/fine, save money. These are available in either type of stone. Use light machine oil to lubricate the stone when sharpening, and wipe clean after use. Occasionally scrub the surfaces with white spirit. Always keep it stored in its wooden box (usually supplied with the stone) to avoid damage to the surfaces.

Use a flat strip of wood rather than the oilstone to practise sharpening. Take the gouge in the right hand with the handle held against the ball of the palm and extend the index finger along the blade (a). The first and second fingers of the left hand are placed across the blade a short distance up from the cutting edge (b). Reverse these instructions if you are left-handed.

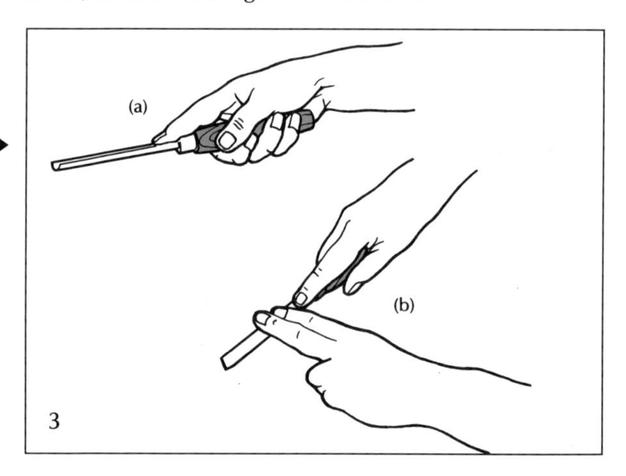

3

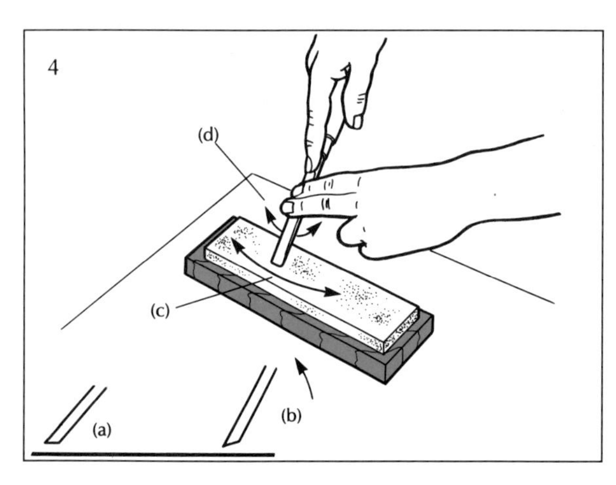

4

Hold the gouge lightly and rest it on the wood. Note that it sits on the back bevel (a). Slightly raise the right hand so that the gouge is resting just behind the front edge (b). Press down with the two fingers of the left hand across the blade. Move the left hand from side to side and let the gouge travel over the wood (c). Whilst in motion, twist the right wrist from side to side so that the whole of the sweep comes into contact with the wood (d).

India stones are made from aluminium oxide and do not give as fine a finish as natural Arkansas ones which are a better long-term buy. Oilstones made from carborundum do not wear well. Combination oilstones are available with both fine (a) and coarse (b) surfaces. Japanese waterstones produce a very fine cutting edge, but their use is somewhat specialized. Slipstones, available in sets (c), are needed to hone the inside sweep of a gouge. It is best to buy a set of Arkansas ones. Light machine oil is required, or a proprietary make of honing fluid.

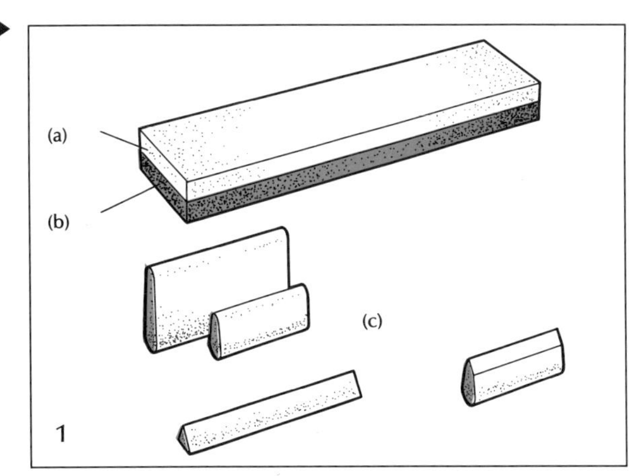

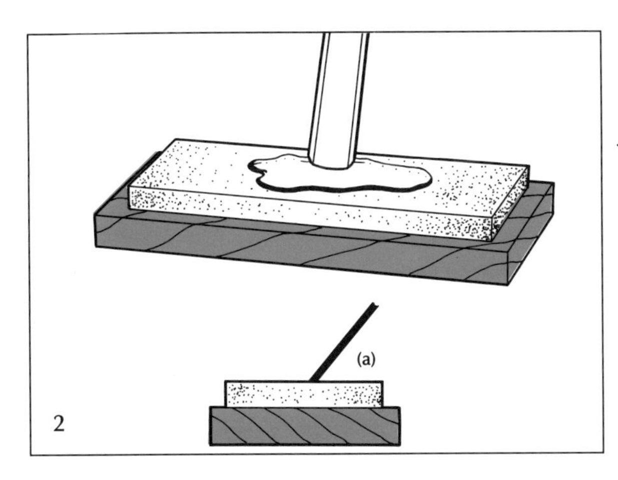

A few drops of oil or honing fluid, are applied to the surface of the oilstone. The gouge is held and laid on the stone as previously described. It is raised to an angle of about 40 degrees (a). At this point the edge of the gouge will squeeze the oil out of the way. Note when this happens, then proceed to move the gouge across the stone whilst twisting the handle from side to side.

If carried out correctly, the honed edge will appear as a narrow band about $\frac{1}{32}$in (1mm) wide and this width should be even across the cutting edge (a). Variations will be due to insufficient twisting (b). When honing reaches the edge of the blade, a burr will be felt on the inside. The lack of this burr means the cutting edge is not sharp, due to the gouge having been at too low an angle.

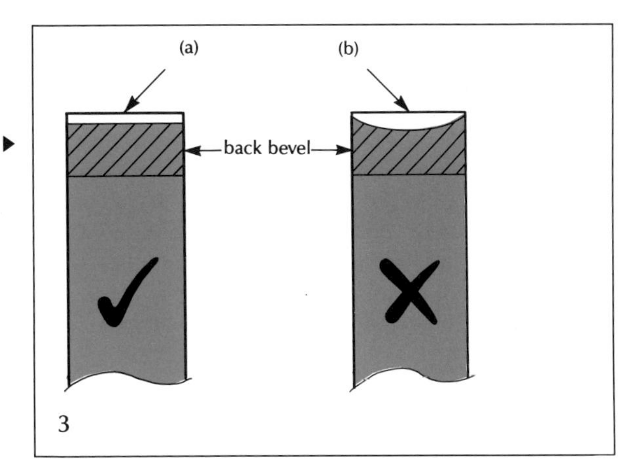

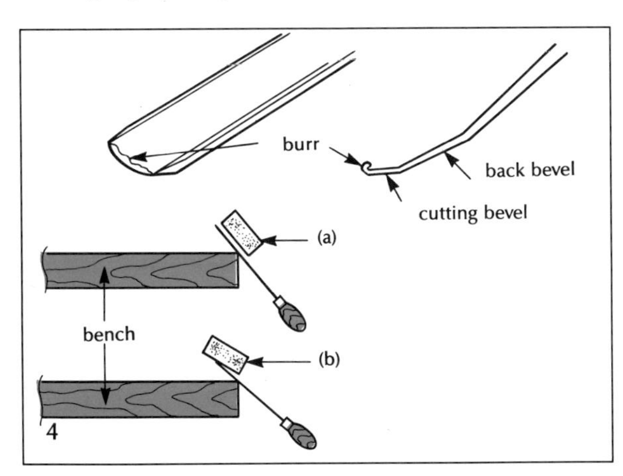

The burr is removed with a slipstone of suitable size and shape lightly lubricated with oil (b). Hold the gouge firmly against the side of the bench and slide the slipstone back and forth on the inside of the blade. Usually the slipstone is held flat to the blade (a), but if it is angled slightly a small bevel will be produced (b). Many woodcarvers prefer this, especially for relief carving, as it makes it possible to use the gouge upside-down.

It is vital to keep both forearm and gouge in a straight line avoiding any change of angle. Any vertical movement of the hand holding the gouge will cause the bevel to become rounded and it will blend in with the back bevel. The operating height of the oilstone is important. It should not be too high. The angle of the gouge needs to be near to 40 degrees (a). Position the oilstone relative to your own height by mounting it on a shelf.

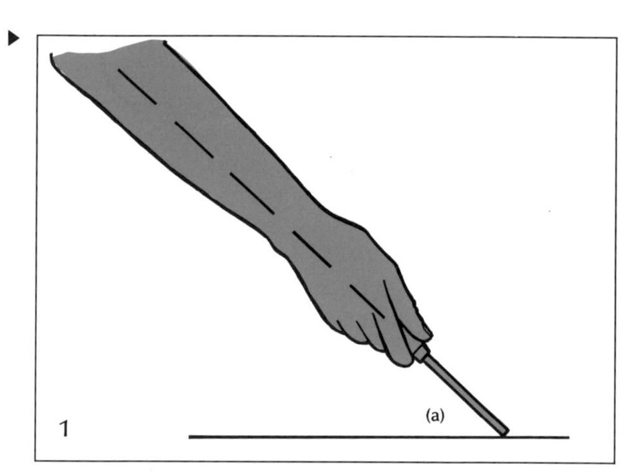

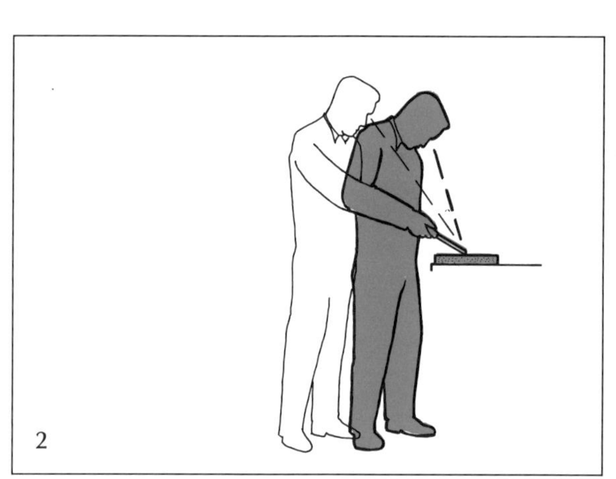

Although the arm is kept straight, one does not want to stand too rigidly. The action of honing needs to be fluid. If the elbow of the gouge hand is kept near the hip it is easier to maintain a constant angle. Sight down on the gouge. Do not stand too far back.

The gouge will traverse the surface of the oilstone in a slight arc (a). This is correct. Rather than the simple back-and-forth motion, some carvers prefer to use a figure-of-eight action (b), claiming that this evens out the wear of the stone. Some difficulty may be experienced at first in controlling the twisting action with this method.

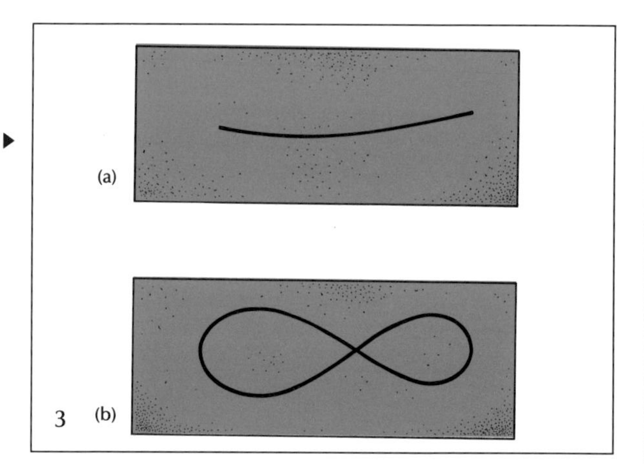

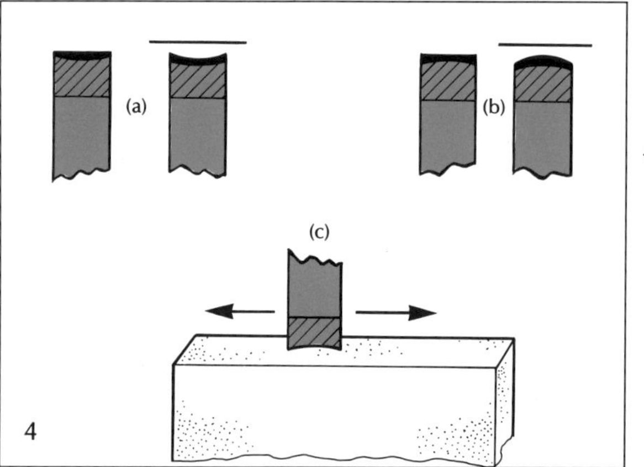

Use a ruler to check the shape of the cutting edge, which needs to be as straight as possible. Excess wear to the edges or to the middle should be avoided. Early stages of incorrect wear can be detected along the line of the honed bevel. (a) indicates the effect of insufficient twisting of the gouge during honing. (b) shows the effect of too much rotation. Both are common faults. Restore the cutting edge by rubbing it on the side of the oilstone, keeping the gouge vertical.

Final sharpening is carried out with a leather strop. You can buy specially prepared strops or you can use any piece of leather having a nap or rough surface measuring about 9 × 3in (230 × 75mm) – smooth leather does not work well. Fine-grade polishing compound is required to buff the bevels to a mirror finish. Ready-prepared paste can be bought, or it can be made from rouge powder and a little tallow or petroleum jelly, and rubbed well into the leather.

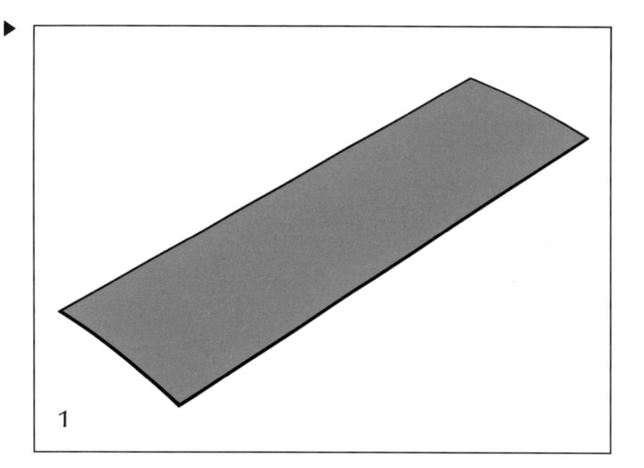

1

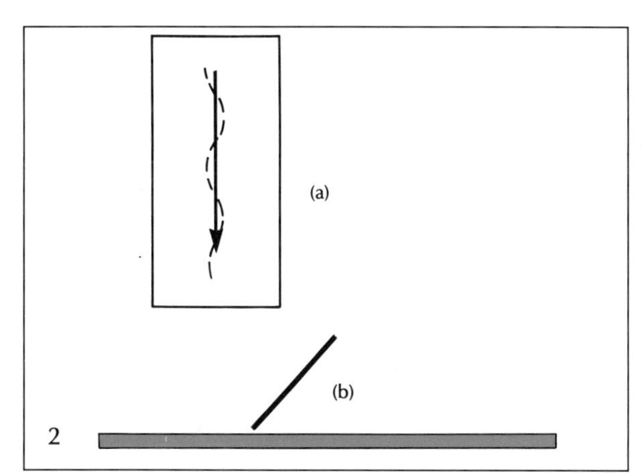

2

Place the strop on a flat surface and draw the gouge towards you along its length, using a twisting action so that all of the sweep comes into contact with the leather (a). Maintain the gouge at a constant angle to avoid the two bevels becoming rounded together (b). Strop the back bevel by using a more shallow angle. Frequent stropping will maintain a keen cutting edge.

To polish the inside of the cutting edge, make up shaped pieces of wood (bamboo works well) covered with suede leather (rough side up) and apply a small quantity of strop paste. You will need a number of the sticks to suit the various sweeps.

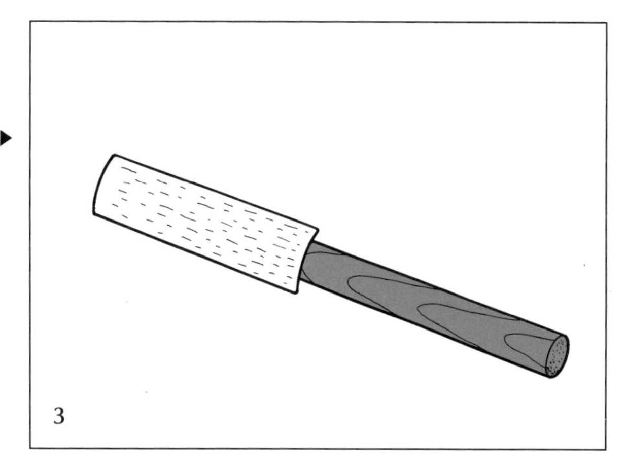

3

4

A rotary strop can be made from a washing machine motor with a wooden disc fitted to the spindle. The disc is covered with leather and strop paste applied. Care must be taken always to trail the gouge or it will jam into the disc and cause a bad accident. Indicate clearly the direction in which the disc rotates.

CHISEL, V-TOOL AND VEINER

A woodcarving chisel has bevels on both sides (a). To sharpen, use the oilstone lengthways on (b). Keep the angle at 15–20 degrees (c) and count the strokes on each side to keep the bevels equal. Strop to remove any burr.

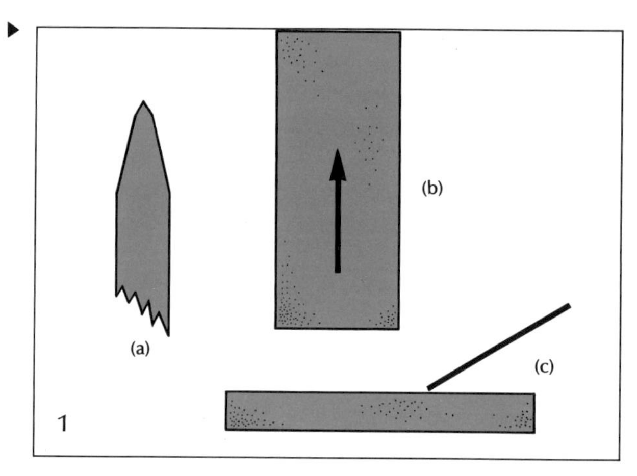

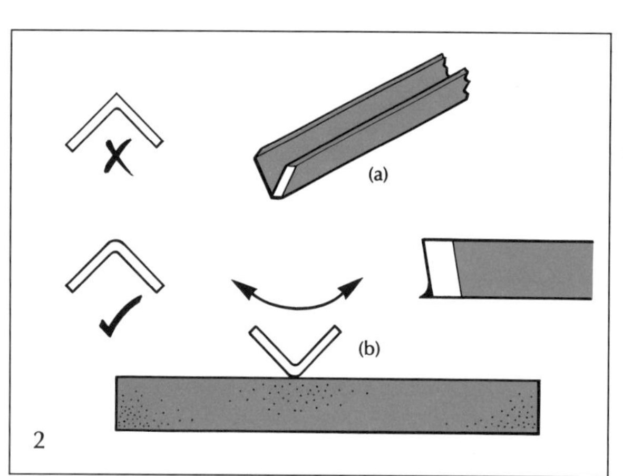

Sharpen the V-tool in the same way. Note that only the side walls have chisel-type cutting edges. The underside does not have a knife-edge; it is rounded like a small gouge (a). When the sides are honed, a point may be produced, rather like a hook, where the two sides meet. Remove this by using the rocking motion that is used with a gouge (b). Do this gently.

The No. 11 veiner is U-shaped. Sharpen as a gouge. The extreme twisting can be difficult. Start slightly off-centre to the middle of the sweep and rotate outwards, each side in turn, counting the strokes. Then hone the middle portion gently. Avoid flat spots. Keep the honing angle low.

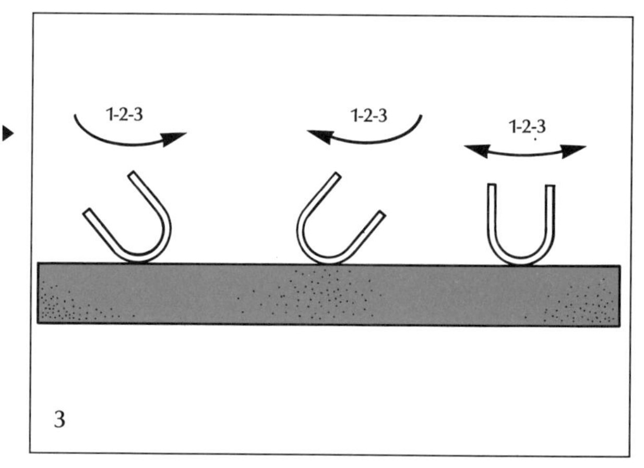

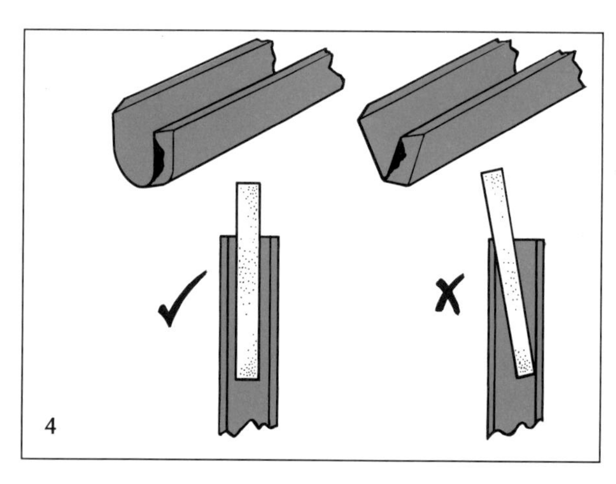

Care must be taken when using a slipstone to remove the inside burr from a V-tool or a No. 11 gouge, as the sidewall will be damaged if it is held off-centre. Keep the slipstone in line, not angled. The burr can be removed by making a few cuts in the end-grain of scrap hardwood.

When sharpening it is important to remember that the cutting bevel must come into contact with the oilstone. Difficulty may be encountered with curved gouges and spoon-bits, as one must compensate for their shape. If due care is not taken, honing will take place behind the cutting edge. The usual effect is that the cutting bevel becomes too long and consequently the steel too thin.

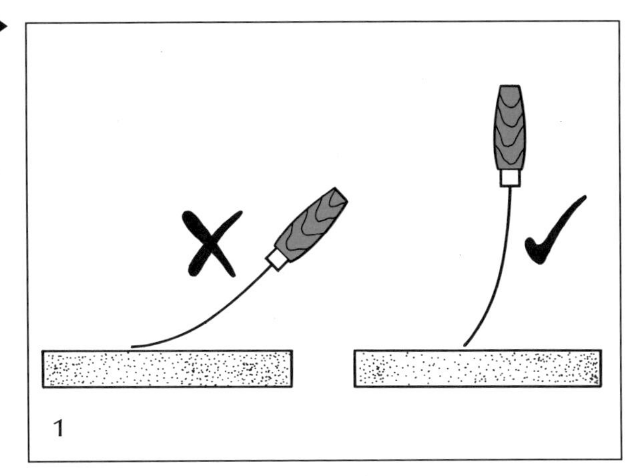

A curved gouge needs to be raised to an angle approaching 60 degrees. This may mean placing the oilstone at a lower level than usual. It should still be possible to hold the gouge in the normal way.

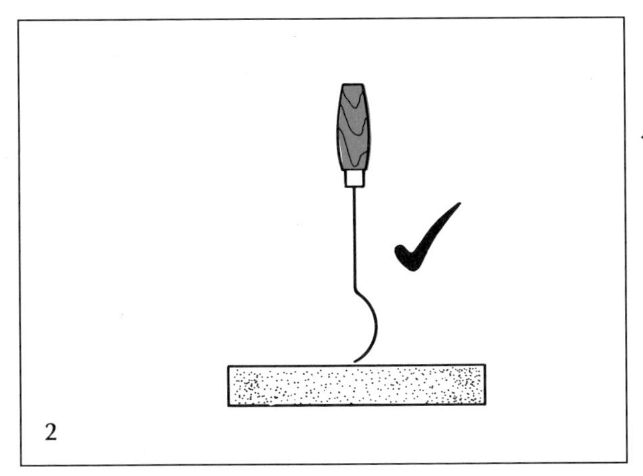

A spoon-bit gouge will need to be held almost perpendicular. If the gouge is gripped along the shaft instead of the handle being held there will be less chance of it wobbling. Hold the shaft as you would a pencil.

A back-bent gouge needs to be held at an angle so low that usually the handle is a little below the level of the stone.

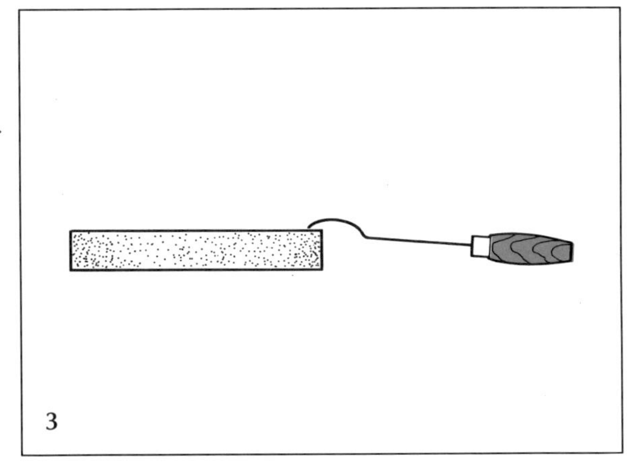

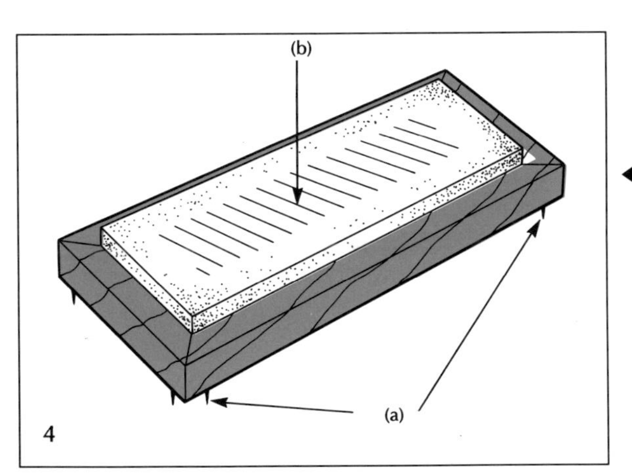

Oilstones are very fragile and should always be in the bottom section of the box when used. To stop the box sliding about insert small panel pins into the underside of each corner (a) and cut back about ⅛in (3mm). Eventually an oilstone used to sharpen gouges will develop a hollow to its surface (b). The figure-of-eight motion helps to alleviate this to some degree. Note that flat-bladed tools such as chisels and V-tools need to be sharpened on a flat part of the oilstone. Eventually you should have a special stone kept just for these.

BEVEL ADJUSTMENT

In theory, the angle of the bevels should be 40 degrees (a) for hardwoods, and 30 degrees (b) for softwoods. In practice, one does not need to alter the bevels for different woods, unless a lot of work is to be done with one species. The angle of cut and how the gouge is used, that is hand pressure, is more important. The gouges which do the hard work need shorter, stronger, bevels than those used for paring and more delicate cutting by hand, but do not be too extreme.

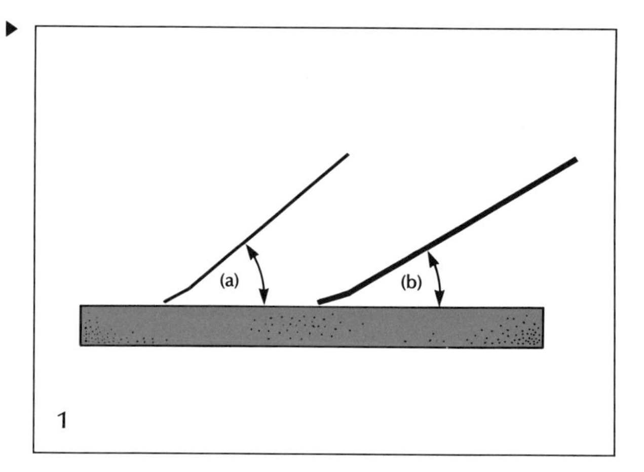

1

The back bevel should be less acute in angle than the cutting bevel. With each sharpening, the angle between the two becomes steeper, and after about the fifth honing the back bevel will need some slight adjustment. Use the same technique as for the cutting edge, but keep the handle lower so that only the back bevel is in contact with the oilstone. Try and follow the original angle.

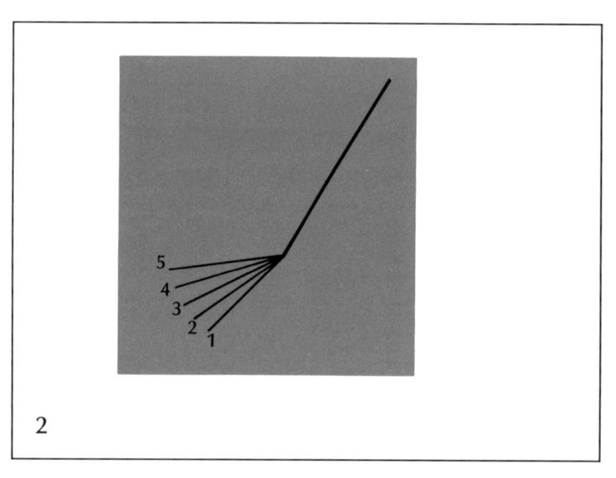

2

When making adjustments remember that the longer the bevel the thinner the steel and the weaker it will be. A useful guide is that the bevel length should never be greater than the width of the gouge blade. The bevel length is shown (a), the thickness of bevel (b) and the angle of cut (c). A short inside bevel improves the cutting quality (d).

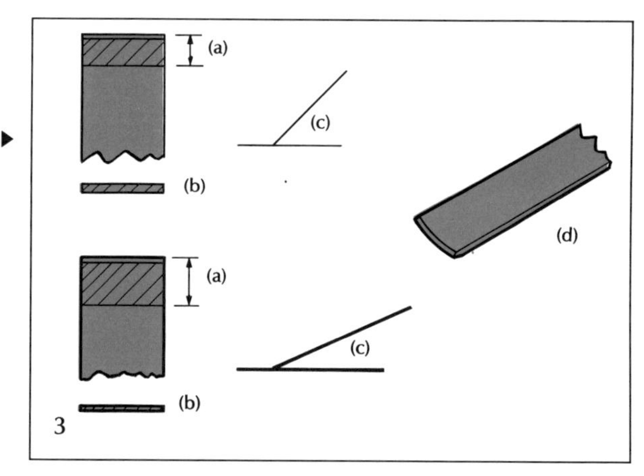

3

If the back bevel is too short and at too steep an angle it will cause the gouge to lift when cutting. The same happens when the cutting bevel and the back bevel become rounded together. The gouge will appear to be blunt, but it will be the back bevel which requires attention, not the cutting one.

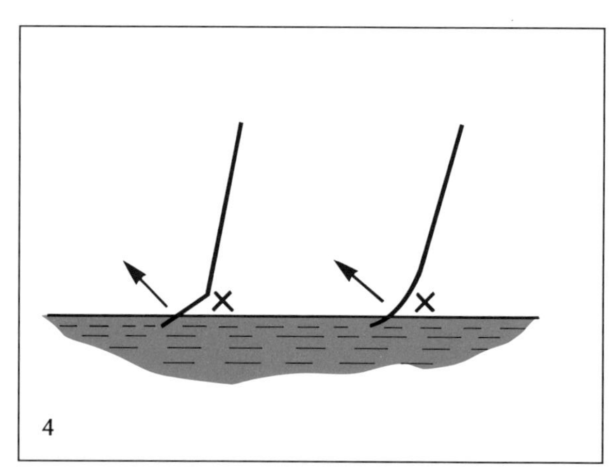
4

The cut of a gouge is curved. This means it becomes wider as it goes deeper into the wood. But to work correctly, it is important to know which part of the edge cuts first. Failure to appreciate this will certainly result in poor workmanship.

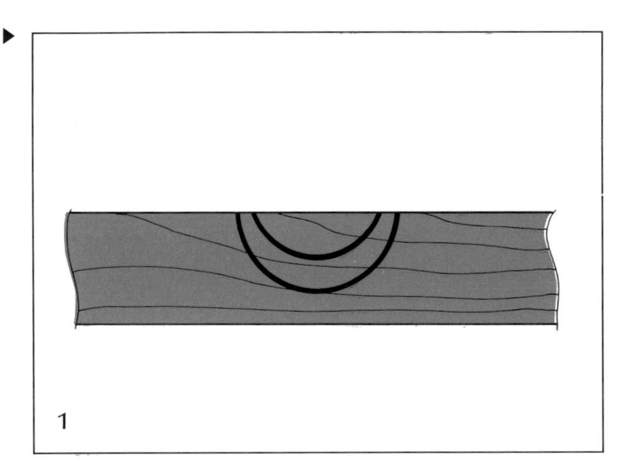

If the profile of the end of the gouge is a true vertical, or if the bottom lies away from the vertical, the gouge will cut the top layer of wood at a width greater than that being cut by the bottom of the gouge and the result will be a clean cut.

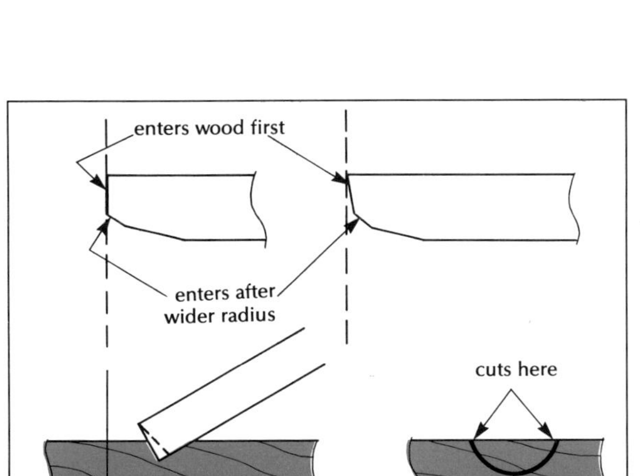

If the profile leans the other way, and the upper part of the cutting edge is back from the vertical, then the bottom of the sweep cuts first, followed by the upper and wider part. The effect will be that the wood tends to split out instead of being cut cleanly. This also applies to V-tools and veiners.

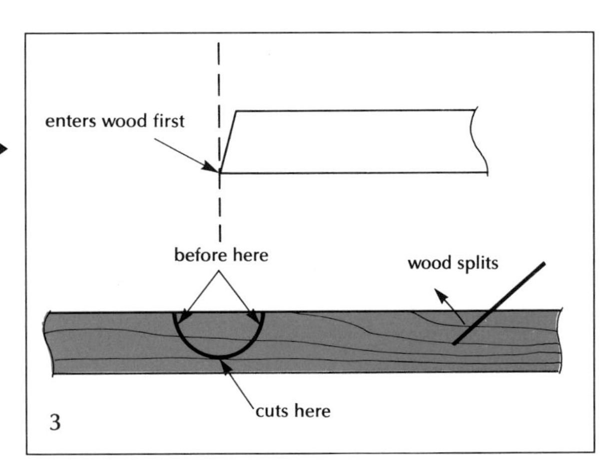

Remedial work to adjust bevels is best carried out using a coarse oilstone. Unless you are skilled at grinding, do not use a high-speed bench grinder as the friction created can easily destroy the temper of the steel. Waterbath grinders are available which do not cause the steel to overheat, but as grinding is so infrequent the cost would make one something of a luxury. Overheating when grinding will turn the steel blue/black. This indicates a change of temper and the brittle steel will snap.

Position of hands when sharpening a straight gouge.

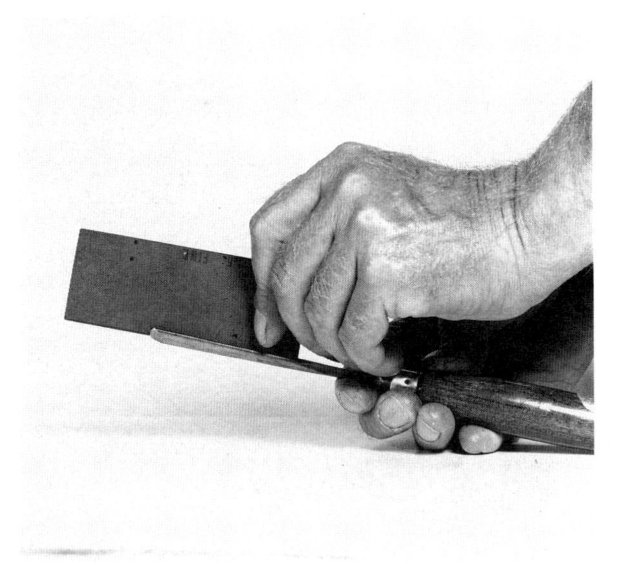

The normal way a slipstone is used.

Slipstone inclined to produce an inside bevel.

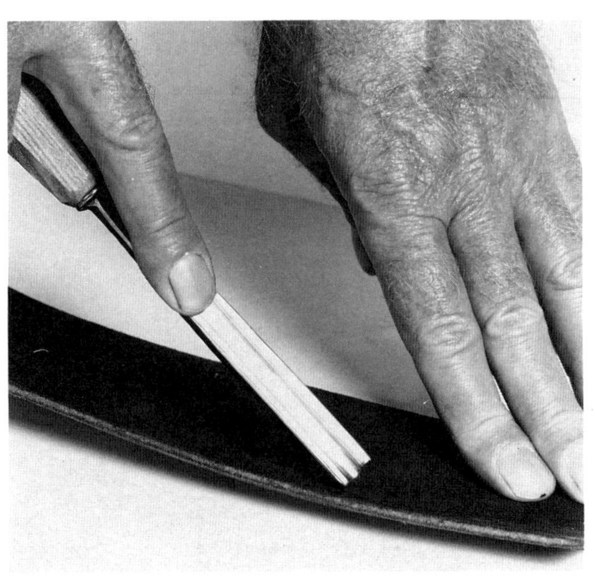

Stropping a straight gouge.

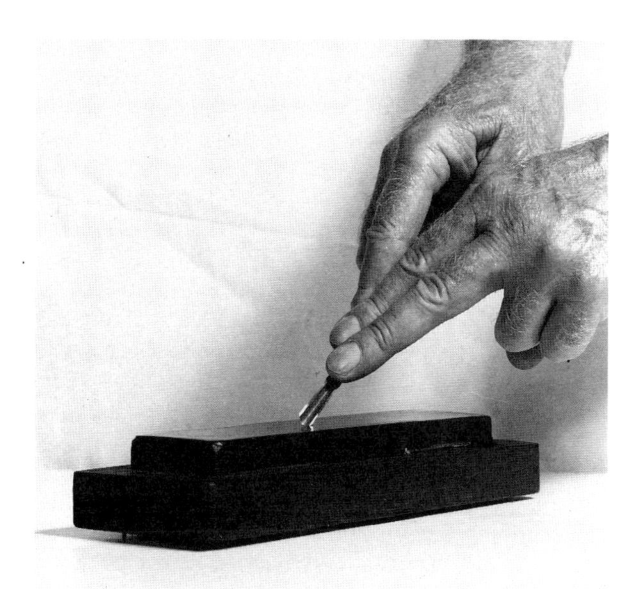

Sharpening the blades of a V-tool.

Rounding the underside of a V-tool.

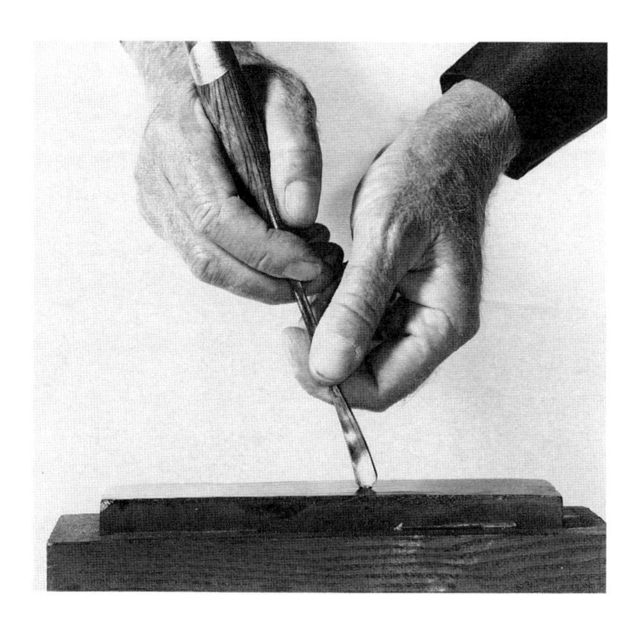

Hand position and angle for sharpening a spoon-bit gouge (front bent)

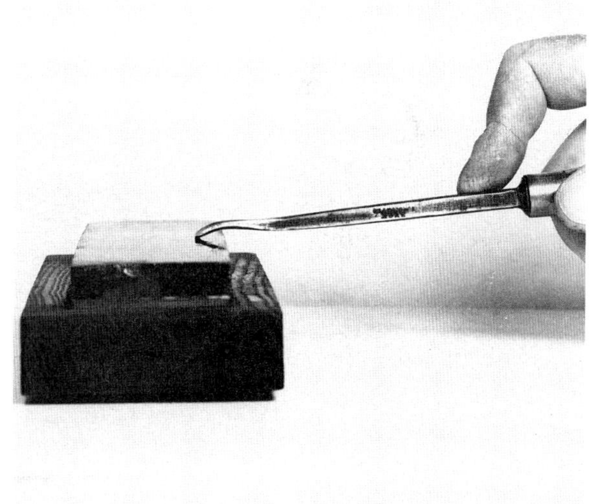

Angle for sharpening a spoon-bit gouge (back bent)

A design should be thoroughly planned. It is a mistake to rush ahead without thinking through the basic idea. Remember that woodcarving is the gradual removal of material and once the wood has been removed it cannot be put back again. When you start to carve you may find this inhibiting, but in actual fact the amount of wood which is taken off with each gouge cut is very small. The major errors occur at the design stage, or in the initial sawing of the wood.

Three-dimensional design is certainly the more difficult. A drawing for relief carving is easier to achieve, since to a great extent it is two-dimensional; the arrangement of the various levels of the relief can, if the design is fairly simple, be worked out as the carving progresses, or, better still, sectional sketches can be made. Coming to terms with a three-dimensional form can be daunting, especially if the project is ambitious.

The first requirement of three-dimensional sculpture is to reawaken your ability to think three-dimensionally. A child, starting to walk, learns that objects stick out by bumping into a chair, a table leg or a door, but in adult life we seem to think in two dimensions rather than in three.

In sculpture, the third dimension is a reality, as it is to a lesser degree in relief carving. In sculpture the object has a front, a back and two sides and, usually, each will blend into the other to create a flowing form. None of them are separate entities. That would be two-dimensional.

Early attempts at three-dimensional work frequently result in four-sided carvings in two dimensions. If you can retain the image in your mind, you are far more likely to carve it correctly. This image, though, has to be a three-dimensional picture.

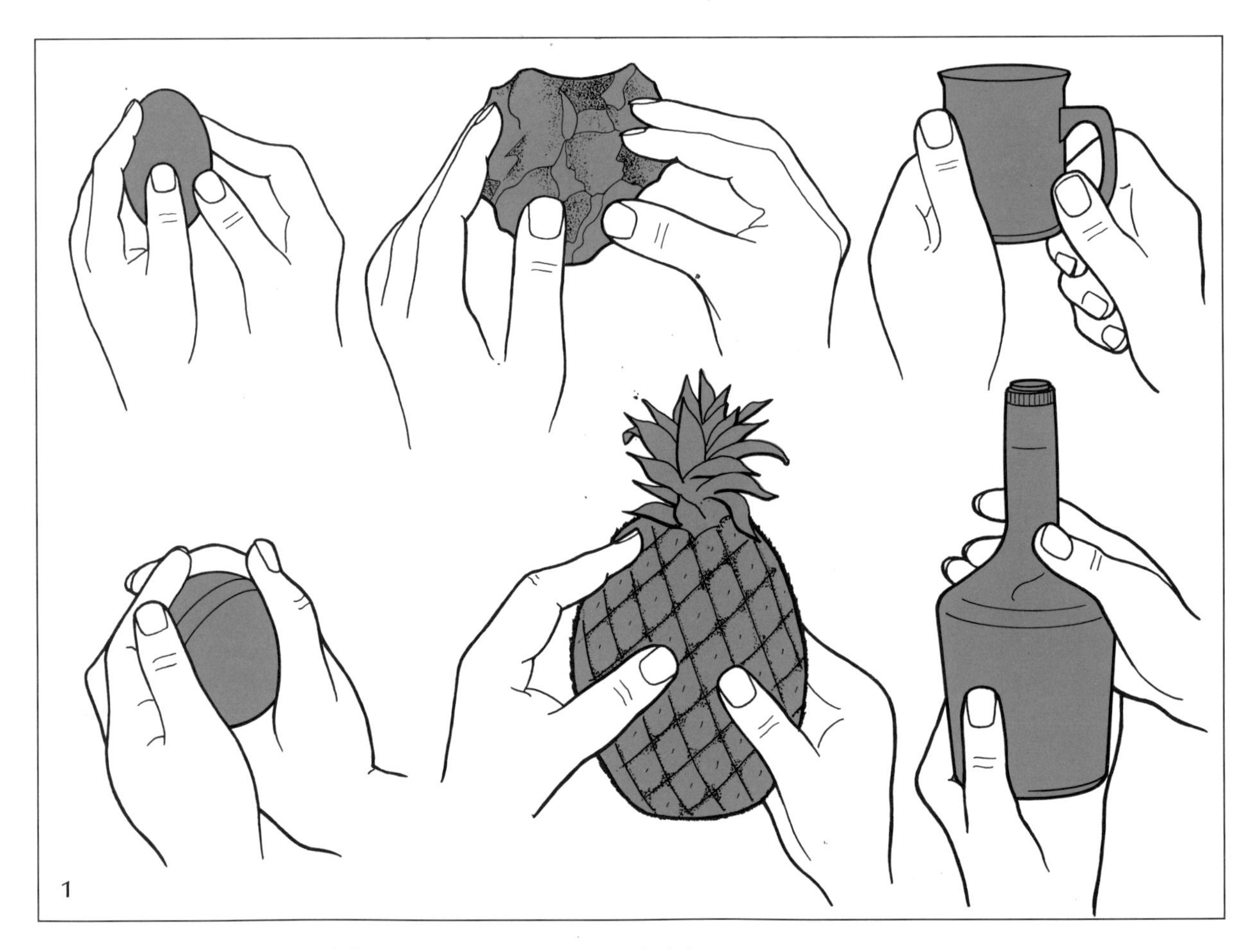

Improve your three-dimensional thinking – close your eyes and feel shapes.

Try this simple experiment. Take an egg; look at it and turn it slowly around so you view it lengthways and from its ends. Now close your eyes and visualize the egg turning, noting the way the shape changes. Then take the egg and, still with your eyes closed, feel its shape; feel the contour, how it tapers and visualize what you are feeling. This is three-dimensional thinking.

2

3

Think of the sides of a fish. Mentally view the fish from head to tail. Are the sides flat or curved? Flat sides would indicate only height and width – this is two-dimensional. Curving sides would have height, width and depth – this is three-dimensional thinking.

Think of a leaf. Is it flat with only two dimensions or does the surface undulate, dipping down on one side perhaps? If you can 'see' the shape, albeit dimly, you are thinking in three dimensions. If you are thinking in three dimensions, you will carve in three dimensions.

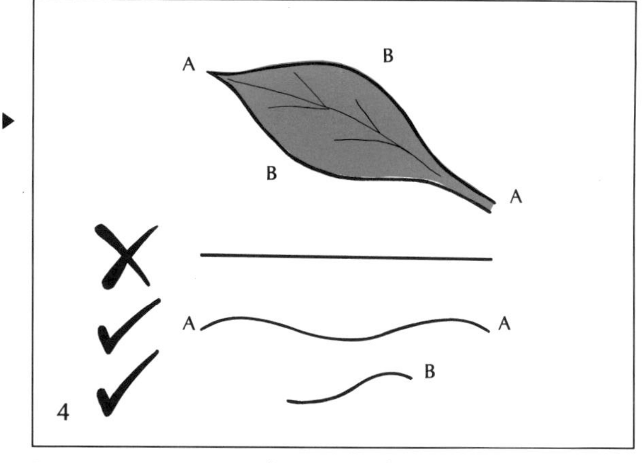

4

Perspective is a two-dimensional way of portraying the third dimension. It is an illusion of depth. Whilst it is used in relief carving it is not part of three-dimensional sculpture where depth is a reality. This needs to be borne in mind when using illustrations for inspiration or for guidance, where certain elements may be foreshortened to create perspective. Only take what you need from the subject. Avoid facsimiles. Remember the limitations of the wood. The perspective view is shown (a) and the plan view is shown (b). Remember to make allowances for perspective.

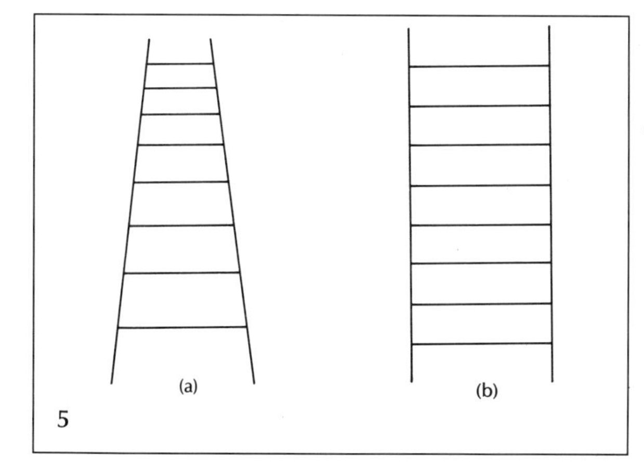

5

Most people experience difficulty in expressing their ideas on paper. The important point is that a three-dimensional carving should 'live' and not be just a static block of wood. Flow of line is therefore essential.

It is a mistake to try and reproduce every detail of the original. By applying too much detail, such as all the feathers of a bird, or all the scales of a fish, such a confusion of lines and cuts can result that the basic construction of the design is diminished. To a great extent it is far better to use a simple form, and utilize the lines of grain of the wood to advantage, rather than to over-texture. Some of the great works of sculpture have very simple lines.

Think of sculpture in wood as the simplification of a design relying to a very great extent on the natural beauty of the wood; and of woodcarving as the skilled technique of texturing and embellishment. The essential thing is to produce a carving where the surfaces (planes) relate to each other and flow together.

Copy carving is seldom a satisfactory way of starting as you will not 'see' the design with the eyes of the original artist. Further, when trying to copy a china ornament, one must remember that the medium is different. What can be done in clay may not be possible in wood, although later, you may need to make a trial model in clay to work out a design problem. These models are known as maquettes.

Initially it is best to start with a simple shape such as a small bird, an owl, or perhaps a fish or dolphin. With the help of a reference book or photographs you can judge the proportion of head to body and form some idea of the anatomy. If you can stylize the design, so much the better.

Life and movement, especially with natural forms, can be introduced by designing the shape around the letters C and S and working from a centre line. If you can write these letters you can certainly draw their shapes; stretched, upside-down or at any angle you like, to create an attractive flow of line. Look first at the centre line running through the body. Once this is fixed you can build up the outline.

Use graph paper for the final drawing and start with the profile or side view. It is always best to have the actual carving block by you so that you can check dimensions. Make sure that you have enough wood. A useful guide for calculating a cube is length (or height) multiplied by ⅔ equals width and depth. In simple terms, you should multiply the longest dimension by a factor of 0.6 in order to calculate the other two dimensions.

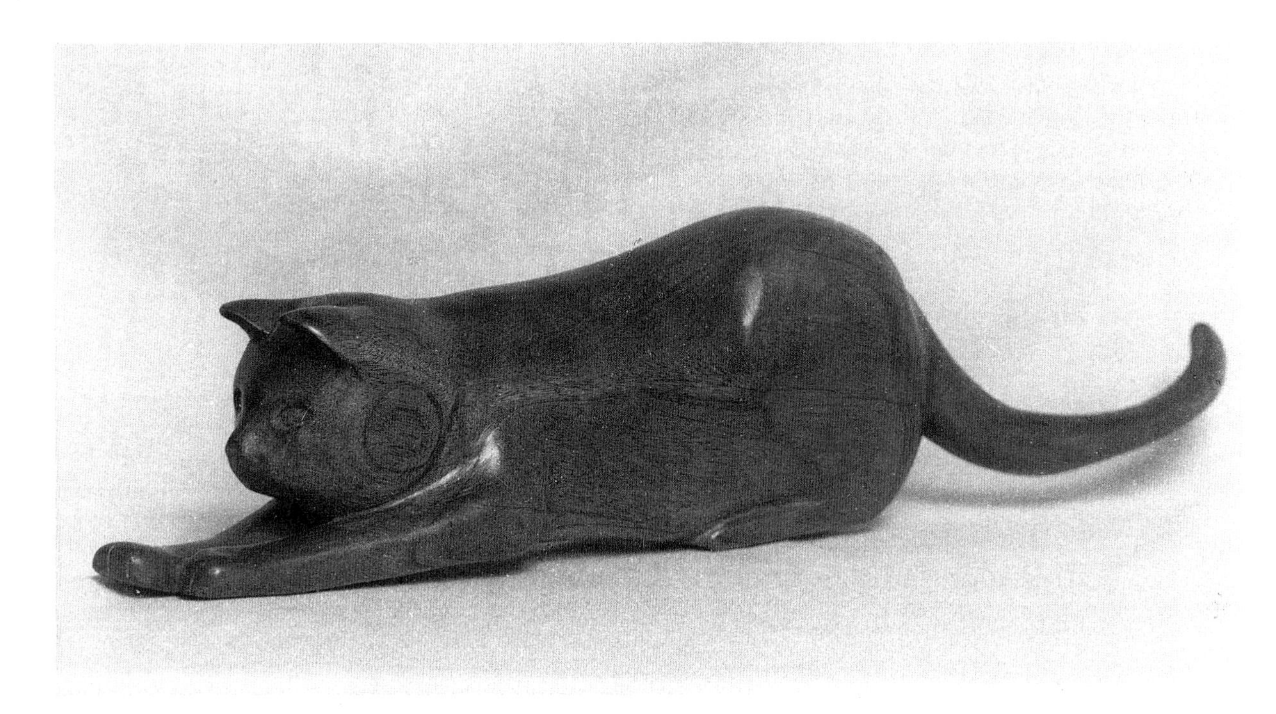

A simple carving of a hunting cat done in reclaimed mahogany. The overall length is 24in (600mm).

(Steps 1–4) Practise drawing a stretched letter 'S' lying on its side. Overdraw as necessary until satisfied. Thicken the line of your choice and erase the others. Use this line as the imaginary backbone. It will help you to compose the rest of the design. Bear in mind the need for curves to provide a sense of movement.

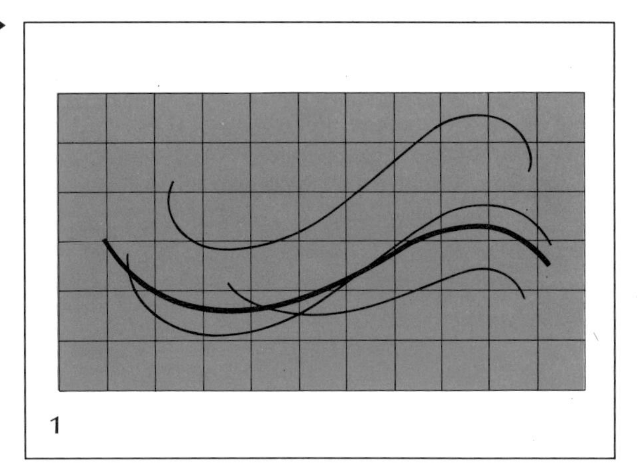

1

2

When you have a centre line with a pleasing flow add the outline using 'S' and 'C' shapes. Repeat using light lines. Thicken up the final lines. Be prepared to use artistic licence to improve the flow of line. This will bring a sense of movement to your work, but remember it should not be an excuse for shoddy work.

Now think of the plan view. Look down on the dolphin from above. Draw the centre line equal to the length of the dolphin. Sketch in half the body shape. If you have difficulty matching the other half, use tracing paper and reverse the drawing with carbon paper. (This can be done when the drawing is put onto the wood.)

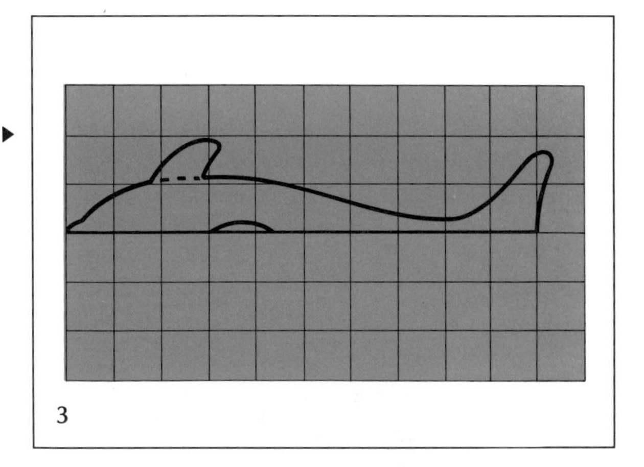

3

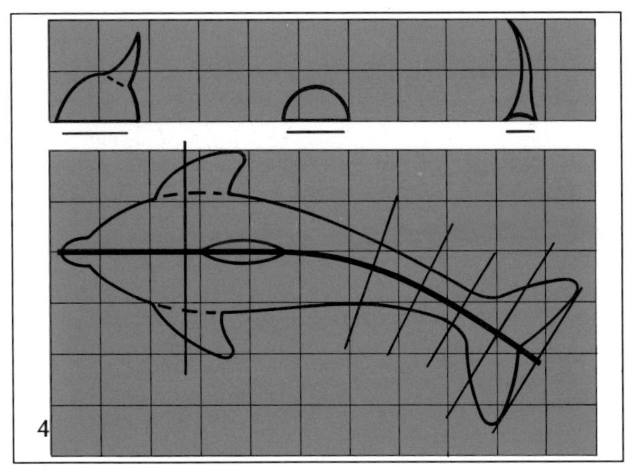

4

If the plan view shape is curved, draw in the centre line and then strike off lines at right angles. These will help to maintain the taper of the body and will keep the tail in balance, and will ensure that the fins are placed at equal points on the body. Also, use these points for sectional sketches.

(Steps 1–4) Try the same procedure to draw a small bird, such as a finch. Use the extended letter 'S' for the body centre line. Sketch circular shapes for the head and body. Note their proportion; the ratio is about 1:2.5. However, remember that it pays to work oversize, so allow plenty of wood for both the beak and for the back.

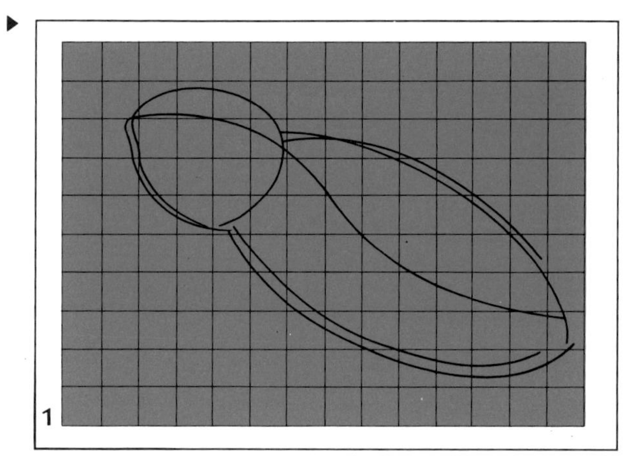

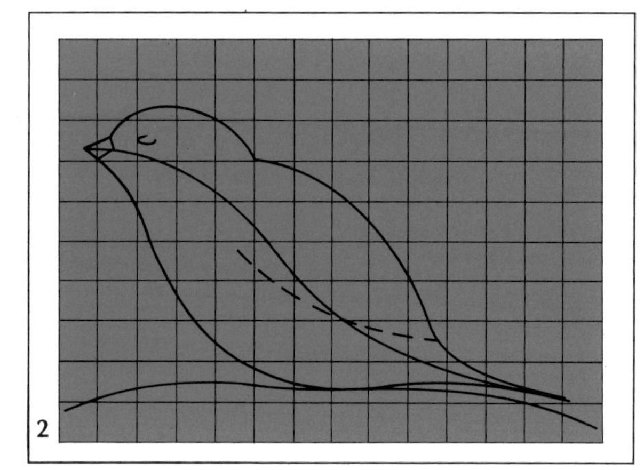

Using 'C' and 'S' shapes, sketch in the outline and firm up final lines. Omit legs and feet, which to be realistic will be difficult to carve. Detail the wing line. Do not forget that the wings curve over the back as well as lie on the sides. If you add a slight upturn to the tips it will impart life and movement.

Incorporate the design of a suitable base. Note that the height of the base plus the bird will be about two-thirds of the length. Multiply the length by 0.6 to check this. Avoid a top-heavy look. Make certain that the bird will sit level, and avoid any possibility of its slipping backwards.

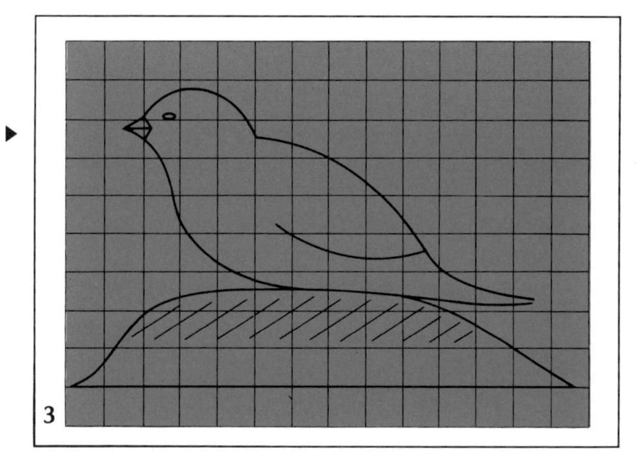

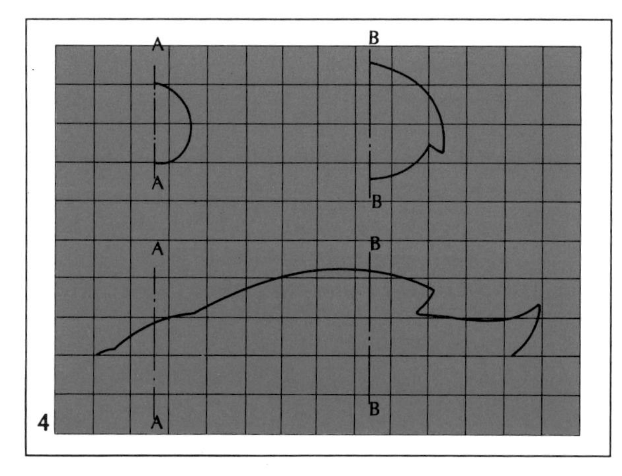

Using a straight centre line and the same scale, draw in one half or all of the plan view. Note that a portion of the wing is seen from above. It is not just on the side of the bird. Sketch sections. These will help you to build up a mental picture of what you will be setting out to achieve. They will aid three-dimensional thinking.

Proportion Make sure you have sufficient wood. For most animal and bird carvings, the sides of the block usually need to have a ratio of 1:0.6. Check the proportion of the head to the body using photographs if possible. Drawn illustrations may contain errors. Always work with a centre line. Use flowing curves wherever possible. ▶

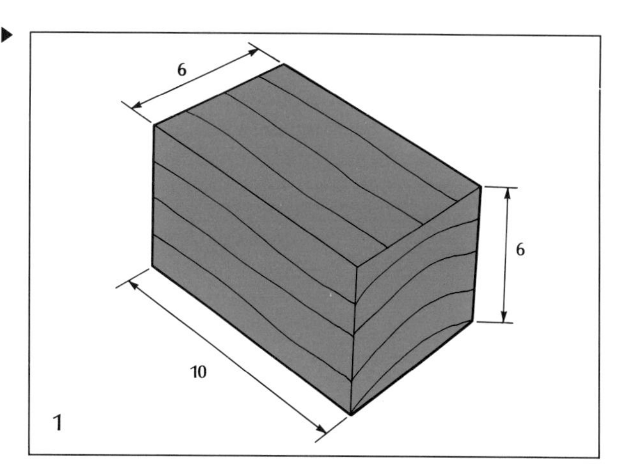

◀ **Three-dimensional Thinking** Visualize what you want to carve. Example: wings wrap around the body of a bird, not set just on the sides. Fins of a fish angle out from the body – they are not flat. Look at as many illustrations as you can during the planning stage. Then build up your own personal design.

Draw Sections Sectional drawing helps to improve three-dimensional thinking. It will help you to see the subject in your mind. It is far better to make mistakes now than when you are carving. ▶

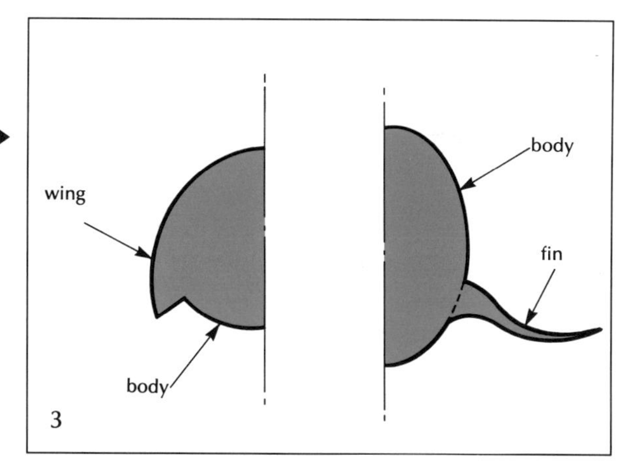

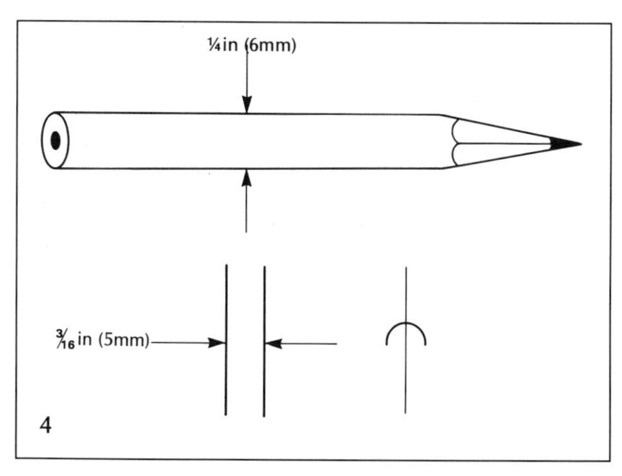

◀ All curved surfaces require more wood than appears in two-dimensional drawing. It pays to start oversize. Example: measure the width of a pencil and draw it to size. Now bend the paper and see how the size contracts. Remember the golden rule: having wood to spare is like having money in the bank.

The actual styles of relief carving are described later, the main points of design being similar in each case. Relief carving is like drawing in wood, but it has the added dimension of depth. To start with, avoid small detail because it is tricky to carve and a wide range of gouges may be needed.

1

2

The essential of all relief carving is to avoid too much plain background. For plaques, let the design determine the actual overall size of the panel. Proportion is important. Pictorial scenes will need a ratio of 1:0.6. Floral designs can be narrower.

Use squared graph paper and wherever possible draw with flowing lines, starting with the main centre line. Overdraw, then thicken up the curve you want. Keep the design simple. Too much detail can become confusing. With floral designs draw in the main stem first to give balance to the picture. Then draw the branches and/or leaves. Note that branches seldom taper. The thickness reduces at a fork. Sub-branches are then thinner.

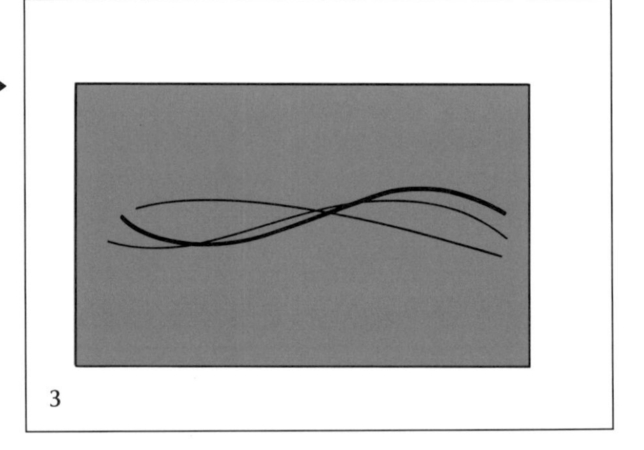

3

It is important to design the layout with some reference to the width of the gouges you will be using, otherwise small details may be difficult to finish. The tool width is critical. Also, the degree of finesse will depend greatly on the choice of timber.

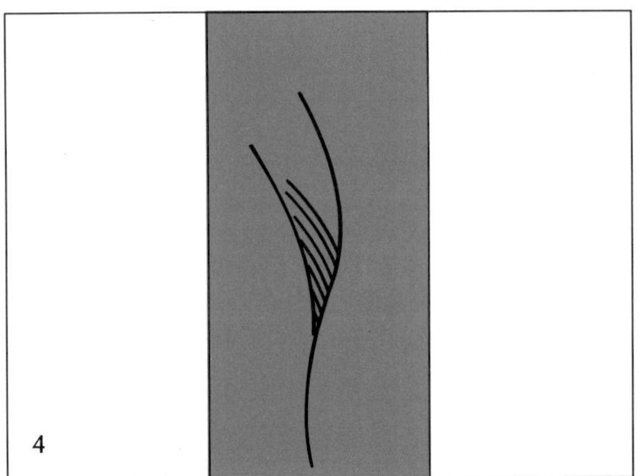

4

(Steps 1–4) Start by planning the total depth of the relief. ▶ A maximum of ½in (a) or 10mm (b) will be sufficient to achieve good contours. If the relief is too shallow, little spare wood will be available to correct errors. But if there is too great a depth, a lot of time will be spent removing the background. Also, difficulty may be experienced initially in working the lowest levels.

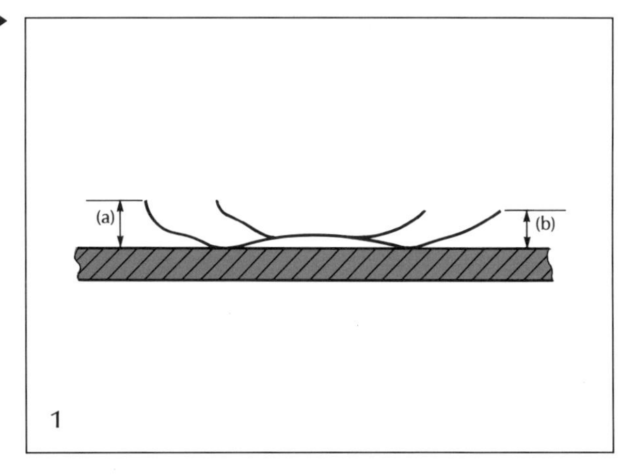

A
A
A
B
B
A
section A-A
section A-A
section B-B
2

◀ Consider the contours you will need. A relief should not be flat. In this type of carving much depends on shadows and the reflection of light. Sectional drawing will help to create undulating surfaces. With leaves and flowers two sectional views are best.

You may find it helpful to colour in the design to ▶ indicate where there is a change of level, for example, red for high spots (a), blue for mid-level areas (b), green for low areas (c).

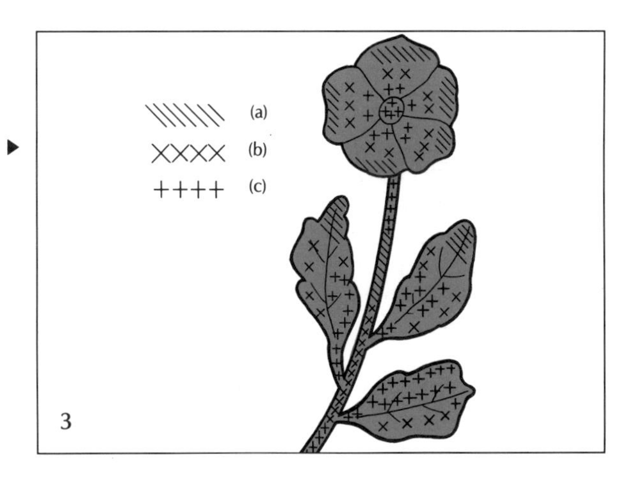

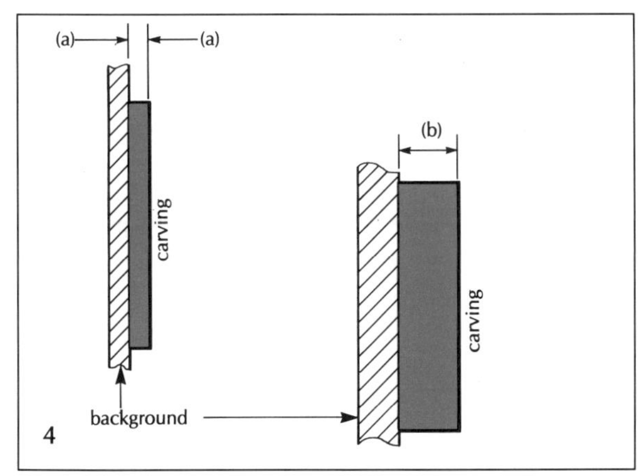

◀ Complex or repetitive patterns are best carried out in shallow relief: ¼in (5mm) maximum (a). Solitary, or single designs, are usually executed to a greater depth or high relief: ½–¾in (10–20mm) (b). When carving deeply it is essential still to retain sufficient depth to the background or an unbalanced effect will be created.

Historically, relief carving was without doubt the most widely used method of carving wood, reaching its heyday in the eighteenth and nineteenth centuries. Principally it was used in church decoration, on room panelling and on furniture. Apart from its continued use in church work and civic buildings, relief carving went into decline at the start of the twentieth century and by the post-Edwardian period it virtually ceased except for small decorative work on furniture, most of which was done by mechanical means.

There are, however, indications that a revival is beginning. Commercially produced hand-carved furniture is now available. Whilst current labour costs would prohibit the wide use of exotic carving in the style of, say, Grindling Gibbons, one hopes that interest will continue to grow.

There are in fact six variations of decorative carving, and while only two may be of immediate interest, we should take a brief look at the various styles.

All relief carving relies for its effect on the reflection of light and the creation of shadow areas. On old relief carvings it is usually possible to see that high spots were burnished and that stain was applied, to under areas of leaves for example, to increase the effect of light and shade. The effect is just as important today, even if staining is not used. To achieve this the carver must be conscious of how the light will fall on the work when it is displayed.

A traditional Scottish spinning stool built of oak. Note the low-relief detail on the back and seat.

The variations are:

Incised (a) Used mainly for chair backs and seats where a flat surface is required. Produced by cutting grooves with either a V-tool or No. 11 gouge.

Modified Incised (b) This is similar to incised but the edge of the design is rolled over with a No. 1 or No. 2 chisel to catch the light.

Pierced (c) Was used extensively for screens and cabinet fronts. Relies on the artistic design of the pierced voids. Remaining areas would be carved in relief.

Intaglio (d) Produces negative designs which are used for such items as butter moulds. Can be used to effect with low-relief carving, that is when part of the design is cut into the background.

The two most *popular* styles are:

Low Relief (e) Patterns worked to a depth of about ¼in (5mm). Mainly used for decorating furniture, also wall plaques and house signs. Ideal for repetitive designs. Also known as Bas Relief and sometimes incorrectly as base relief.

High Relief (f) Deeply carved, even to the extent of three dimensions. Should be used when the design is one main feature and not a complex pattern. Depth is usually greater than ½in (10mm) and, when incorporating three dimensions, will be much more. Spectacular effects can be achieved but it can be very time-consuming. High relief is used for perspective work.

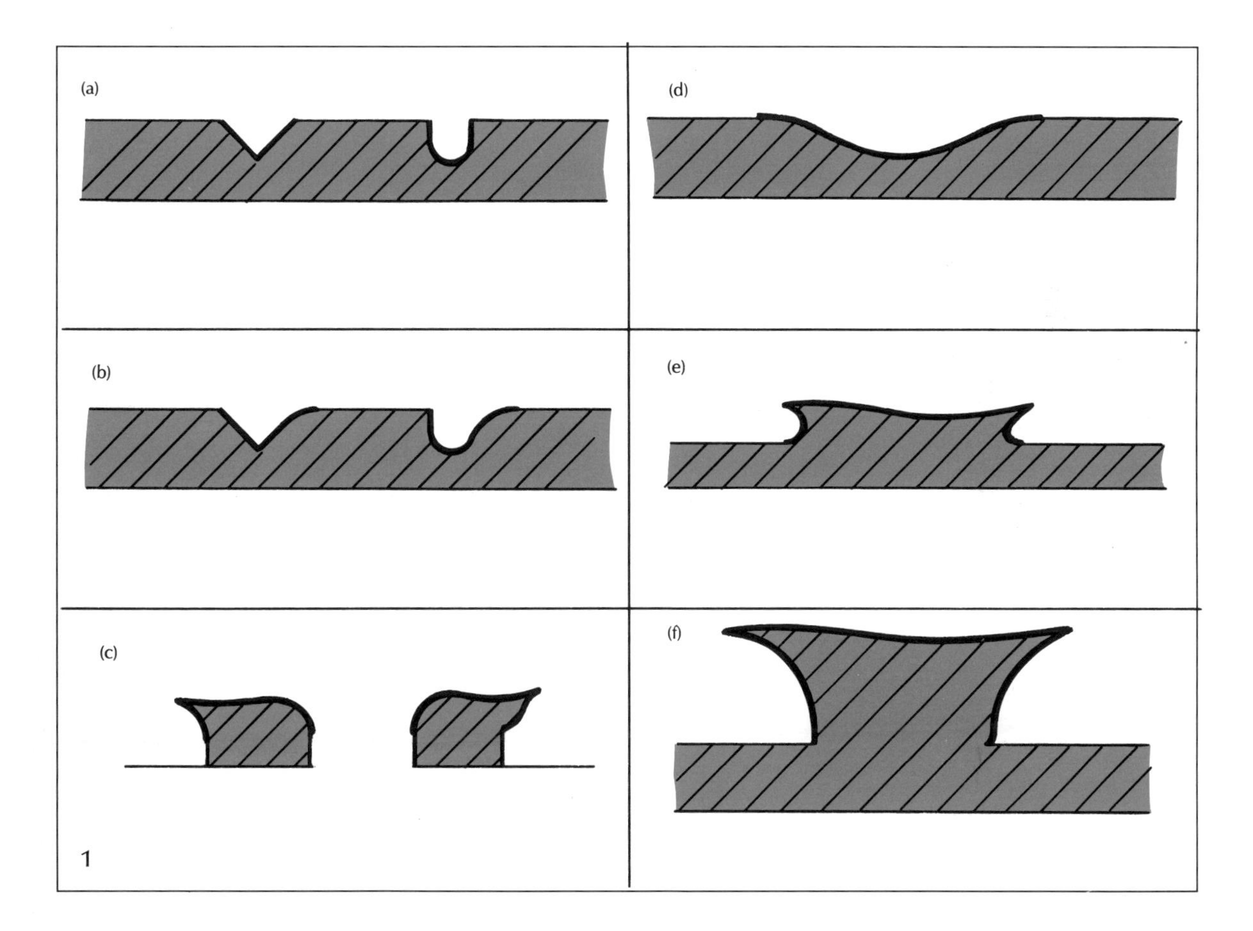

Boards for relief carving should be planed and thicknessed. A good timber supplier will do this. Check planks with a straight edge for warping or twisting (a). It is best if the carving block is prepared by having the timber planed on all sides, as this makes it much easier to put the drawing on to the wood. Make sure that the block stands vertically at 90 degrees (b), or the final carving may have a tilt.

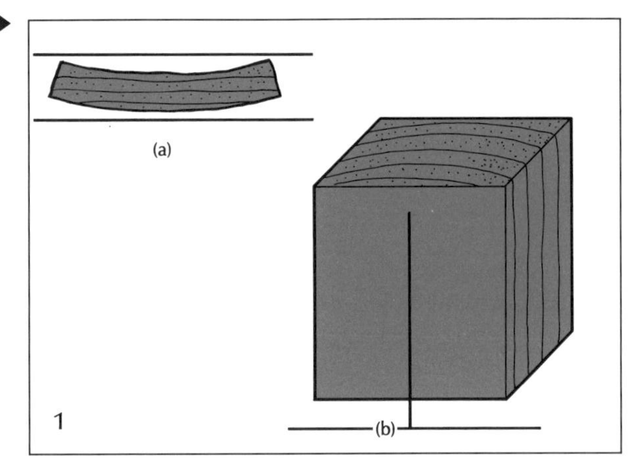

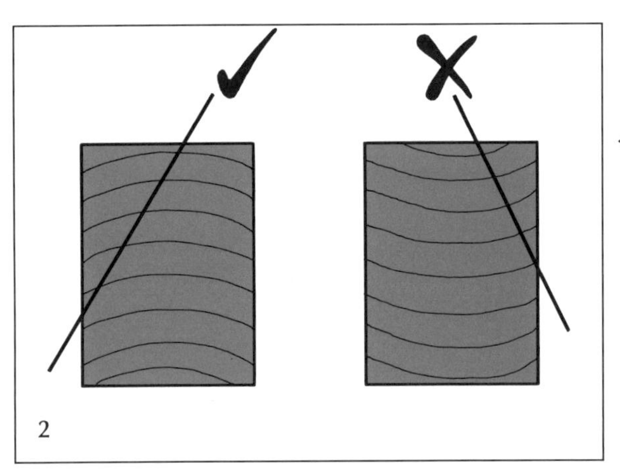

Determine which way round the wood needs to be. Relate the annual rings of the carving block to the convex curves you wish to produce. If you use the rings sympathetically the carving will look better. Bands of grain will be wider when the wood is carved with a shallow angle to the annual rings.

When cut 'through and through' into planks, the annual rings try to flatten out and this can cause the surface to cup and become concave on one side and convex on the other. If the rings face downwards (a) the opposite surface tends to cup. If this surface is used for the carving the edges at right angles to the rings may curl up. Use the surface with the rings facing upwards (b).

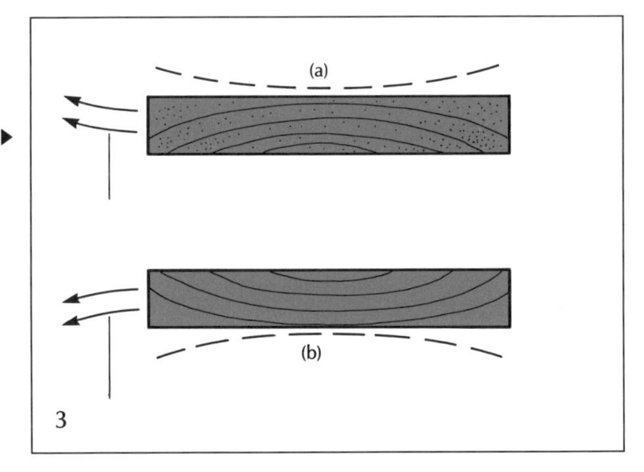

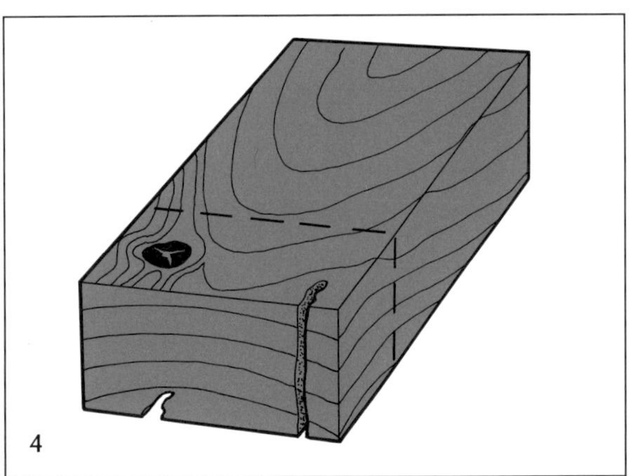

Examine the wood for flaws such as splits and knots. Wherever possible cut back beyond them. It may seem wasteful to scrap some of the wood, but in the long run it is worth it. End-grain splits may not be fully visible until the wood has been worked and, if you have not taken the precaution of trimming back at the outset, little or nothing can be done about them later.

Relief Carvings

(Steps 1–4) Always allow some waste wood at either end to facilitate clamping (a). If G-cramps are not used this will not be necessary. The waste area can be stepped below the carving level (b).

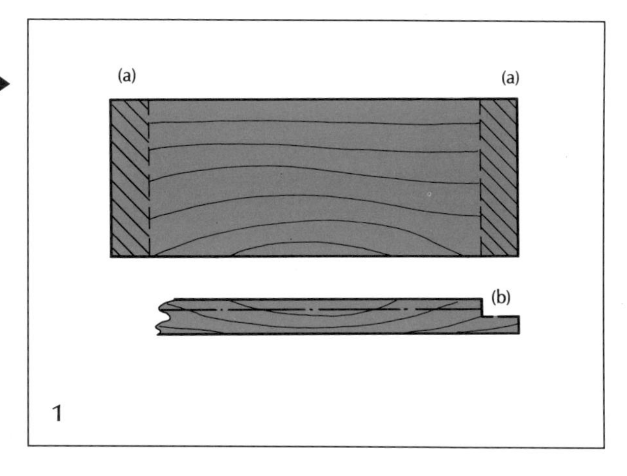

Find the mid-point (a) of both the wood and the drawing. Make location marks. Make sure you have the wood the way up that you want it. In your eagerness to start carving you can easily overlook this vital point.

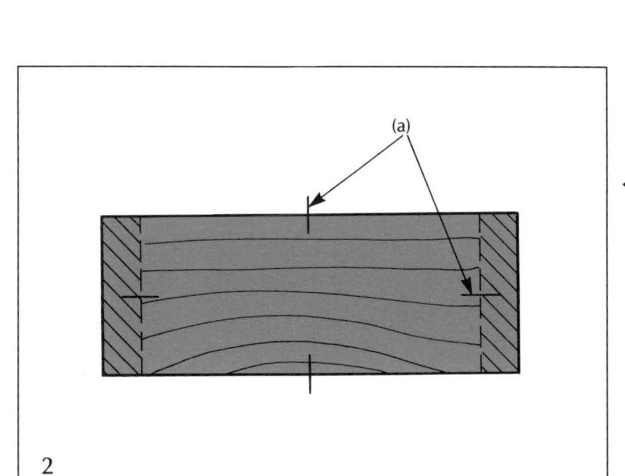

Using masking tape on one edge to hold it down (a), position the drawing (b) and a sheet of carbon paper (c) on the wood (d). Check that the location points line up. Use pencil grade of carbon paper to obtain the imprint. Use a ballpoint pen to obtain a sharp imprint.

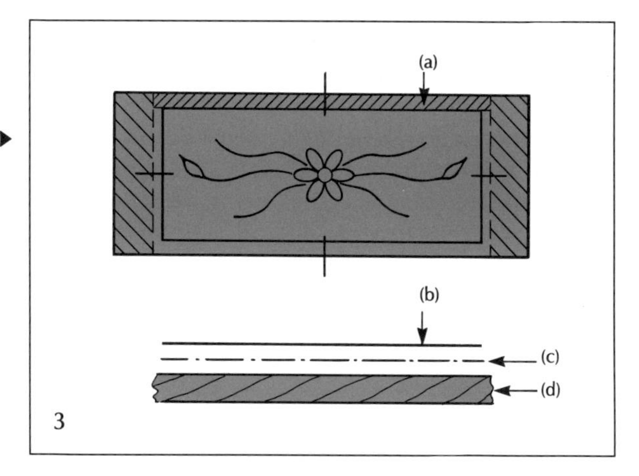

If it is not possible to use carbon paper the drawing can be 'pounced'. To do this, perforate the lines of the design. Fine powder or charcoal dust can then be rubbed into the paper and through the holes, imprinting on to the wood. The same effect can be achieved by dotting the holes with a felt-tip pen.

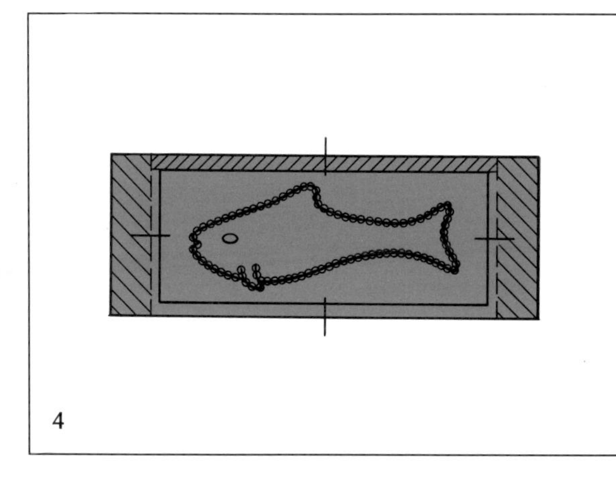

Sculpture

(Steps 1–8) The main drawing is usually the profile (a) (side-on) view, but with certain designs such as upright figures, both animal and human, a frontal view (b) may be better. The initial sketching should guide you.

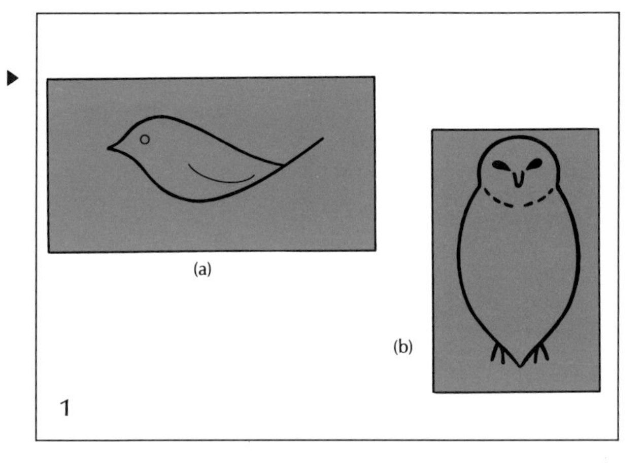

2

Check the block for faults and decide which way round it needs to be. For example, a bird carving will require the bands of grain along the back. Therefore the annual rings will need to be convex and at right angles to its length.

Be sure that sufficient wood has been allowed for the base and for holding in the vice if this is necessary. It is a common fault to find, as the carving progresses, that there is not enough wood left to create an attractive base.

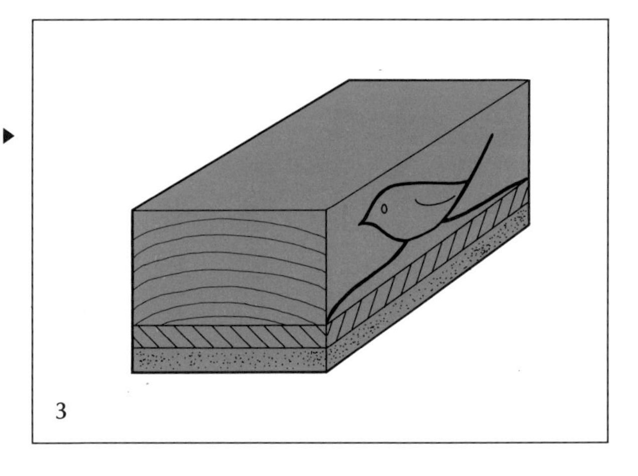

When using a carpenter's vice with a gape less than the width of the wood the end of the block can be reduced in area (a). If it is octagonal in shape the block can be turned round whilst carving (b). A false base can be screwed and glued in place, but it is less satisfactory.

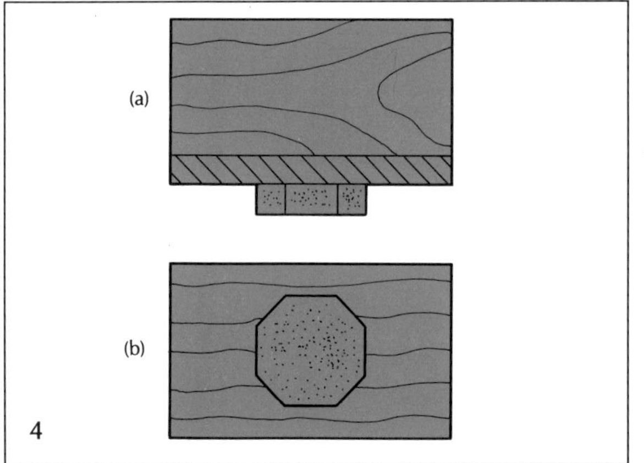

Drawings will need a clearly marked centre line. The wood will also need a centre line (a). It is a lot easier if the block has been prepared and trued-up in the first place. With irregular pieces, make quite certain there will be enough wood all round to produce the carving.

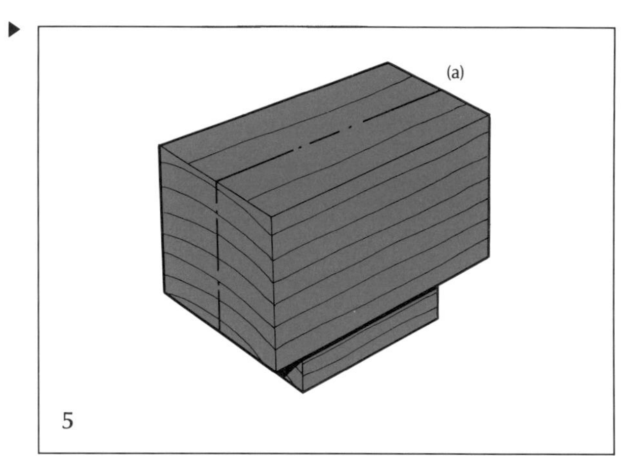

5

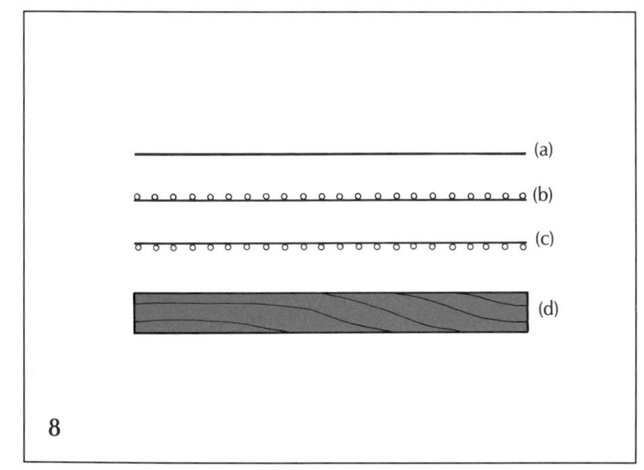

6

The drawing and the carving block will need locating marks. These should be drawn in ½in (10mm) from the corners and in each direction. Make sure that those on the wood line up with those on the drawing.

Position the drawing on the wood and secure with masking tape (a) on one edge. It is easy to make a mistake at this stage so check that the drawing is correctly located. It should line up at the locating marks and at the centre line.

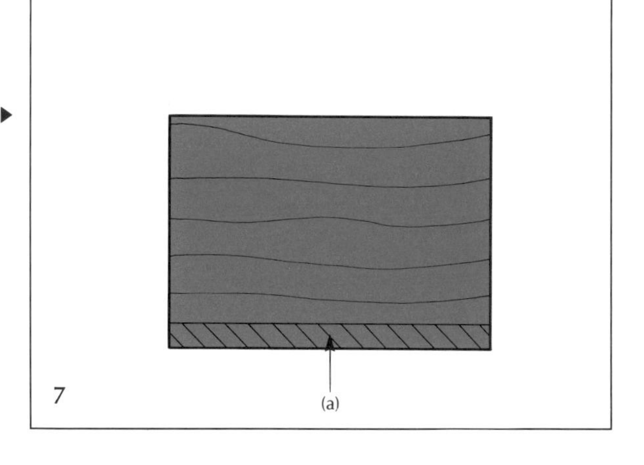

7

(a)
(b)
(c)
(d)

8

Note that two sheets of pencil grade carbon paper are required. Beneath the drawing (a) the first sheet (b) is inverted so that a carbon imprint comes out on the back of the paper. The second sheet (c) provides the imprint on to the wood surface (d). In order to cut the wood accurately a second imprint is required on the opposite side and this is done with the reverse (carbon copy) of the drawing. When making the second imprint, it is essential to make sure that the alignment is correct.

All carving can be reduced to three basic shapes:
1. Flat – produced with a No. 1 chisel (a),
2. Concave – produced with gouges Nos 3–11 (b),
3. Convex – produced by using a gouge upside-down (c).

Used in varying combination of cuts, and with the tools at various angles, virtually any shape can be made.

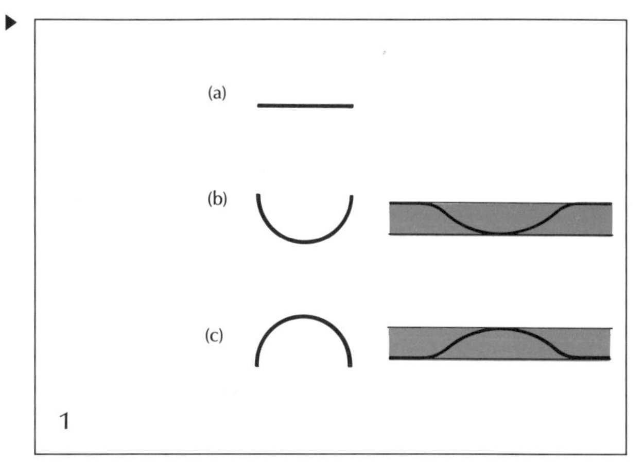

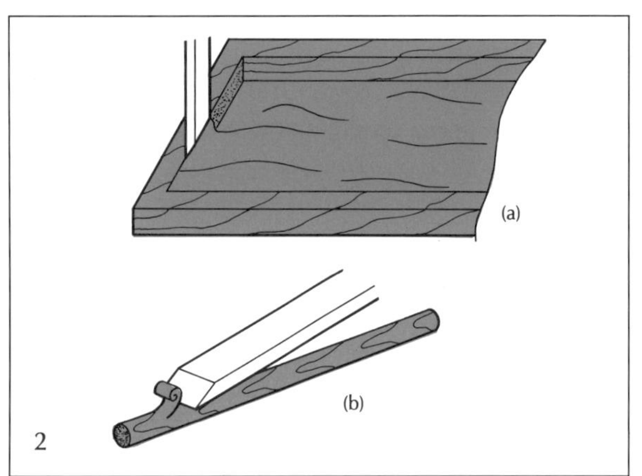

No. 1 and No. 2 chisels are used for cutting down into the wood (a) (border edges in relief carving) and for small detail requiring the use of a flat tool. They can also be used for shaving wood (b).

A No. 3 gouge, inverted, will cut shapes with a radial curve or dome (a). Examples are the head of a bird, nuts and berries. When used normally the cuts will be slightly dished. On a flat surface these will produce an attractive tooled effect (b).

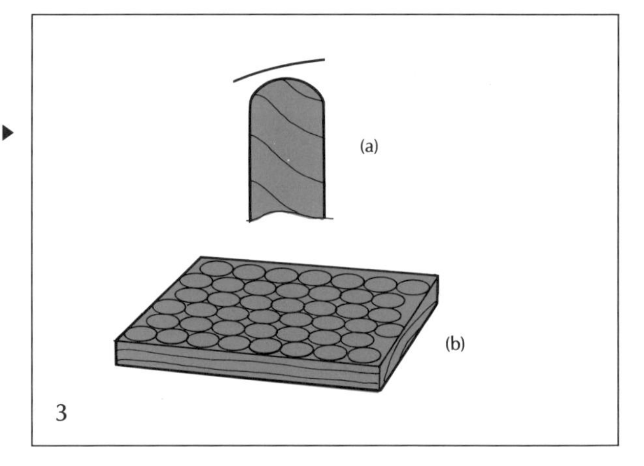

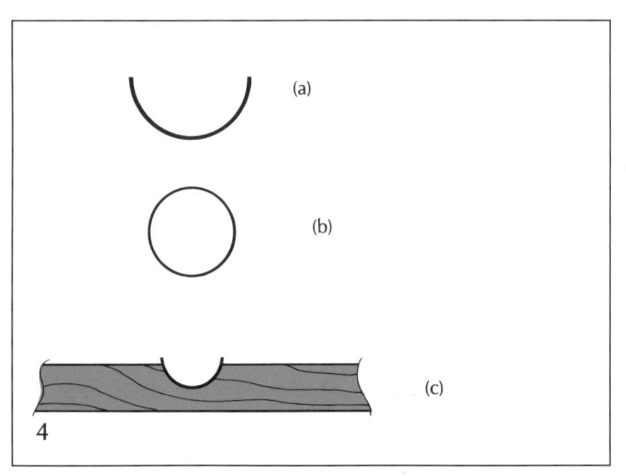

Concave shapes are cut with the higher-numbered gouges. Note that the No. 9 gouge is semicircular (a) and rings can be formed with this tool such as the outline of eyes (b). This gouge will cut deeply and quickly remove waste wood (c).

With any gouge the depth of cut should be no more than about two-thirds of the sweep. If a gouge is allowed to cut so deeply that the side walls become buried they will act like wedges and the wood will be split out not cut out (a). There is also the danger, if too deep a cut is made, that the gouge will become embedded in the wood and maybe snap. V-tools and veiners can break easily, if driven in too deeply.

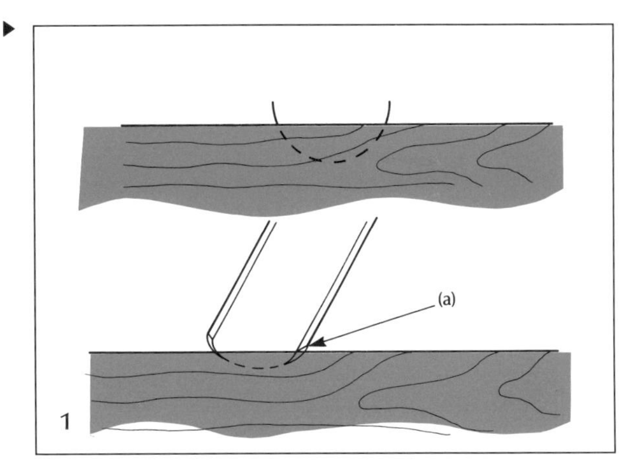

All cuts should be made at a constant angle. Do not start a cut then lower the handle as this will cause the wood to split out (a). It is always better to make a series of shallow cuts than a deep one.

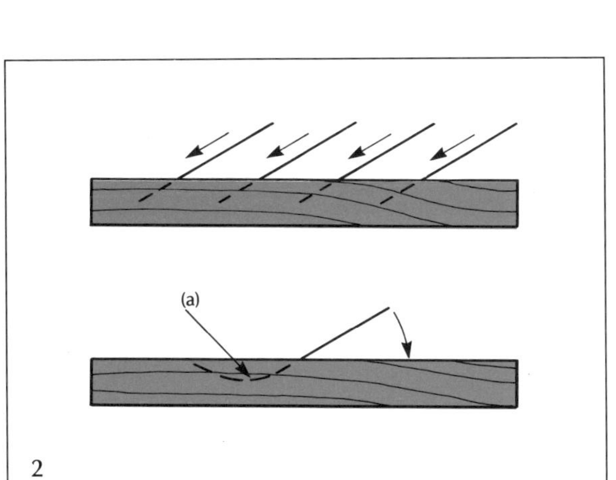

Cut slightly on the diagonal to the line of grain. This will give a cleaner surface with less chance of splits running ahead of the cut. If you cut in-line to grain the wood may split (a).

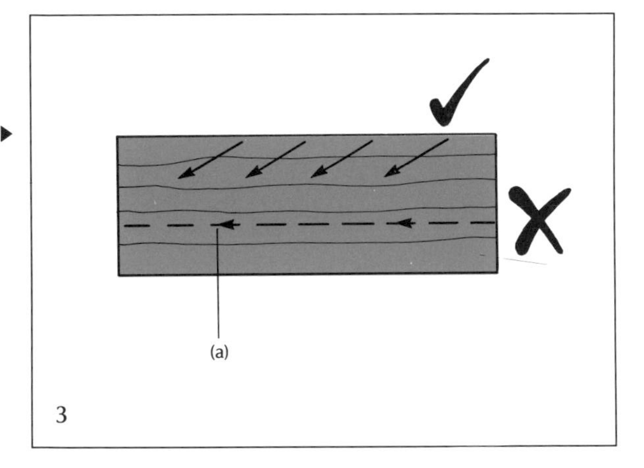

Take off edges by cutting in towards the block, not away from it. If you cut away from the edge, the last part of the wood has nothing to support it against the force of the cut, and it will split off. Only use minimum force when working along the edge to avoid fracturing the wood.

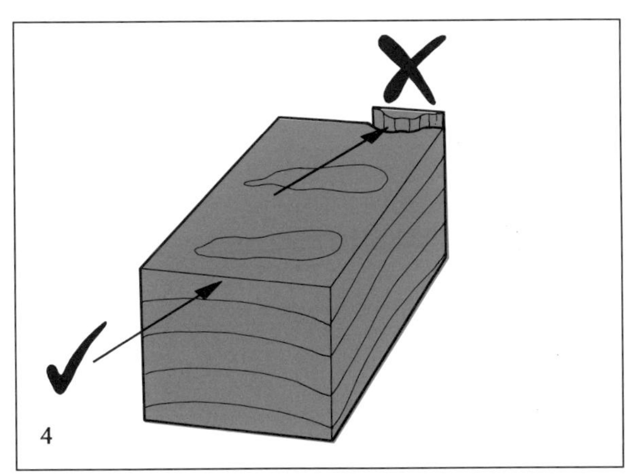

CUTTING WITH A GOUGE

Wood lies in layers and will always cut more cleanly in one direction. This will be seen in the cuts, which are shiny one way and dull the other. Change direction to suit the lie of the grain. This applies to all woods, but especially those with interlocked grain. Remember that cutting against the lie of the grain produces a rough cut (a), cutting with it produces a smooth cut (b). Therefore always cut with the grain and not against it.

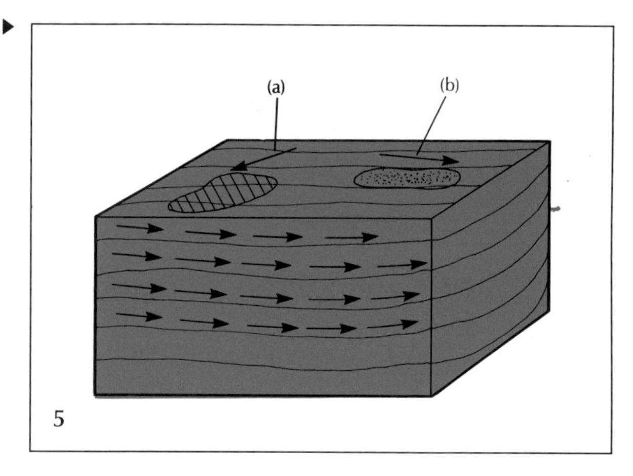

5

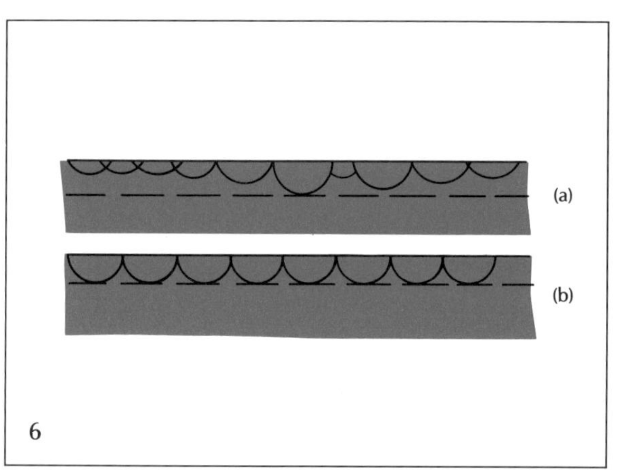

6

Try to cut to a constant depth. This will save time when you get to the finishing stage. Remember that the deepest cut you make will become the datum line (a) and that all the surrounding wood will have to be finished to that level (b) otherwise there will be hollows in the surface.

Always cut in a downhill direction on any curved surface. If you try and go uphill the gouge will catch the grain and cause a split (a). Keep the gouge edge in contact with the wood by raising the handle to compensate for the curve.

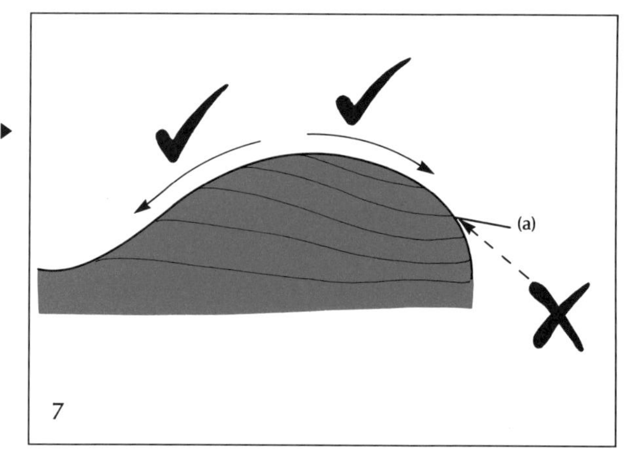

7

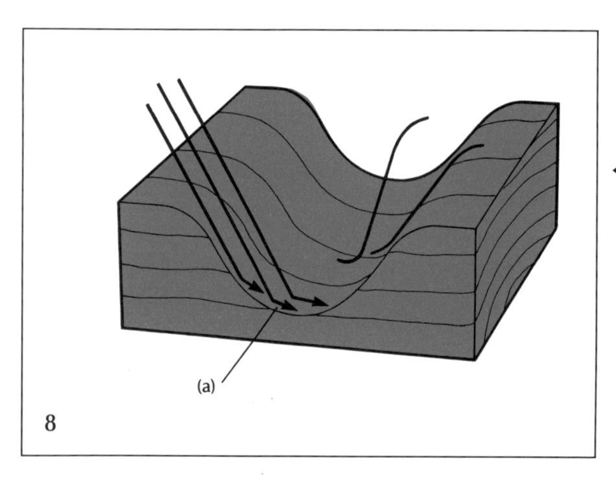

8

It is difficult to cut a steep recess or hollow with a straight gouge, as the angle will be too acute; the gouge will jump over the concave surface. This is known as bottoming out (a). Use a curved gouge (Nos 12–20) or a spoon-bit gouge (Nos 24–32) for these areas. Often a twisting, scooping action will be needed. This can be achieved by rotating the gouge handle.

A curve drawn on wood will have basically two types of angles relative to the line of grain. In one area it will have a shallow or obtuse angle, under 45 degrees (a), in other parts it will be acute or steeper (b). Note that the position of these angles changes depending on the direction in which you follow the line of the curve, that is from the right or from the left.

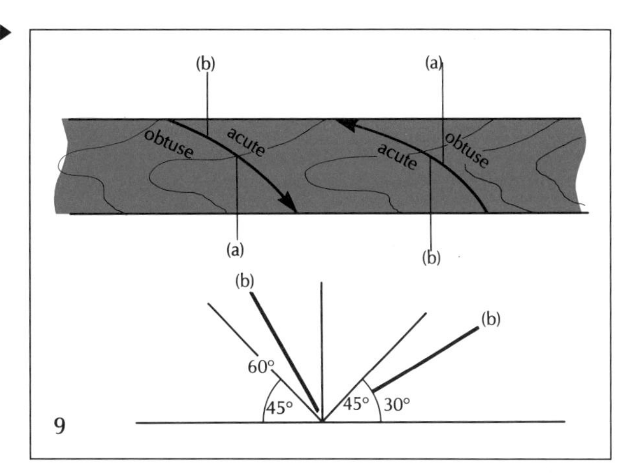

To achieve a clean cut one must pay attention to the angle of the blade of the gouge relative to the line of the grain. The steep angle – acute – should always be in the waste wood.

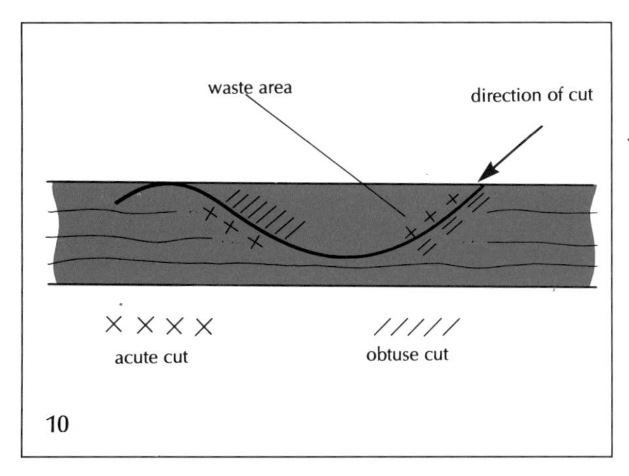

The acute angle cuts against the line of the fibres of the grain leaving a rough surface. Look at the surface of the cuts as you make them. If they are smooth you are cutting in the right direction; if rough, try cutting the other way. Attention to this detail is particularly important in relief carving.

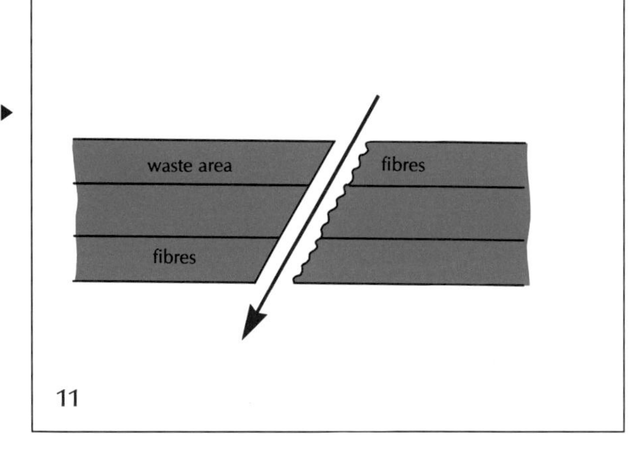

If the wood has been cut in the wrong direction the fibres of the wood will have been distressed and will tend to break off. When incising a line with a V-tool or veiner it is sometimes necessary to make the cut in both directions, tilting the gouge slightly against the shallow angle.

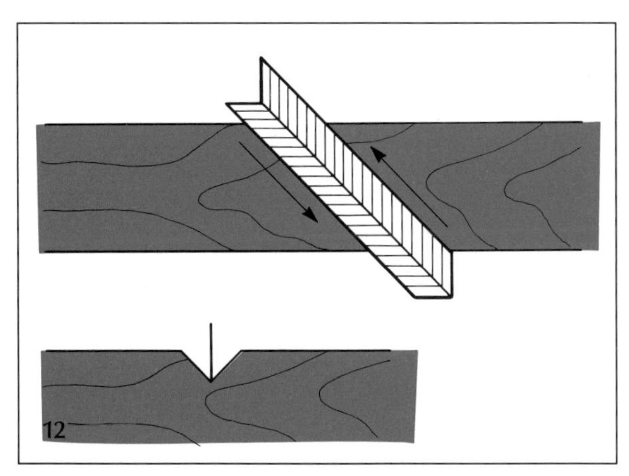

If you are a beginner try a simple relief carving first, then move on to three-dimensional work.

(Steps 1–16) As very shallow relief carving has little or no margin of error, start with a design permitting a depth of about ½in (10mm). Use a close-grained wood which is not too hard, such as lime. Have it planed and thicknessed to ¾in (20mm). Ends can be stepped for clamping (a). The length and width depends on your choice of design. If you follow the example on page 74, you will need a piece 12 × 4 × ¾in (300 × 100 × 20mm). Check the end-grain to determine the working surface (b).

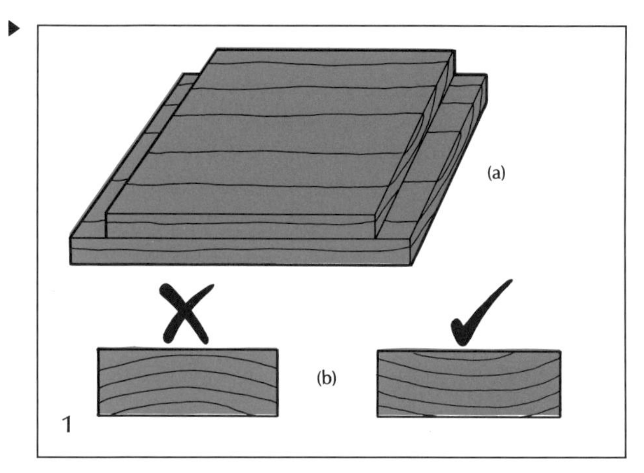

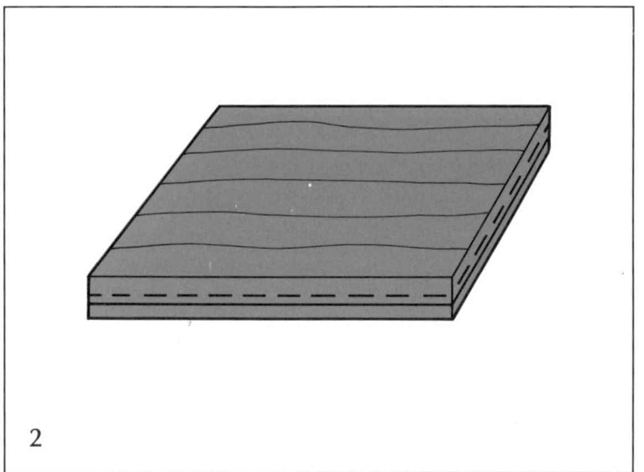

Decide on the depth of the carving. This should be about ½in (10mm). Mark a line at this level below the working surface on all the edges. This is the final level of the carving. Dot in a second line slightly above the first line. All carving is initially carried out to this depth, which permits a margin of error and also ensures that no downward cuts penetrate the final background.

Use carbon paper to put the design on to the wood. Avoid having a border which would make it difficult to check the background depth. It is easier on first carving to remove all waste (a). But, if preferred, the background can be dished and not taken to the edge (b).

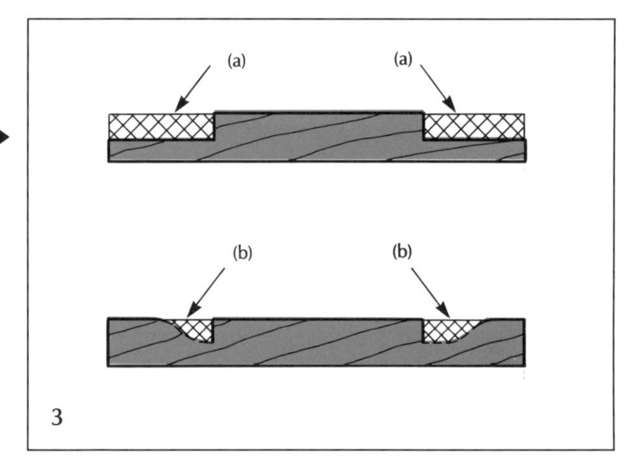

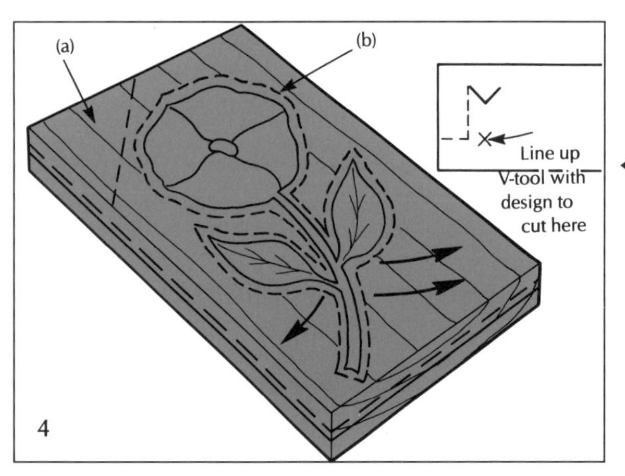

Large areas of waste wood can be sawn off, but take care not to cut deeper than the dotted line (a). Use the V-tool to cut round the design, working in the waste wood about ⅛in (3mm) from the line of the design (b). Cut to a depth of about ⅛in (3mm). Delicate areas can be left in block form, while you work around the main area. Remove the waste wood using the ¼in (6mm) No. 9 gouge, or No. 11 veiner, working away from the design across the grain and down to the depth of the dotted line.

Set in to the design with vertical stop-cuts using a gouge having a sweep similar to the design. Note: convex curves can be cut with a No. 1 chisel, and concave curves can be made with a gouge having a greater sweep than the actual curve. Always cut cross-grain areas first. This prevents the wood splitting at the sides of the gouge, which would happen if you cut in line with the grain.

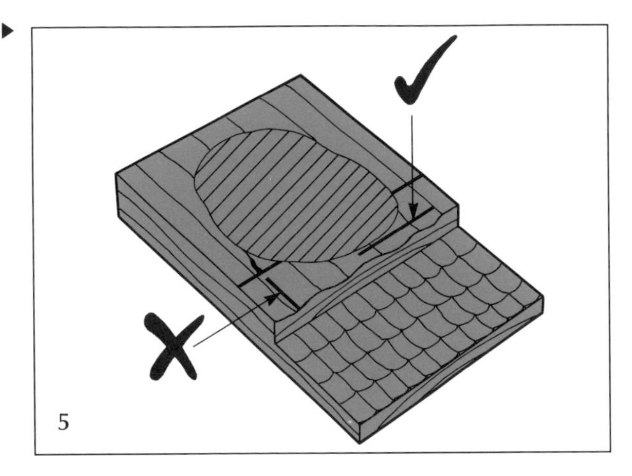
5

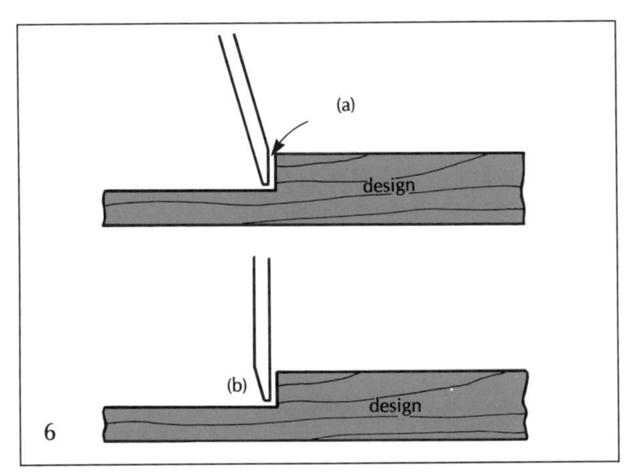

6

When using a gouge with the bevel towards the design lean the gouge outwards slightly, so that the bevel is vertical (a), otherwise, as the cut is made into the wood, it will slope away from the design. Keep the gouge vertical when the bevel is facing outwards (b).

To obtain accurate downward cuts hold the gouge low down the shaft, using the first two fingers and thumb. If held by the handle it is more difficult to be accurate. Sloping sides to the cuts can inadvertently be made, which will result in possible reduction of the design area later on.

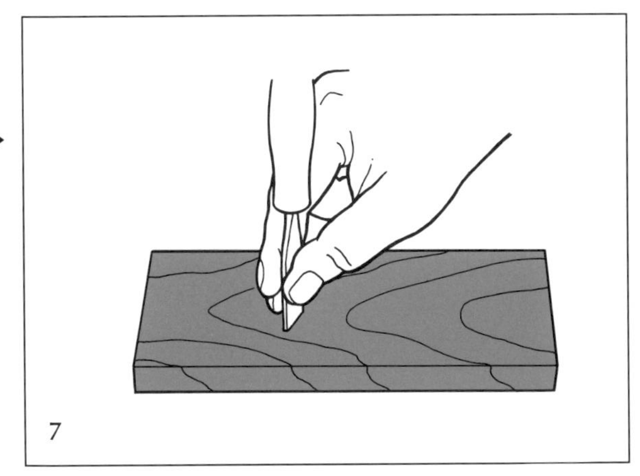
7

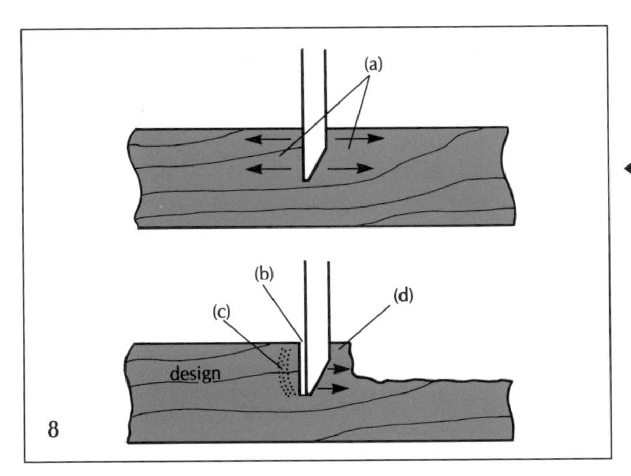

8

When the gouge enters the wood vertically it acts like a wedge and the fibres are displaced on either side (a). These tend to fracture when the gouge is removed. This is prevented by starting the stop-cuts in the waste wood and working back to the final line (b). This way there is no pressure on the design and the fibres remain undamaged (c). On subsequent stop-cuts the pressure of the tool is directed into the waste area only (d) leaving a clean cut on the design side. Always start stop-cuts in the waste wood.

When cutting convex curves, use a flatter gouge or chisel and pare back to shape. Flat cuts can be made with a No. 1 chisel (a) whilst a No. 3 gouge can be used for curving cuts (b). When cutting concave curves use the correct sweep, or one more curved, and pare back (c).

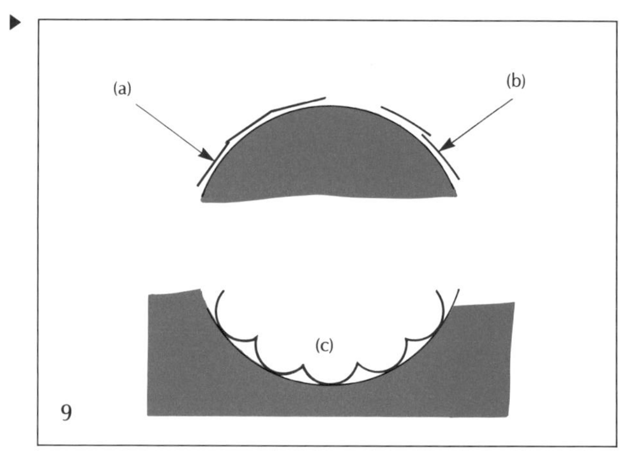

9

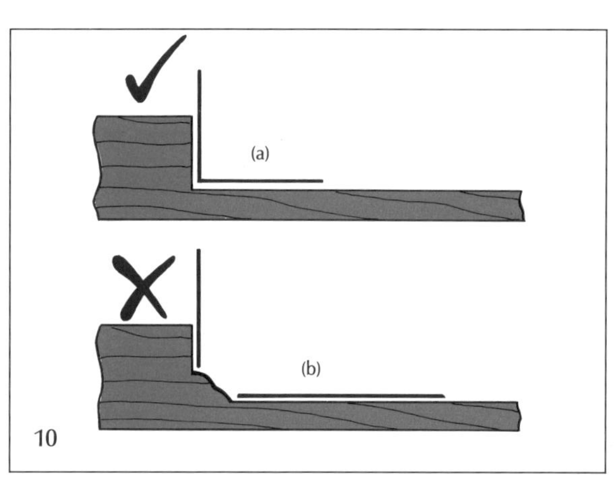

10

Always make stop-cuts to a uniform depth. The waste wood will come out cleaner. Avoid breaking out the wood on the slicing cut. Sharp tools used at the correct depth will cut cleanly (a). The more accurate the cutting, the better the finish will be. Badly sharpened tools and inconsistent cutting will break out the wood (b). When using a mallet, note the sound of the impact blows. This will help you judge the depth of cut.

Ensure that the background is kept as level as possible. Groundwork is best carried out with cuts diagonal (a) or at right angles to the grain (b). If you cut to the edge of the wood it will usually break off as there is nothing to support the pressure of the cut (c). Work in from the edges (d).

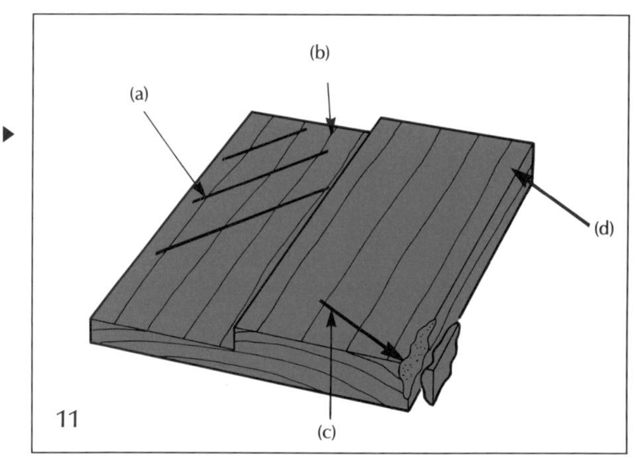

11

Test the level of the background by touch. Note, it usually tends to rise up near to the design. A piece of plywood with a hole drilled at one end to take a pencil makes a useful depth gauge. Slight variations in level will be taken care of when the final groundwork is carried out.

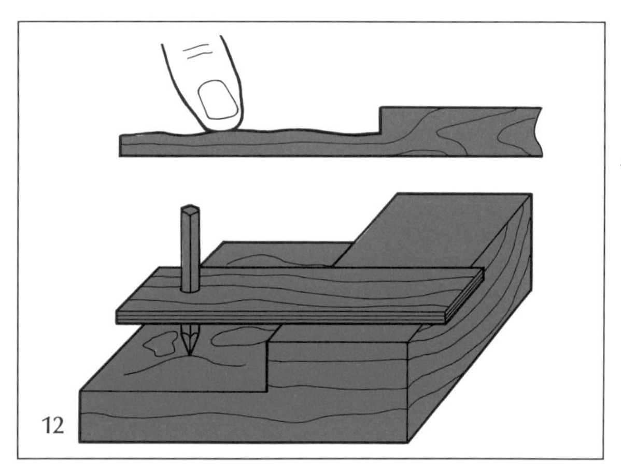

12

Reflection of light and shadow areas (a) are very important in relief carving. Periodically test the effect you are creating by standing the panel upright with some side lighting (b). Remember there will be more reflection when the carving is polished. The more the surface area of the design undulates, the better the effect will be.

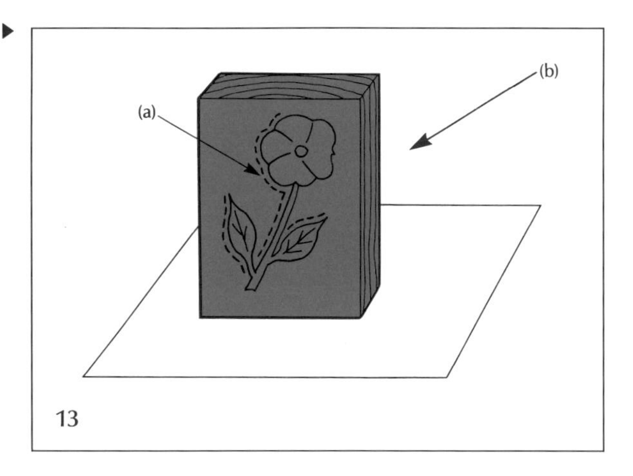

13

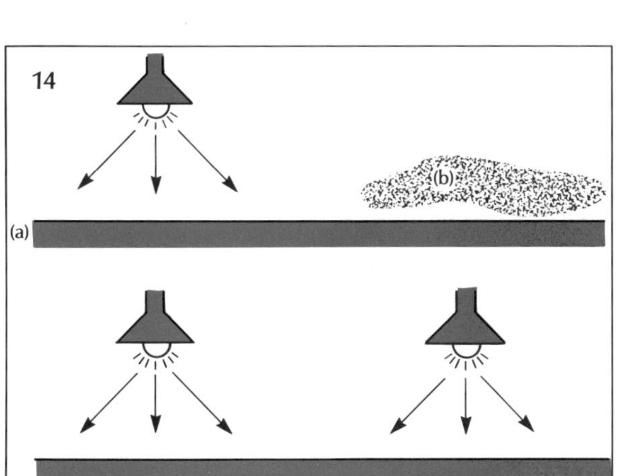

14

Good workshop lighting is essential above the working surface (a). Natural daylight and standard light bulbs cast shadows (b) but fluorescent lights are too flat and shadows will not show up. Ideally two light sources focusing on to the work surface are better than one.

Avoid flat surfaces as these will look uninteresting. Any blemish will be obvious. Sanding will produce a 'dead' look with minimal reflection (a). If small gouge cuts are left showing, each will act as a facet and reflect light, bringing life to the work (b). Stems of plants will catch the light better if they are carved to a slight ridge and not rounded over (c).

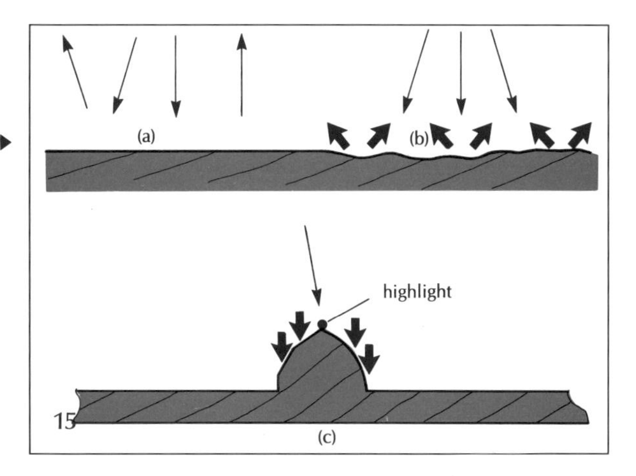

15

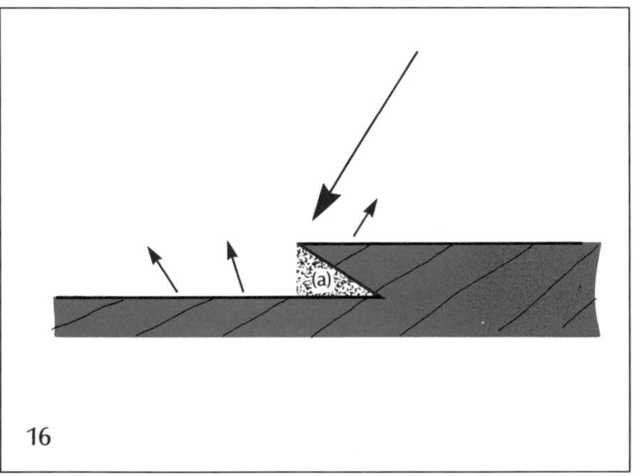

16

Shadow is produced by undercutting (a). This is normally done where areas of detail need to be 'lifted' off the background, as for example in the case of leaves. Cut the sidewall at an angle of about 30 degrees. There is no need to cut in too deeply or the detail will become too fragile. Undercutting is carried out when the final groundwork is being done and after all contour carving. Use a No. 1 chisel, or No. 3 gouge; note the small dog-leg tool No. 52 for future purchase. The background can be lightly tooled with a No. 3 gouge for a ripple effect.

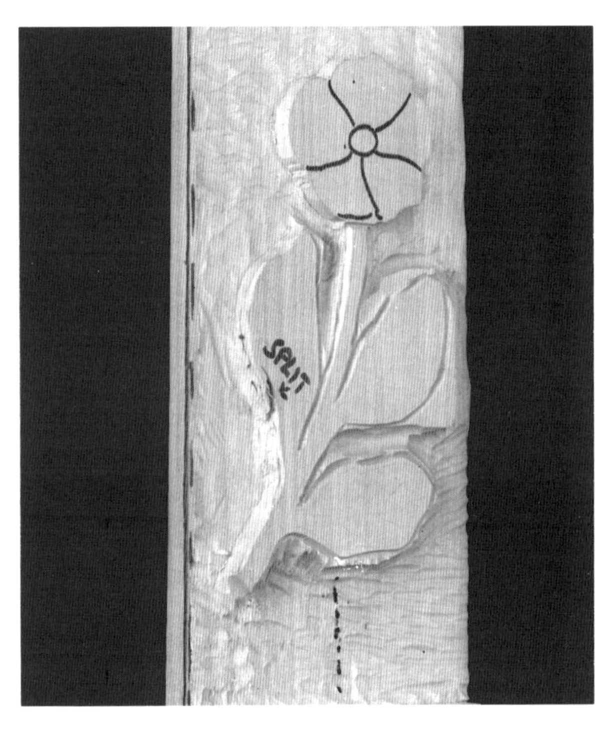

(a) Relief carving design applied to wood.

(b) Background removed.

(c) Modelling of design.

(d) Finished carving.

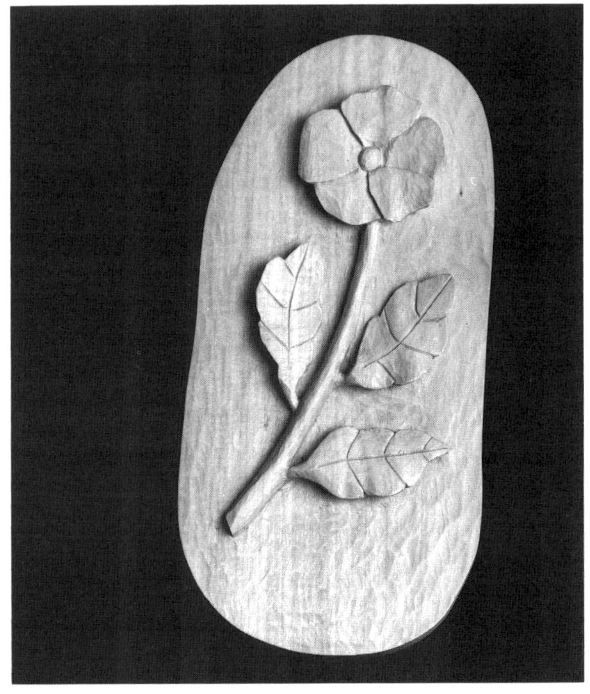

(*See photographs on page 74*) A breakdown of the stages of a low-relief carving. Some examples of common faults have been included. The wood is lime, 12 × 4 × ¾in (300 × 100 × 20mm). Note that the design has been applied to the wood and incised with a V-tool (a). Background depth and first working depth have been marked on the sides. Consider the proportion of height to width. Do you feel the design would look better if the wood was wider?

Much of the background has been removed (b). The flower has been stepped back to its final size. Background: bottom left has been cut with a blunt gouge; bottom right with a sharp one. Note fractured wood (left side of left-hand leaf) caused by lack of cross-grain stop-cut.

Vertical gouge cut.

Note the gouge is being held vertically. The sweep is cutting a convex curve. The cut on the inside of the blade is more important than the cut of the bevel.

The wood has been reduced to the final level. Modelling of the flower and leaves completed (c). Note that not all the undercutting has been carried out cleanly and that traces of waste wood still exist. This can be caused by lack of attention to detail, or by the gouge being incorrectly sharpened.

Here the design has been carved with greater attention to detail. In order to allow the background to be shaped, a wider piece of limewood, measuring 5in (125mm) width, was used (d). Note that this gives better balance to the design, so be prepared to waste some of the timber. If, when buying, you skimp and do not have wood to spare, it can ruin a carving.

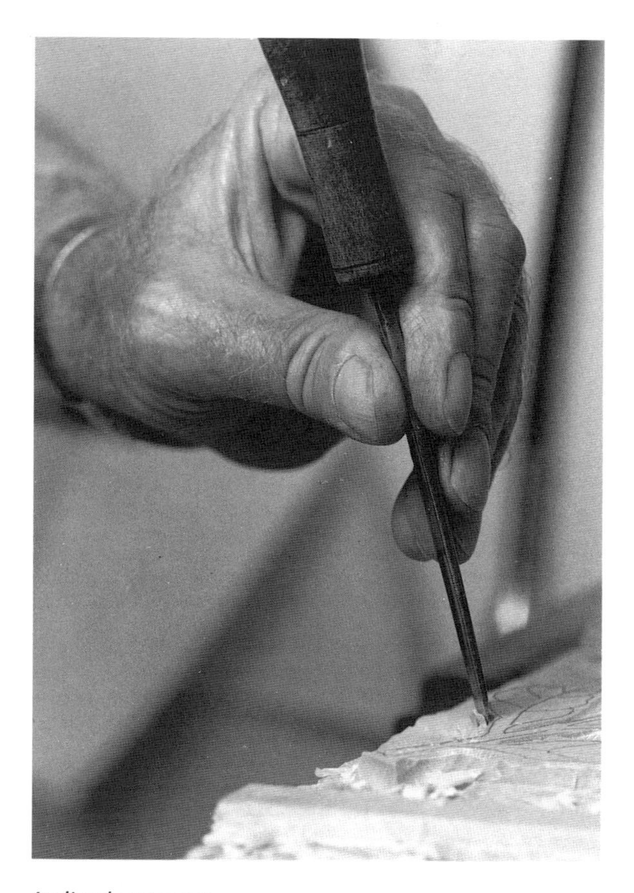

Inclined gouge cut.

Here the shape is concave, so the bevel cut is the important one. The gouge is leaning away from the design to permit the bevel to produce a vertical cut.

(Steps 1–8) Carving in high relief has a main depth from about 1in (25mm) to 6in (150mm) or even deeper. It is best for single subjects rather than for repetitive designs. Very deep relief can be built up with blocks glued to a baseboard. Care needs to be exercised to ensure that they are positioned with opposing growth rings to balance out stress, or severe warping can result. Kiln-dried timber is best, but some shrinkage at the joints can occur. Usually this type of work was gilded or painted.

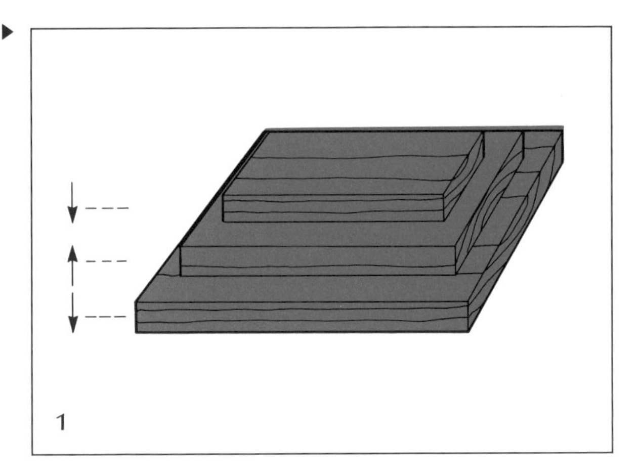
1

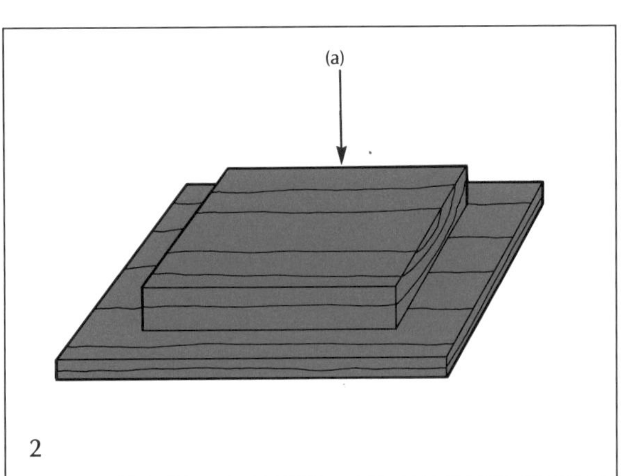

2

In general practice, high-relief carving will be to a depth of 2–2½in (50–60mm) and can be worked in solid timber (a). Do not make the base too thin which would look out of proportion and be structurally weak. A background of ¾in (20mm) thick should be sufficient.

It is not always necessary to remove all the background around the carving area (a). A design with shelving or graduated sides can be both attractive and very practical, since a lot of time removing the background is saved. However, if the slope is too steep (b), some difficulty can be encountered in cleaning up the surface or undercutting parts of the carving. Curved gouges Nos 12–20 or spoon-bits Nos 24–32 may be required.

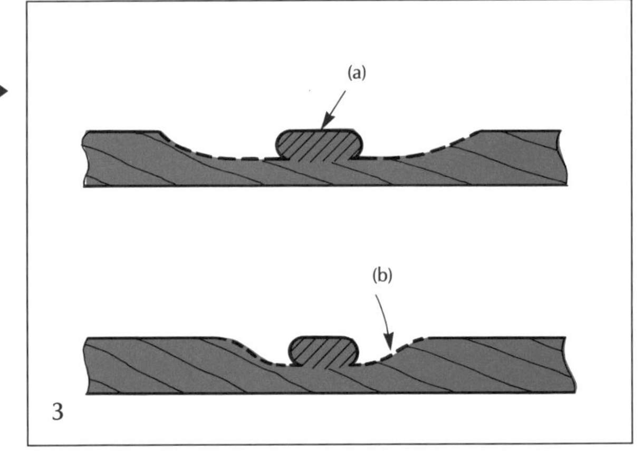

3

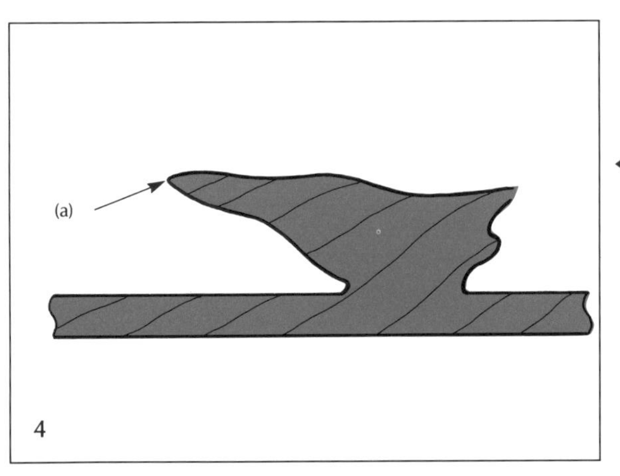

4

Undercutting can be more pronounced than in low-relief work, and if detail can be cut through to lift it from the background, so much the better. Strength can be retained by just thinning the edge of the design, for example the edge of a leaf. This is called feather-edging (a) and will create the illusion that the detail is thinner than it actually is. Remember that relief carving is usually viewed from the front. If the sides of the design are emphasized the carving will become too deep, and will take on a three-dimensional form.

The procedure for placing the drawing on the wood, marking out with a V-tool, and removing the waste is the same as in low-relief carving. However, because of the greater depth, it is very important not to use too much force when working down to the background. Remember that the wood has to absorb the force of the mallet blows (a). If it is excessive, shakes – splits in the wood below the surface – can occur (b).

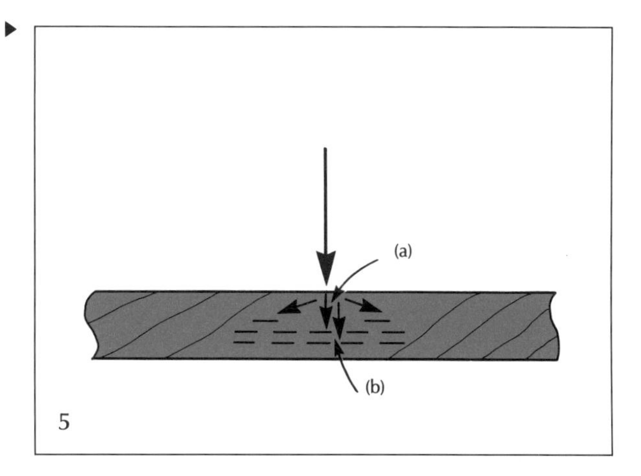

5

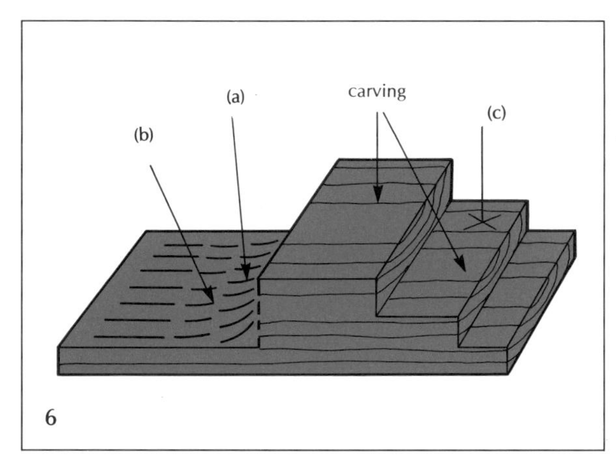

6

The background will invariably tend to rise (a) and be higher towards the centre and in the design area. Care is needed to avoid this, and the background must be levelled up before modelling of the design is started (b). Parts of the design on lower levels can be redrawn on to the wood as the background is removed (c).

Try to avoid placing delicate parts of the design, which are to be raised, on the cross-grain. For example, leaves which come on the cross-grain are best carved near to the background, or their tips should be brought down to base level to provide some strength.

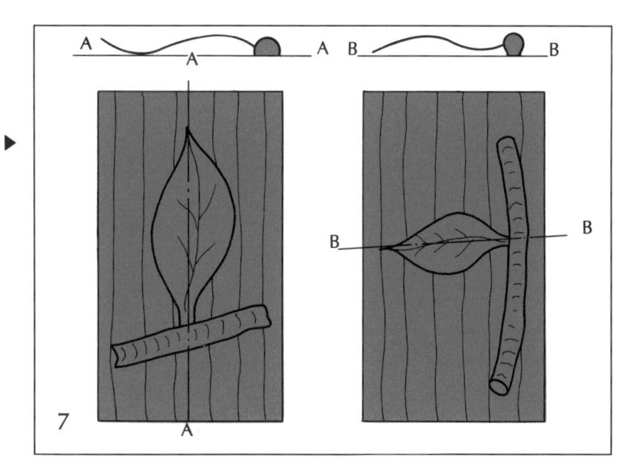

7

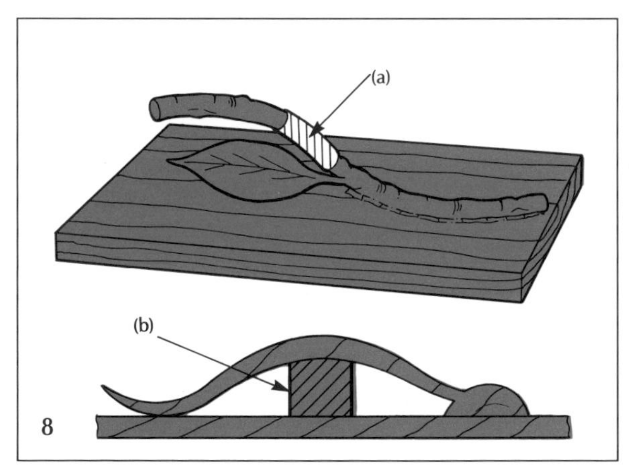

8

Delicate sections may need to be strengthened temporarily with masking tape (a) until the carving is finished. Supporting blocks can be left in place (b) and carefully removed when the stress of carving is finished. To avoid over-stressing, sand from behind where necessary rather than trying to remove all the waste wood with cutting tools.

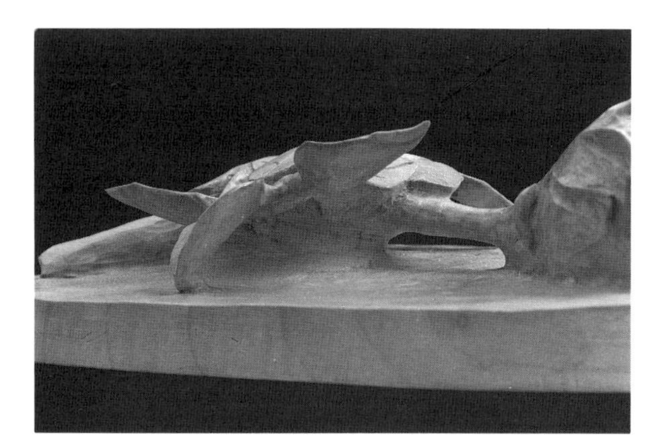

Note the depth of carving.

Sycamore was chosen for this piece. It cuts cleanly and is quite strong on the cross-grain. Lime would have worked equally well. A block 14 × 11 × 3in (350 × 280 × 80mm) was required. It was left in its rectangular shape throughout. The design could have been built up with blocks glued to a backing board, but the effect would not have been the same.

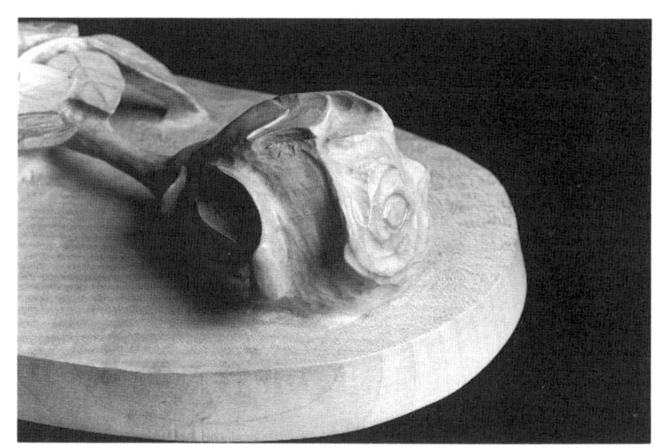

Waste wood was removed by sawing and gouge work.

Once the drawing had been applied, it was deeply incised with a V-tool in the waste. The larger waste areas were then sawn off and the smaller parts removed with either a No. 9, or No. 11 gouge. It is essential to restrict the force used during the roughing out period, or the timber may suffer structural damage.

The position of the stem was fixed before the leaves were carved.

It will be noted that, despite the overall depth being used, some of the high points of the leaves lie on a level close to that of the rose itself. This facilitated matters, as only the stem of the rose had, initially, to be taken down. This was done first, the contour of the flower then being formed. To allow for final adjustment, areas to be lowered were kept oversize. This meant a certain amount of redrawing.

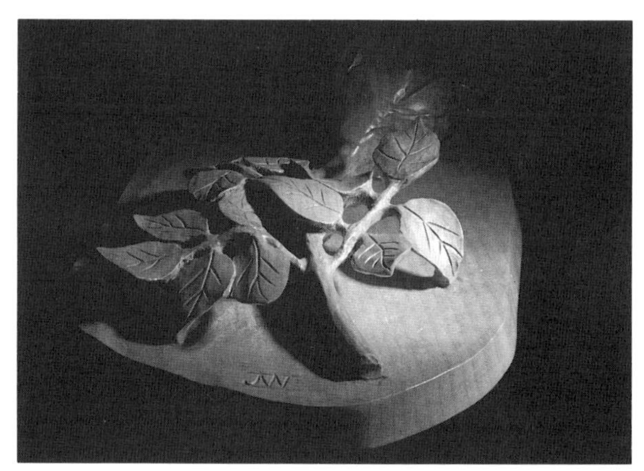

Model the leaves to create interest.

When all the parameters had been located the actual modelling was started. Up to this point the outline of the flower had been flat. It was then shaped to very nearly a three-dimensional form and the stem curved into place. Cross-grain areas of leaves and stems needed supporting pieces left in as long as possible. The leaves were shaped and then reduced in thickness from behind. Finally the background was shaped.

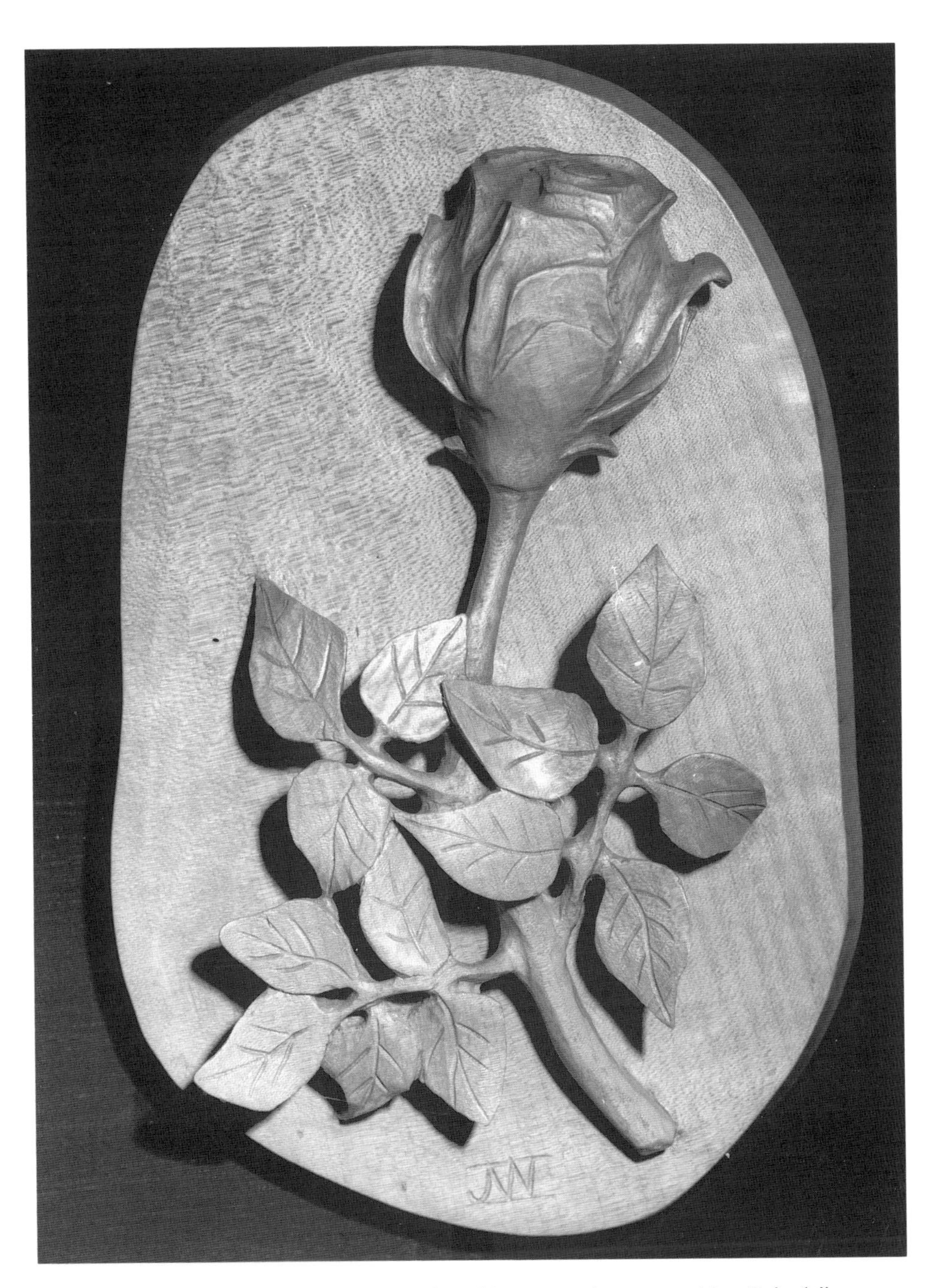

The execution of a carving in high relief such as this rose can be most exciting. To be fully effective, the greatest possible use has to be made of the depth. This means incorporating as many contours as possible. Frequent viewing from the sides helps to achieve this.

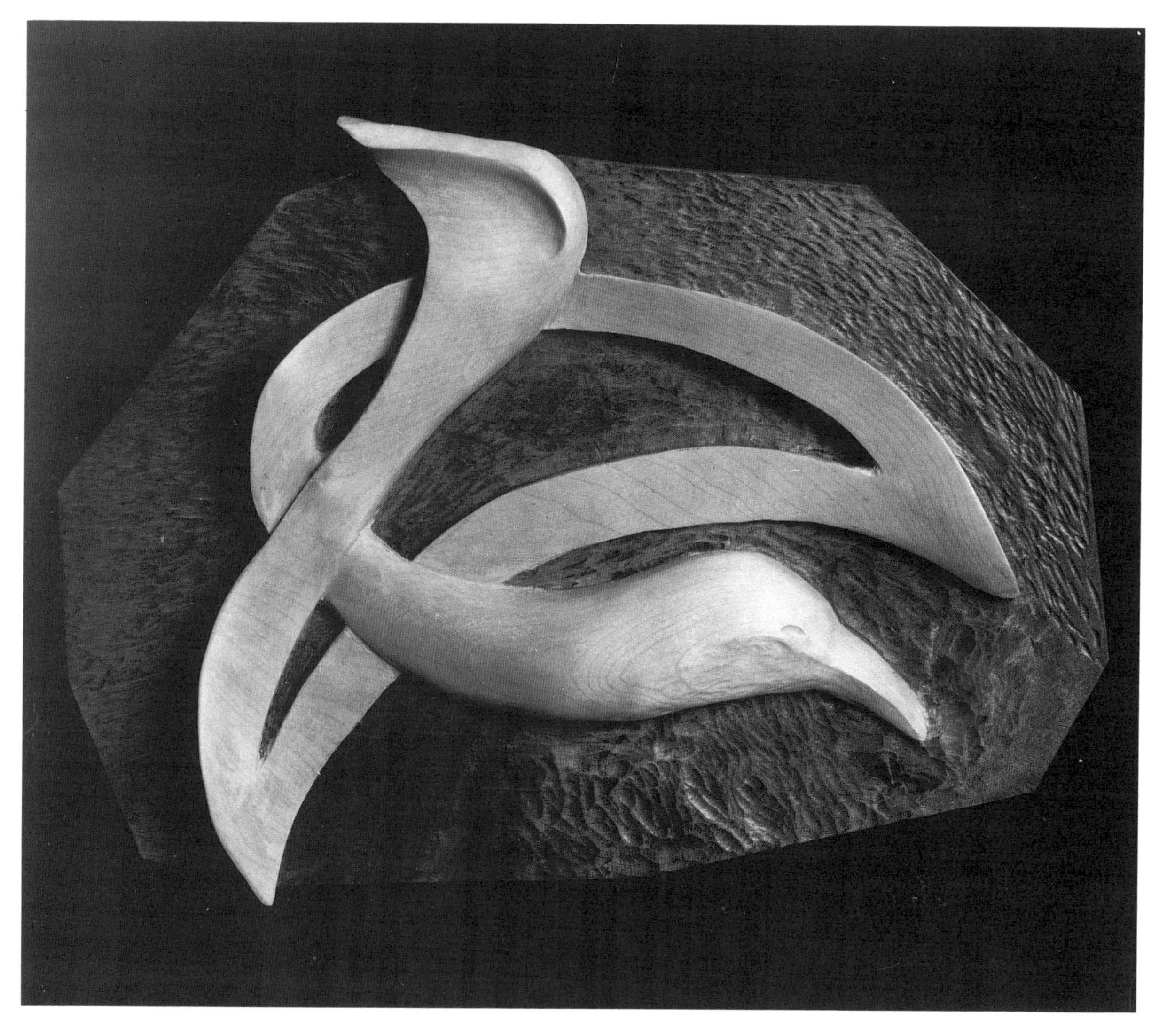

Relief carving: flying bird.

Sycamore was used for this relief carving. Dimensions: 13½ × 10 × 2in (340 × 255 × 50mm). The background was not shaped until the carving had been completed.

A complete contrast was needed between the subject and the background. The bird has a smooth finish, whereas the background has been heavily tooled.

The background was shaped using angles to contrast with the curves of the bird.

The effect of the contrast was further increased by staining the background after the bird had been waxed. This prevented the stain creeping into the white wood.

Relief carving: heron.

This subject was carved from a plank of kiln-dried American cherrywood, measuring 26 × 7½ × ¾in (660 × 190 × 20mm), which had been planed and thicknessed.

As this carving is quite shallow, care was needed to ensure that sufficient graduation to the various depths was achieved. One does not want either to have flat surfaces, or to have to carve much deeper than planned to create the curving planes.

Some thought had to be given as to how to create the effect of water flowing round the legs of the heron. Deep lateral cuts were made to produce this.

Note the treatment of the willow leaves at the top of the panel. This is an example of the use of intaglio carving.

RELIEF CARVING – KEY POINTS

- All relief carving work relies on the reflection of light.
- This means having both high spots and shadow areas. The more contour levels there are, the better.
- When planning the design, use sectional drawings. These will help you to visualize contours.
- Tool cuts on the surface of the wood act as tiny mirrors when polished.
- Excessive sanding will create a dead or flat look.
- Badly cut parts of the background will show when the wood is polished.
- Work to the capability of the structure of the wood.
- If you want fine detail, use a close-grain wood.
- Try to work some of the lowest detail first. This will help to fix areas to be in greater relief.
- As you carve, periodically check the effect by standing the panel upright to see how the light is cast.

(Steps 1–16) The plan was to carve a bird. A finch was chosen, as it has a rounded and compact form, and particularly because it has a short stubby beak, which is less likely to be a problem to carve. A profile drawing was made and this was put on to the wood with carbon paper in the usual manner. The wood selected was lime and the size of the block was 8 × 4 × 5in (200 × 100 × 125mm). The design was incised with a V-tool.

1

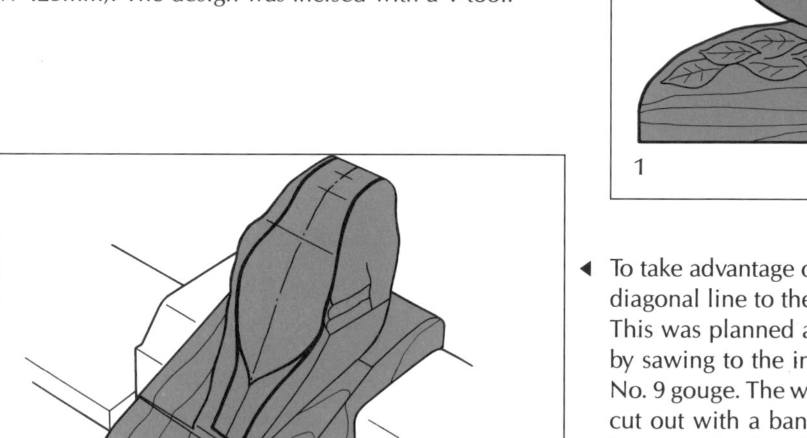

2

To take advantage of the grain, the carving was set on a diagonal line to the base with the head slightly turned. This was planned after the surplus wood was removed by sawing to the incised line and chopping out with a No. 9 gouge. The waste wood at the front of the bird was cut out with a bandsaw, but a coping saw could have been used. The photograph on page 86 shows both methods of waste removal.

As with all figure carving, it was best to start by rough shaping the head. Gouge Nos 5, 7 and 9 were used. The dome of the head was formed with the No. 4 gouge upside-down. The centre line was replaced as it was removed by cutting, and right angle lines were also drawn in to assist with the shaping. Check on the balance by masking out waste wood and redrawing the shape.

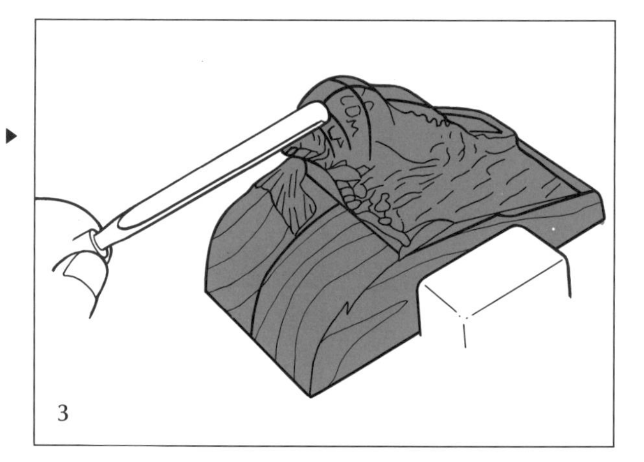

3

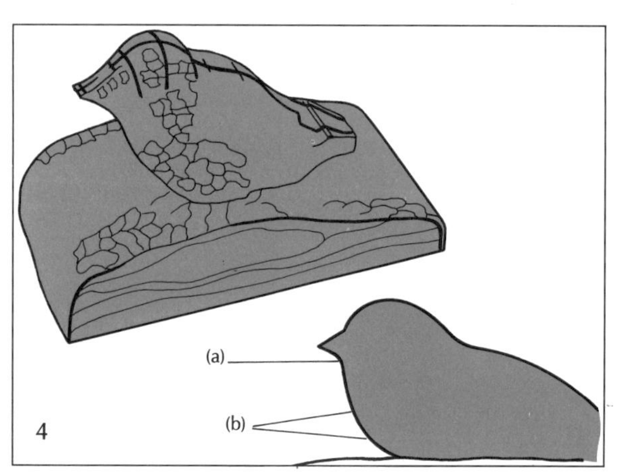

4

The neck, or throat, was carved with the ¼in (6mm) No. 9 gouge (a). Having fixed the position of the head, the next stage was to start forming the breast area. As this is a convex curve the No. 3 gouge was used to make shallow cuts (b). The beak was left full and not reduced to its final size at this stage, as it would have become too vulnerable.

The next stage was to start shaping the back of the bird. Gouges Nos 3 and 4 were used to avoid cutting too deeply. It is essential to work progressively from side to side. Completing one side and then trying to match up the other always causes problems of balance. Check the balance by masking out with the thumbs. ▶

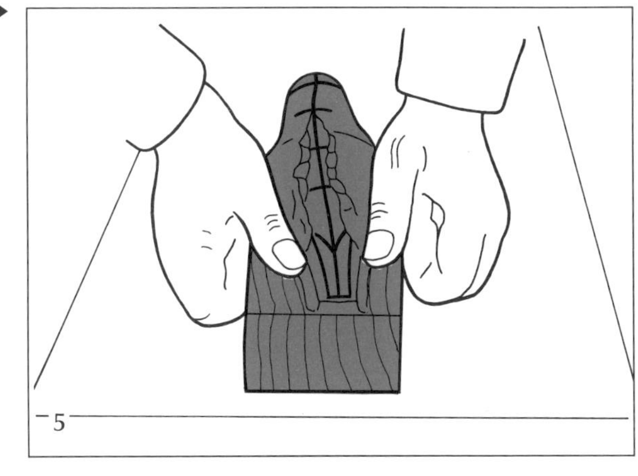

5

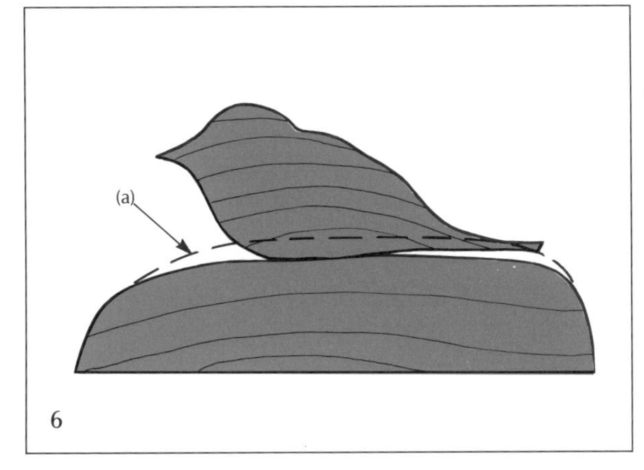

6

◀ Once the main roughing out of the body had been done the plinth line was lowered to allow work on the lower part of the breast and sides (a). Altering the base level like this will allow adjustments to the body to be made as you go along. Do not fix the line where the body meets the base by sawing deeply. The cut may show. Keep the plinth as level as possible at this stage. The No. 11 veiner was used to remove waste where the body joins the plinth.

Having established the shape and curve of the sides, it was then possible to start reducing the breast to its final size. The shape of the wings was then incised on both the sides and the back. Note that only part of the wing is treated like this. The V-tool cut was made in the part of the body which was to be reshaped under the wings and then the wings were trimmed to size. ▶

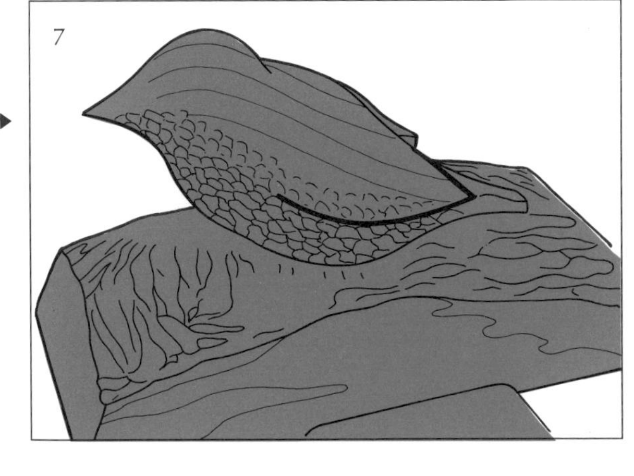

7

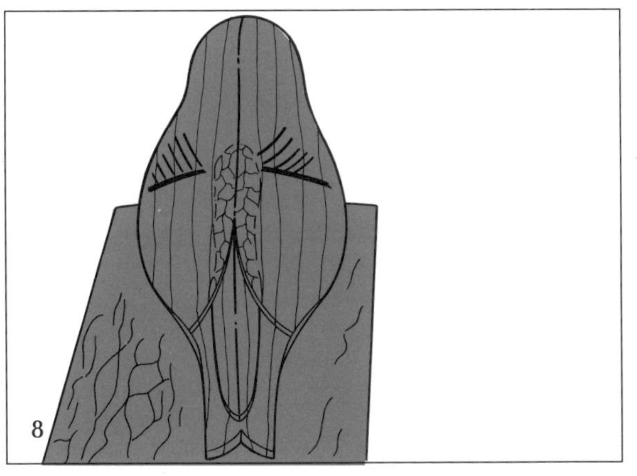

8

◀ The final shaping was now carried out, starting with the head. Details, such as the eyes, were omitted as this is best done after the initial sanding. Mainly gouges Nos 3 and 4 were used and light cuts made. Some rasping may be necessary if you are unable to effect delicate cuts, but do try to keep this to the minimum, as the pleasure of carving is in using the gouges. It was necessary to check the balance of the shoulders carefully to ensure that neither wing was out of true. Note that the centre of the back is dished slightly.

The back of the bird should not present any problem and most, if not all, of the work can be carried out with gouge Nos 3, 4 and 5. In the carving illustrated the wing tips were given an upward flip to create some sense of movement (a). This is a classic example of artistic licence. In real life the wings are straight, due to the shape of the flight feathers. This area is delicate, so cut carefully with a steep gouge such as No. 9 or use the half-round Sandvik Filemaster as a precaution (b).

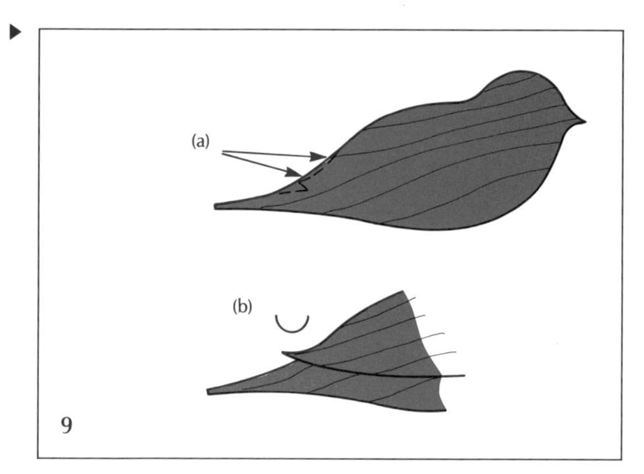

9

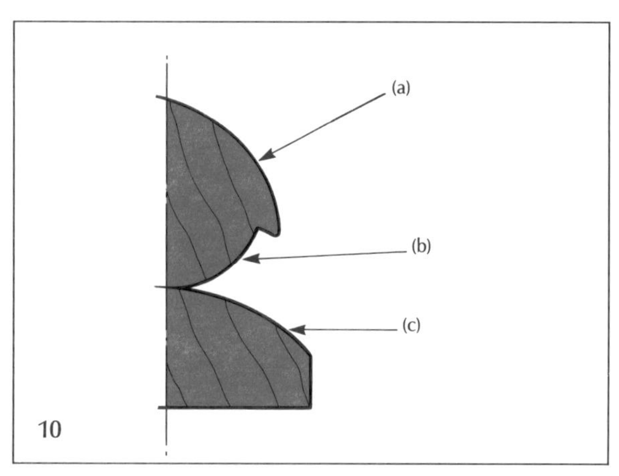

10

It was necessary to pull in the lower edge of the wings (a) and to reduce the body where it runs into the tail (b). The amount of reduction depending on the initial rough shaping. This area should not be too slim as, typically, the finch family have a rounded shape. Legs and claws were not included; they would not be visible in this pose. The base should be shaped (c).

At this stage the decision had to be made whether the wings should be left plain, or if they should be layered. A cape of feathers could be depicted behind the neck. As the final picture shows, the wings in this instance were left plain and allowed to form a smooth shape. The tail can be left smooth (a) or layered (b). It should, however, be gently undercut along the sides.

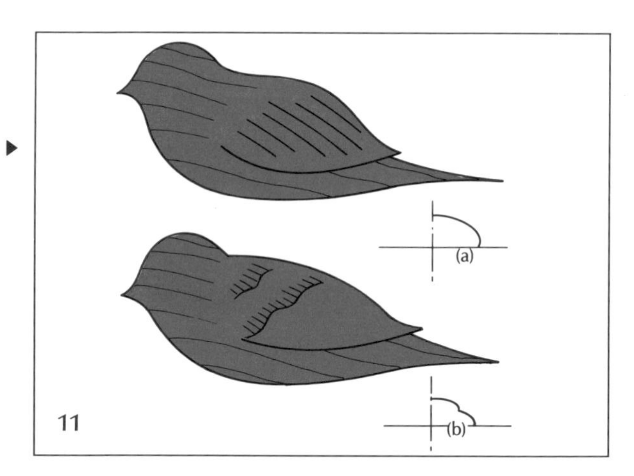

11

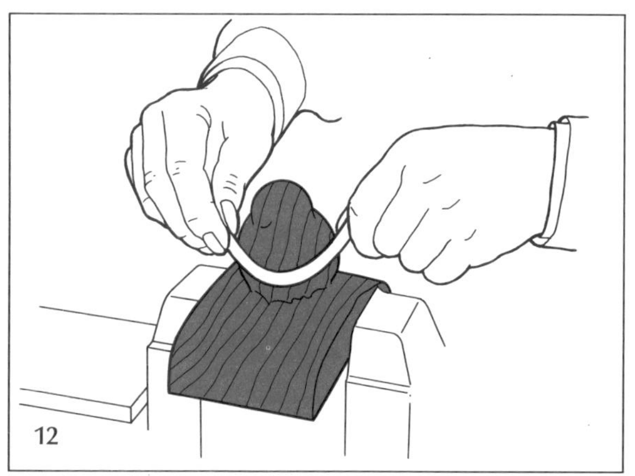
12

The final cleaning up of the bird then took place, using a combination of the No. 3 gouge, fine cut rifflers and 150-grit paper followed by the 250 grade. Abrasive paper can be cut into strips for final shaping. Between stages scraping was carried out. Care was exercised to ensure that the balance from every angle was correct and that no score marks or tears had been left. The base was then levelled. Where the body and base meet was worked with the No. 11 veiner. The rounded cut of this tool creates a better look than that formed with a chisel.

The head, being the smoothest part of the bird, was sanded with 500-grit paper, then the position of the eyes was located. Care had to be taken to make sure that they were equally aligned. The detail of the eye depends on the tools available. It can be carved using a small No. 9 gouge, which being a half-round will form a circle and then the inner part rounded over with a small No. 3, or the circle can be formed with a piece of metal tube sharpened on the edge. If the eye is not considered to be an important feature, it can be shown as a slight hollow cut with the No. 11 veiner, or touched in with a drill. Sometimes beads are used, but they can look artificial.

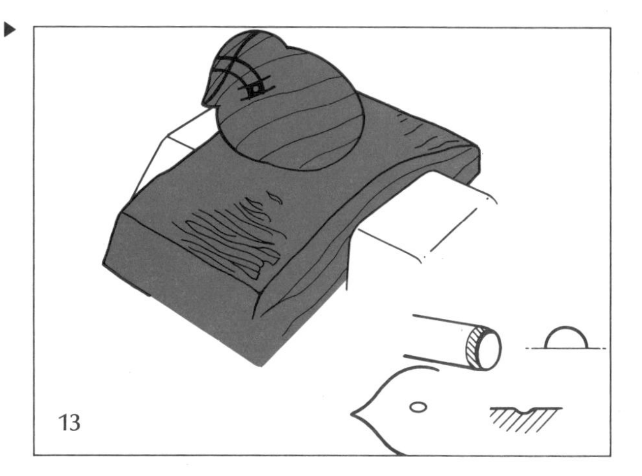

13

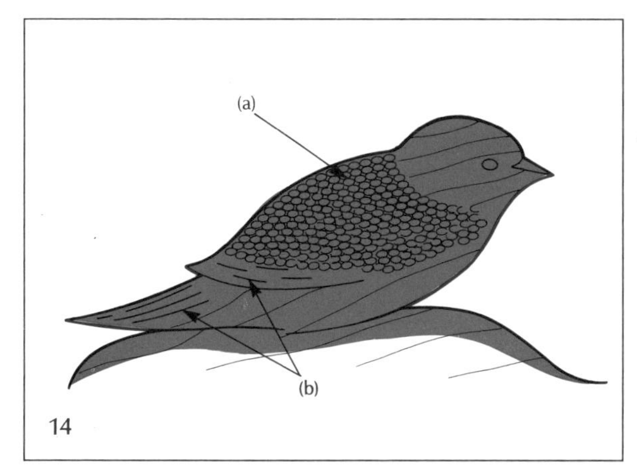

14

As lime is somewhat uninteresting if left totally smooth, and can be easily marked, the body was lightly textured with a No. 3 gouge (a), kept well stropped. The surface was then rubbed back with 500-grit paper. The V-tool was used to incise a few lines on the wing tips and over the surface of the tail (b).

Up to this point the base had been an oblong block. It was now randomly shaped on the bandsaw (a coping saw could have been used). To provide a contrast to the bird the upper surface was carved with leaves in low relief. Alternatively the base could have been rough cut with the No. 5 gouge, or cross-hatched using the No. 11 gouge. Leaves were chosen as being sympathetic to the subject.

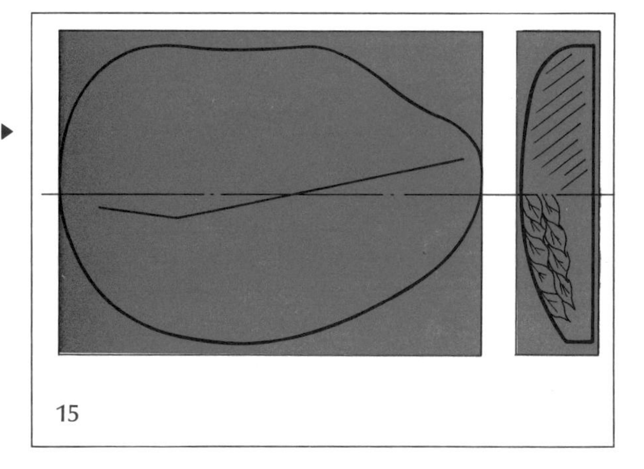

15

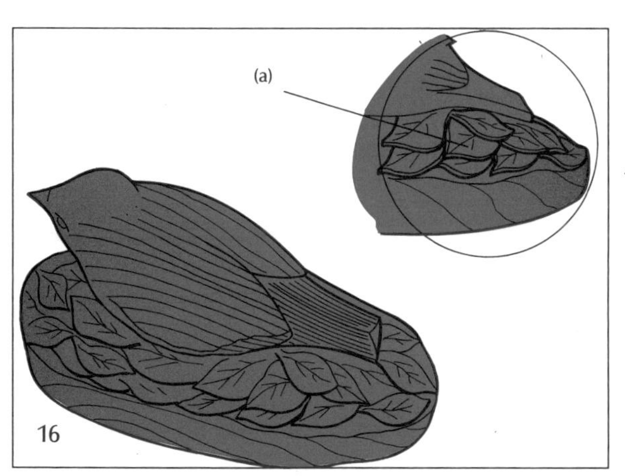

16

It is important that the leaves are placed in a random fashion, or the effect will look contrived. The No. 11 veiner was used to outline their shape and to remove interspacing wood. The leaves were to be on varying levels (a). When doing this type of carving keep on the move, doing five or so leaves on one part then going to another section. This creates a more varied impression. Each leaf was gently hollowed and the veins put in with the No. 11 gouge, or, by lightly cutting with the V-tool. *See* photograph on page 86.

Removal of waste wood.

Finished carving.

Finch on Leaves

On the left side of the photograph above, the waste wood has been removed with a bandsaw – a coping saw could have been used. On the right, vertical saw cuts were made first and the waste then removed with a No. 9 gouge. Wood, bottom right, could be kept as a fixing point.

The photograph (left) illustrates the completed carving. Note the lightly tooled finish on the body of the bird.

The leaves provide sufficient contrast visually to separate the bird from the base.

Only clear wax was used as a surface treatment, the wood having a natural honey colour. This was applied after very light sanding with worn 500-grit paper.

Kitten-cat. Pitch pine.

Kitten-Cat

This photograph illustrates the use of a strong grain to accentuate the line of form.

The wood used was pitch pine, reclaimed from a 150-year-old dockland beam.

Note the use of curving surfaces. Grain lines will always follow either a concave or a convex curve.

The carving was given a smooth finish, since tooling would have detracted from the beauty of the wood. Being resinous, an oil finish was applied.

Seated Figure

The concept was a placid, seated figure. The wood chosen for this carving was wild cherry, as the dark grain lines would be effective in creating the look of fabric.

Note the use of a small No. 11 veiner to texture the hair. Otherwise detail was kept to the minimum. For example, the arms blend into the fabric draped over the lap of the figure without any definition of hands.

When carving in this style it is essential to think of the subject in broad terms, relying on the sympathetic flow of form to create the picture, rather than becoming involved with minute detail.

The general shape of the carving, depicting quietness and repose, allied to the grain and colour of the wood, dictated a smooth finish. The carving was finished with Danish oil.

The overall shape of this carving is typical of the use of flowing lines, as described in the section on design.

Seated figure.

Sleeping Duck

The wood is elm. Dimensions are 9 × 5 × 5½in (230 × 125 × 140mm).

The piece was first shaped to the plan view, the position of the head and beak were then fixed, keeping them oversize and trimming back to the final position.

The attractive grain of this wood clearly dictated a smooth finish.

The carving was oiled and later waxed.

Sleeping duck.

Seabird

This carving in lime is suggestive of a seabird, such as a gannet.

As lime is a bland wood, different types of tooling were employed. The only part of the carving which was kept smooth was the beak. A contrast was formed between the body and the base by using different gouges. Strong V-tool cuts were made to emphasize the strength of the wings with some of the cuts curving in sympathy to the line of the body.

After tooling, the carving was lightly sanded with 500-grit paper. The wood was then sealed with well-diluted shellac, followed by further sanding using worn 500-grit paper. Any heavy traces of shellac were removed with methylated spirit. Neutral-coloured wax polish was then applied.

Seabird.

Wading Bird

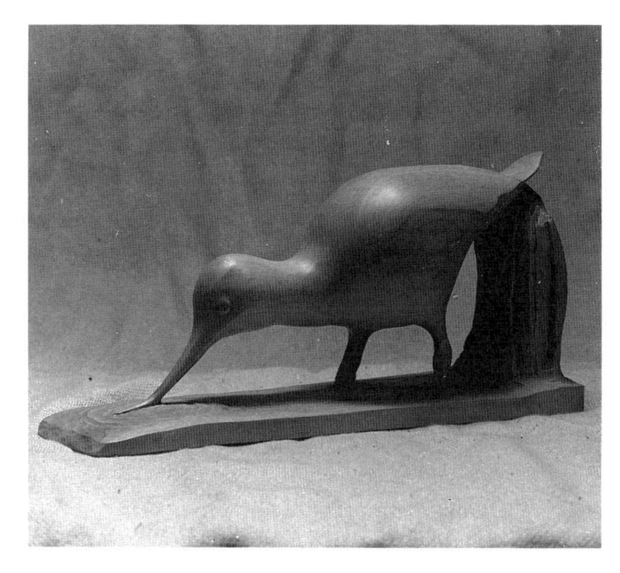

Wading bird.

Any carving which is going to require delicate cutting is best carried out in lime, as it does not easily fracture.

All birds, especially long-legged wading ones, present a structural problem. To be lifelike the legs must be thin, and are therefore weak. This was overcome by having the bird in a wading situation with only the upper half of the legs visible – typical of birds such as the avocet.

The strengthening block at the rear was retained, but the finish contrasts with the smooth body lines. Slight ripple cuts were made on the surface of the base to simulate flowing water.

The carving was finished with shellac and clear wax. Dimensions: 12 × 4 × 5½in (305 × 100 × 140mm) high.

Fish

Fish.

Fish usually present a mounting problem, if they are to look alive when a plinth is used, as it detracts from the sense of movement.

To overcome this the lower (pectoral) fins were kept very much oversize during the work, and only trimmed back once the final centre of gravity had been established by standing the fish on the edge of a table and letting it come to its point of balance.

The profile drawing had been placed diagonally to the line of the grain. Pitch pine, reclaimed from an old beam, was used. By carefully positioning the drawing, full advantage was taken of the distinctive grain.

A smooth finish was chosen. Owing to resin still being in the wood – surprising after over a hundred years – diluted matt polyurethane varnish was used prior to waxing.

Hen

Hen.

Walnut was used for this carving. Dimensions: 6 × 6 × 4½in (150 × 150 × 112mm).

This carving illustrates how it is possible to extract only certain elements of the original subject to create a design concept. Some influence of early Mexican carvings was used.

The tail was featured by bold V-tool cuts, and the remainder was left with a tooled finish applied with a No. 3 gouge. To give presence to the carving a shallow, angular base was included.

Walnut responds well to an oiled finish. Three coats of Danish oil were applied. The first two were buffed with fine wire wool. This did not flatten the textured surface, which would have been the case if abrasive paper had been used.

Green Woodpecker

Green Woodpecker.

The wood used for this carving was walnut.
Dimensions: 18 × 14 × 4in (460 × 360 × 100mm).

Being an expensive timber, wastage was kept to the minimum by making the carving from two pieces. The bird and branches were carved from the main block; the base from its off-cut. The head was turned. This allowed the beak to lie along the back preventing any possibility of accidental breakage.

Carving the overlapping and twisting branches can prove daunting at the outset. It is simplified if two colours of chalk or felt-tip are used when marking out. Then it should become fairly simple to plot how each one twists and overlaps the other. It is vital to work them oversize at the outset.

When complete the carving was glued to the base using dowels. The required holes were located by firstly drilling the branches at their point of contact with the base. Small panel pins with their heads removed were then inserted into the holes and used to mark the base with the position to drill for the dowels. The carving was finished with Danish oil.

Owl

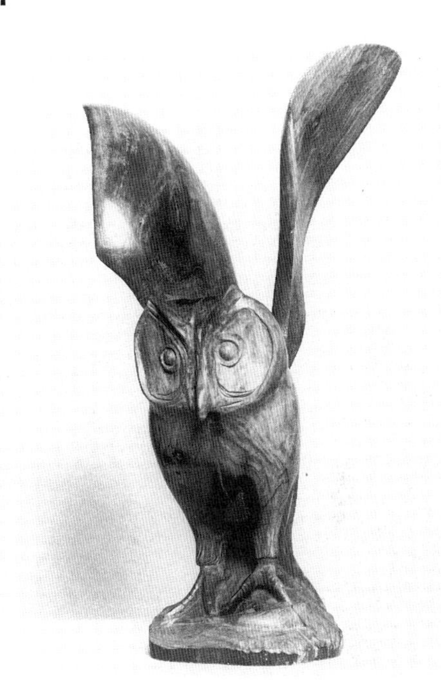

Owl.

Yew was used for this carving. Height: approximately 16in (400mm).

The problem when carving any bird with outstretched wings relates to the lie of the grain. For optimum strength it must run the length of the wing. Working from a sawn block may not achieve this, but it can be overcome if a forked branch is used.

It is essential the two sub-branches, to be used for the wings, emanate equally, or misshapen wings can result. This means starting with a piece of wood far larger than the final carving. Otherwise the aerodynamic contour of the wings will prove impossible to achieve.

As this work constitutes carving what is virtually a log, some splitting can happen. Keeping the body diagonal to the centre core may help to reduce this.

(Steps 1–8) Figures which are basically upright in stature can present certain problems if the carving is mostly carried out from the side views. The effect will be a carving which, whilst having good two-dimensional form, will be rather insubstantial when viewed from the front. Be sure to view the carving from the front periodically.

1

2

A lot of the work needs to be done facing the front of the carving. The overall shape can be rough cut from profile drawings, and some slight rounding over of the edges is helpful, but it is best not to develop the shape of the body too much until the head and its features have been set in, working oversize as usual.

In general a head is spherical in shape and the initial carving must try to create this (a). Frequently the amount of roundness is underestimated, resulting in a flat-faced appearance (b).

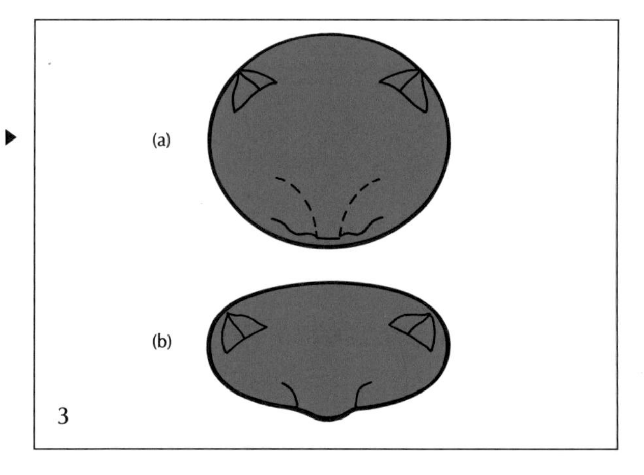

3

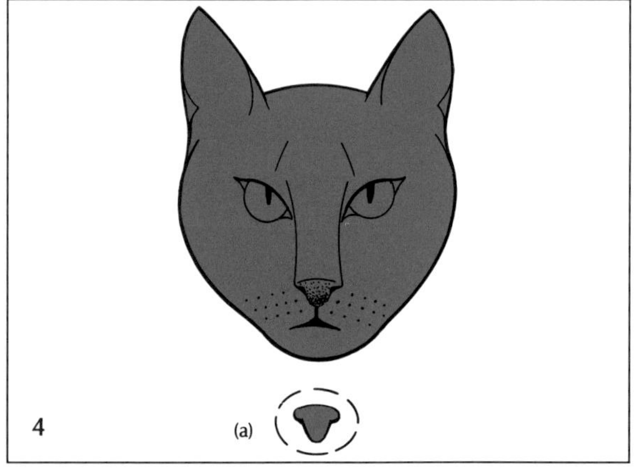

4

First locate the tip of the nose (a), as this always stands out, and in most cases no other feature is at this level (except sometimes the tip of the chin in the human face). In general terms, decide which part of the carving stands out furthest. Light gouge cuts into the wood are all that is necessary at this stage.

Now it is simple to incise two lines with a V-tool for the position and length of the nose to the eye sockets. Use a centre line (a) but be sure these lines are set in the waste area to start with. It is best to have some room for manoeuvre.

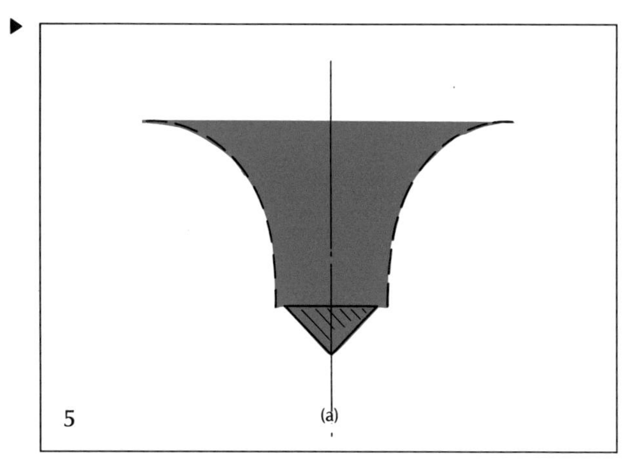

5

1 2 3 4 5

6

It should now be possible to visualize the different levels needed to create the other facial contours. Again, proceed with caution. If you are too hasty and do not think out your plan of action, mistakes will happen.

While working back from the main frontal extremity – the nose in this case – one must keep the spherical form and not flatten the shape. The centre line is shown (a).

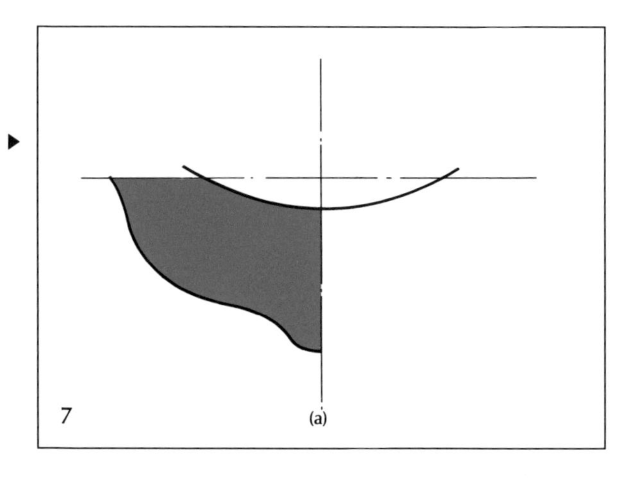

7

Be aware that the eyes are not only forward facing. They are located on an orbital plane relative to the main shape of the head. In simple terms this means that the eyes are capable of some side vision as well as looking to the front.

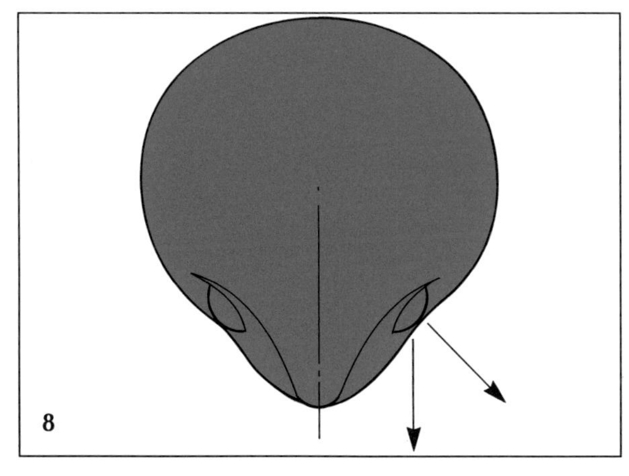

8

(Steps 1–8) To carve any object, animal, human or otherwise in a reclining position, one must first consider the plan view and look at the total area of space it occupies, that is the floor space taken up by, say, an animal asleep and curled up. If one were to draw round the sleeping body, the result would be a picture of the area occupied, something like this illustration, with the head at (a) and the tail at (b).

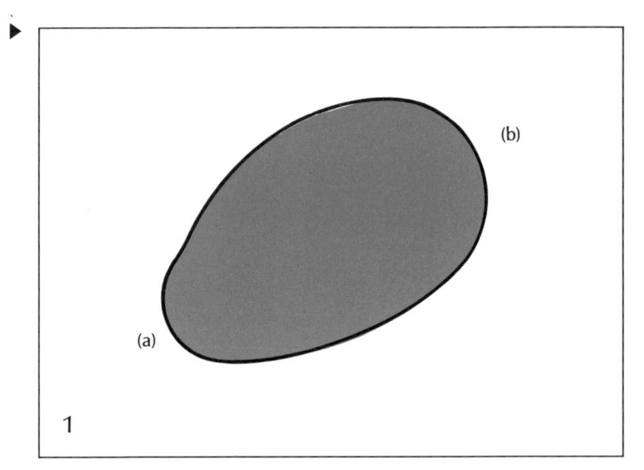

A

A

section A-A

2

Next, one must produce sketches of the side view and sectionally at the highest point (A-A). From these three drawings it will be possible to calculate the amount of wood needed to produce the carving.

Cut the block to the plan view, removing the waste wood. Work oversize at this point, since it can be hard to visualize accurately the true shape of the body.

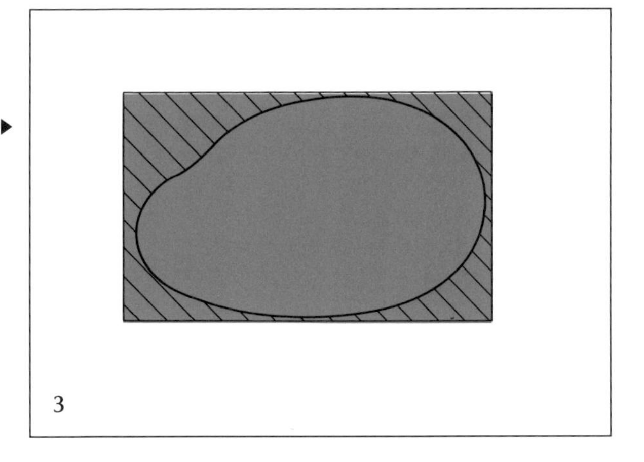

Consider the proportion of head to body. Draw this on to the wood. White chalk is best to start with, as it can be easily washed off should you change your mind. Remember to take into account any turning of the neck. When satisfied overdraw with felt-tip.

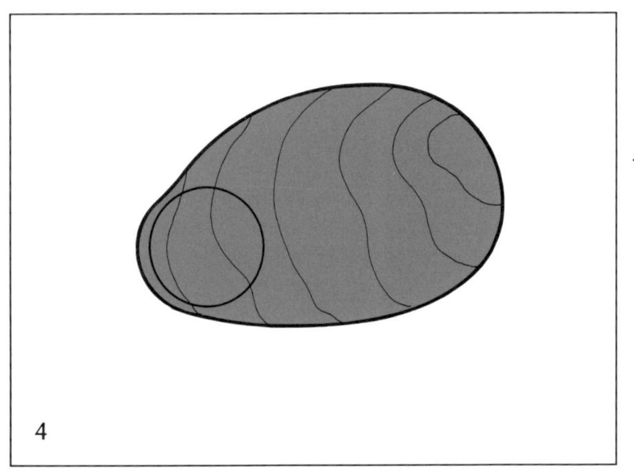

Using the plan drawing, roughly mark in where the main features occur: the ears (a), the nose (b), the tail (c), the hind leg (d) and the front leg (e). To start with you may experience some difficulty in transposing a body shape on to a flat piece of paper. Concentrate on the main features – arms, legs, head, etc. An animal study may prove easier than the human form.

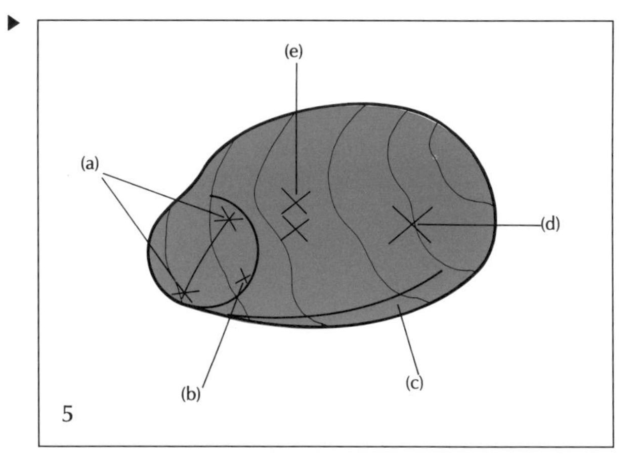

5

The next stage is to mark up the wood, working from the plan drawing, so that the surplus wood can be removed. Try doing this with coloured chalk. You will need three colours to indicate height, width and depth. Start with the head. Mark in the probable position of the nose, then the main features such as ears, forehead, etc. V-tool cut the main lines.

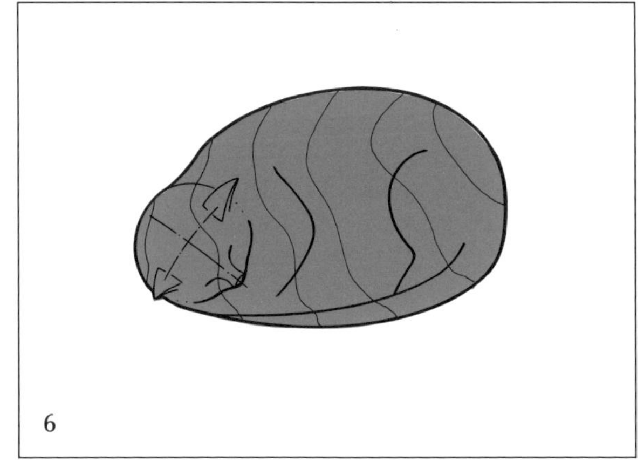
6

Using a saw, make shallow cuts (a) to remove some of the surplus wood. Go carefully, or you may cut off too much. Form planes equal to the main features. Even a slight change of surface level with a No. 4 or No. 5 gouge (b) will be sufficient. It is important to keep the carving oversize at this stage.

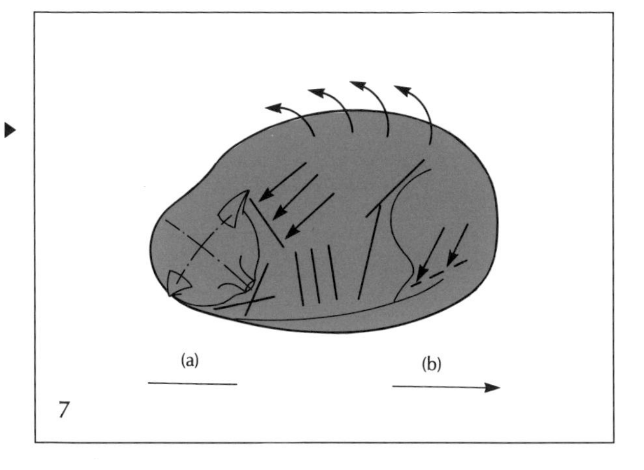

7

Now start to convert the flat planes to curved surfaces with contour gouge cuts. Start with the head and mark the position of the ears and nose. Continue, working all over the carving to maintain uniformity.

8

Finches on branches.

Finches on branches

Lime was used for this carving, which measured 12in (350mm) in length and 5in (130mm) high and wide.

Most carvings, whether they are free standing, or mounted on some form of plinth, are composed of a single element. This could be a bird, an animal, or the human form.

A more complex carving will prove to be an interesting exercise, since it will require a good deal of three-dimensional thinking.

If you look at the photograph above, you will see that it can be broken up into four main parts: two birds, centre piece and the supporting branches. To add to the interest, the birds are on diagonal lines to the centre line of the carving, and they are on two different levels.

A feeling of space has been created by keeping the central portion low. The visual emphasis is on the birds, the leaves and branches being secondary. If there were too much detail, the impact of the primary elements would be lost.

Try using a more complex composition to provide greater interest to a carving, it is not as difficult as it may first seem. Once the main features have been positioned, the rest of the carving will follow, and should present little difficulty, providing sufficient wood has been retained. Start with a side-view sketch, which should position the main elements.

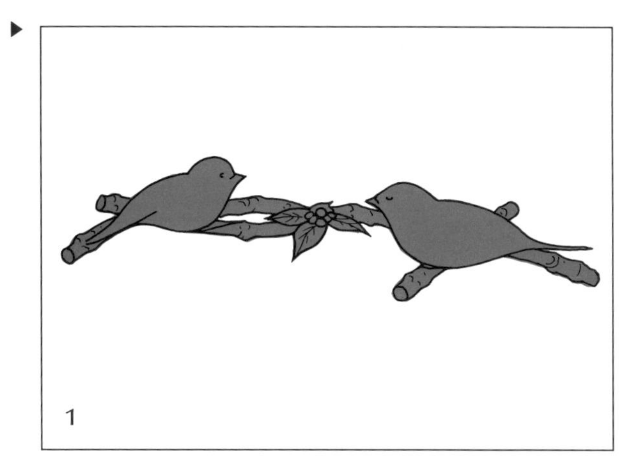
1

2

Sketch out a plan view and, using coloured chalk, separate the main components, i.e. the birds, centre detail, main and cross branches.

Make sure that the wood you select – lime for preference – has sufficient depth to accommodate all the levels required; you do not want to end up with a carving which is too flat. It will be useful to have the wood longer than the carving to provide holding points (a). Direct draw on to the wood the position and angle of the two birds.

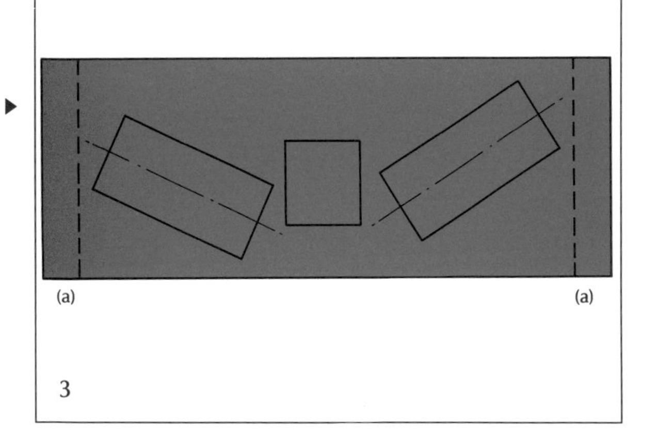

3

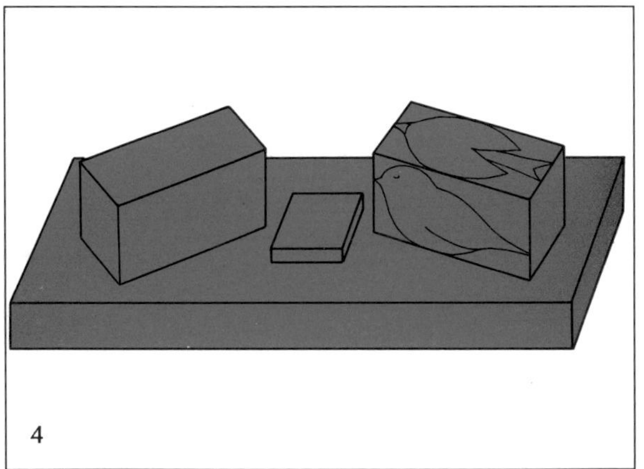
4

Reduce the wood where the birds are to be to two oblong blocks. Do not make these too deep, or you may run into trouble later on when you start carving the branches. Rough out the bird shapes using gouges and a coping saw. As the birds develop draw in the position of the centre detail and the branches, using coloured chalk or felt-tip. Start shaping the branches well before the birds are completed, so that they blend together.

(Steps 1–8) The importance of correct finishing of any woodcarving, in relief or sculpture, cannot be overstated. This not only reduces the surface to a degree of uniformity, but also produces a tactile, silky sheen, which is a joy to see and touch. The style of finish needs to be matched both to the subject and to the character of the wood.

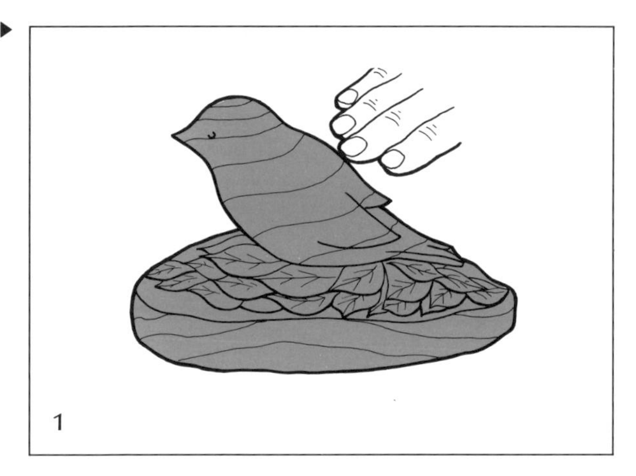

1

Do not rush the various stages of finishing. It can sometimes take as long as the carving. For example, a sculpture of complex form may have to have a perfectly smooth finish. Plan the type of finish well before the carving is completed. In fact, when you visualize the shape, you should know the finish. Note the tooled finish to the back (a) and the leaves on the base (b).

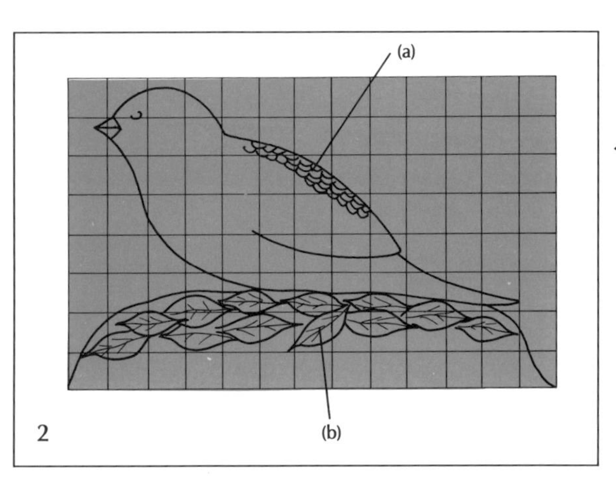

2

Generally, the amount of time spent on finishing is directly related to the sharpness of the carving tools. If the gouges have been kept sharp, and the cuts have been to a regular depth, only light paring cuts will be necessary to produce a clean surface (a). Neglected or blunt gouges give the wood a dull, ragged appearance (b) requiring extensive rasping and sanding.

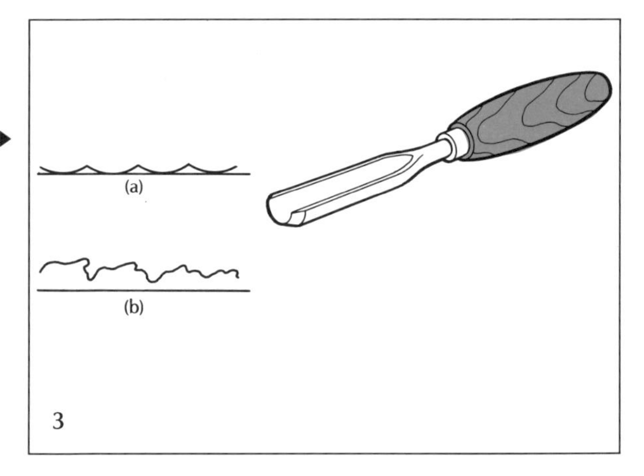

3

When rasps are used to excess, the surface of the wood becomes distressed, as the fibres below the surface are damaged. This will show when the wood is polished (a); light patches are frequently visible, and these are difficult to eradicate with sanding. It is always possible to detect when a carving has been heavily rasped and this is all too frequently the case with the work of beginners. The more practised one becomes in cutting the wood, the better the finish will be.

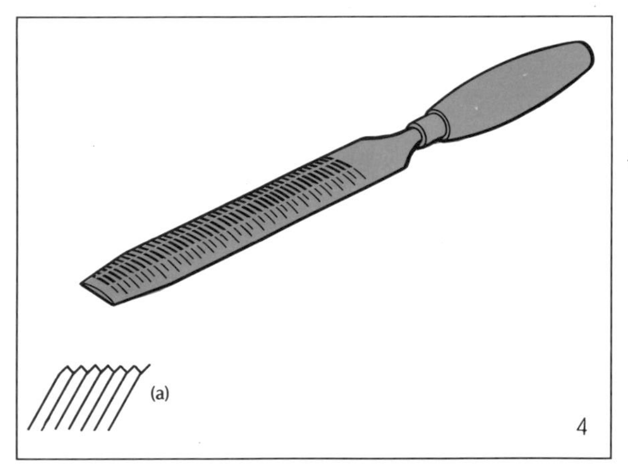

4

Sometimes an irregular surface cannot be seen when the wood is unpolished, but the high and low areas may be felt. Use your sense of touch – it can tell you more than your eyes; it is surprising how even a slight undulation, or excess of wood can be detected with the fingers.

5

Spend time just looking at, and touching, the surfaces. Mark with chalk any areas which still need attention. Look at the carving by both daylight and electric light. Do not be tempted to embark upon major structural changes, as you may well find that you run out of wood.

6

Consider carefully the balance between the grain of the wood and the effect that can be produced by the use of texture. If you have taken the trouble to carve the wood by hand, rather than resorting to using power sanders and grinders, why not let the gouge cuts show? If the surface is ripple-cut with a sharp No. 3 gouge the effect can be pleasing – particularly true in relief carving.

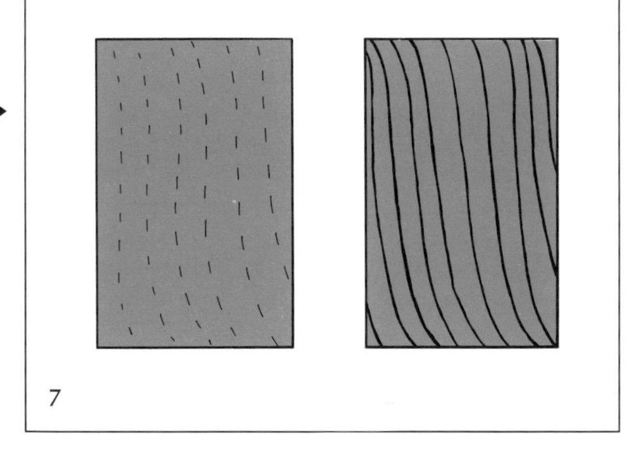

7

The effect of light reflection is important. When a carving has a high gloss any natural blemish in the wood will be exaggerated. Similarly, lack of attention to the sequences of finishing will be highlighted. A smooth surface has to be perfect. A tooled finish allows more latitude, as each cut acts as a facet, reflecting light at a different angle to those next to it – much like a diamond. All woodcarvings, whether they have a smooth surface or a tooled finish, look better with a satin-type lustre rather than a high gloss.

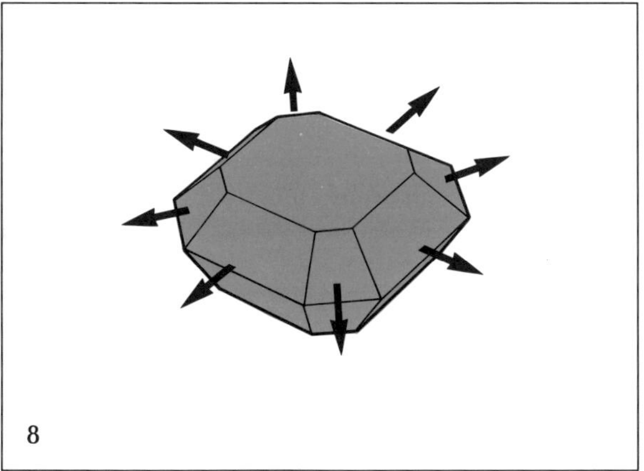

8

(Steps 1–8) The wood must be prepared before it is sanded, or the final texturing applied. This means obtaining an even surface, free of humps or hollows. Do not tackle this just with a rasp. The more that is done with cutting tools, such as a No. 3 gouge (a), or a No. 1 chisel for convex areas, the better the surface will be and the less time it will take to obtain a good finish. Fishtail types are useful for maximum visibility (b).

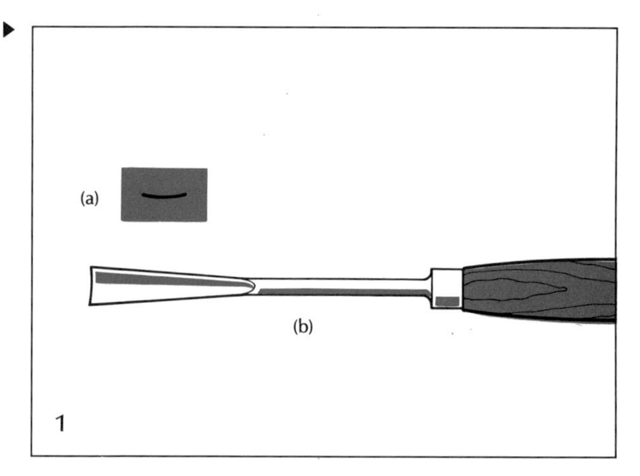

1

By now you will know the lie of the grain. Cut with it to flatten the fibres. Use the gouge with a slight circular movement (a); this gives more control than just pushing the tool forward. Let the hand holding the tool blade apply counter-pressure to the hand holding the handle. Keep the back bevel rubbing the wood and fractionally raise the handle. This will prevent the gouge digging in and will produce light paring cuts.

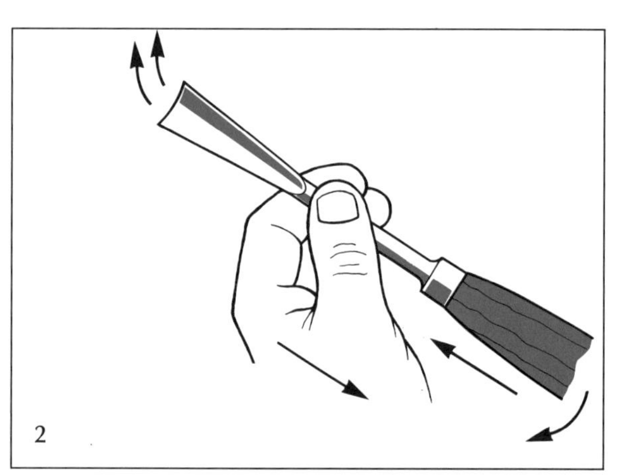
2

Some areas may be difficult to finish with the gouge, for instance where the grain is very twisted, or in small recessed parts of detail. Here a medium or fine-cut rasp or riffler will be needed. Remember that these will distress the wood fibres (a) and that the areas where they have been used will show. This applies particularly to end-grain surfaces which can become pitted or scratched. Smoothing files and rifflers give a cleaner cut.

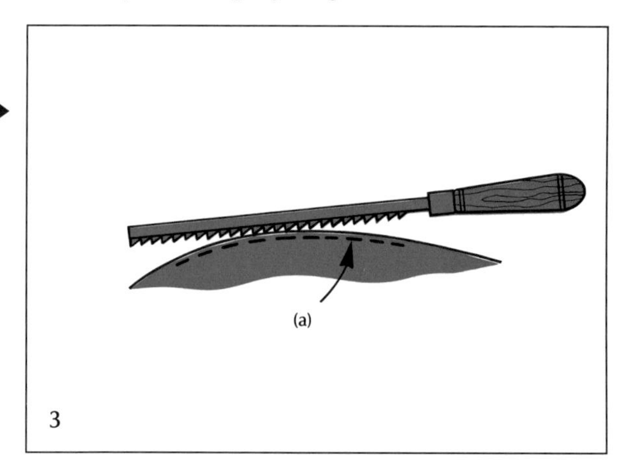

3

Heavy rasping against the lie of the grain will cause the wood to tear, leaving split areas below the surface. Torn grain is sometimes difficult to see until the wood is smooth, but it can usually be felt. These should be cut out and the surrounding wood lowered. It is seldom possible to sand out this type of tear. If the damaged area is very deep it may be necessary to use wood-adhesive, but leave this until the wood has been sealed, or light patches will remain where the glue has filled the cells which will show when the wood is polished.

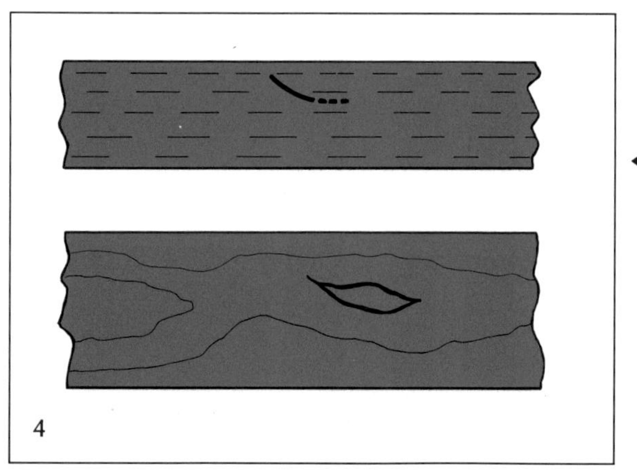
4

The next stage is to scrape the wood. This is a cutting process and should always precede sanding for best effect. The only exception is when very coarse sanding is being used as a shaping process, when the scraping would follow. Cabinet scrapers are made from hardened steel. The types most useful are the 'hollow' (a) and the 'goose-neck' (b). Small scrapers can be made from tempered steel such as old hacksaw blades. Broken window glass can also be used.

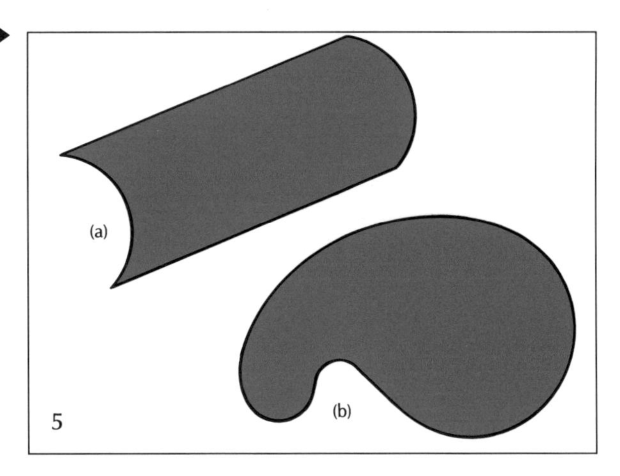

5

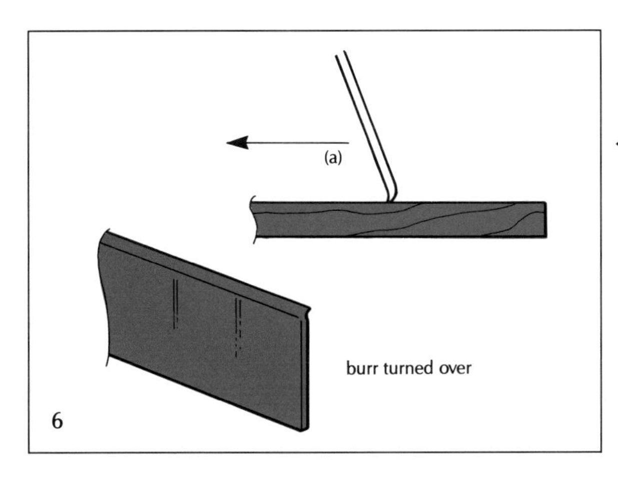

6

A scraper relies for a cutting edge on a burr, turned over on one side, similar to that produced when a gouge is sharpened. They work best when kept flexed with thumb pressure in the middle. Push the scraper in a forward direction, holding it at an angle so that the burr cuts the wood (a).

Start each stroke with light downward pressure to prevent ridging. Increase during forward stroke, then end with light pressure (a). Use in-line or on a slight diagonal to the grain. Flex the scraper with thumb pressure (b). Work with the lie of the grain to flatten the fibres, not against it (c).

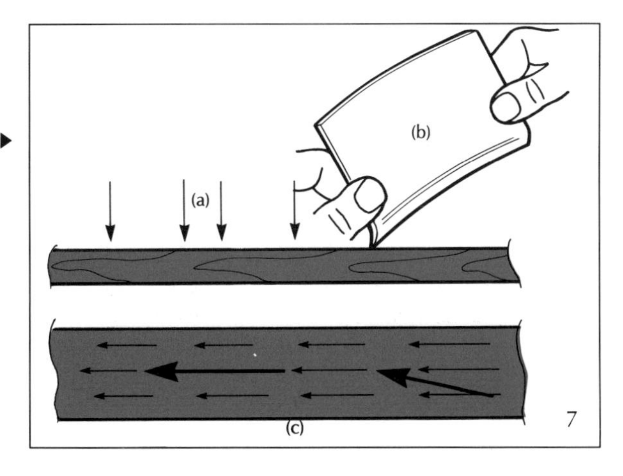

7

8

Scraping can be difficult on woods such as pine, where the changing density from soft areas to resin bands may cause corrugations to the surface unless a very light and even pressure is maintained. If the density varies a lot scraping may not be possible at all.

The scraper is an important tool and it is essential to keep it sharp. The burr is turned over using either the back of a gouge, or better still, a specially made burnisher. This is in effect a hardened steel rod which can be either square in section or round, depending on the shape of the scraper. In appearance it is rather like a knife-sharpening steel, which can be used as a substitute.

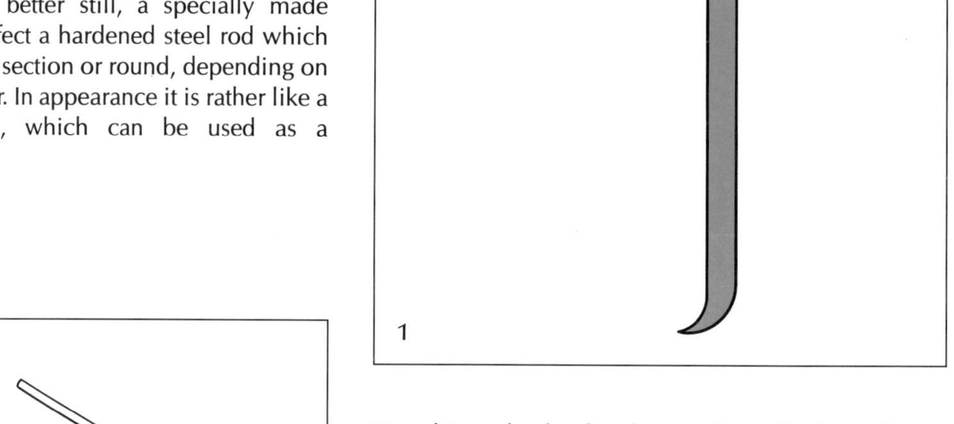
1

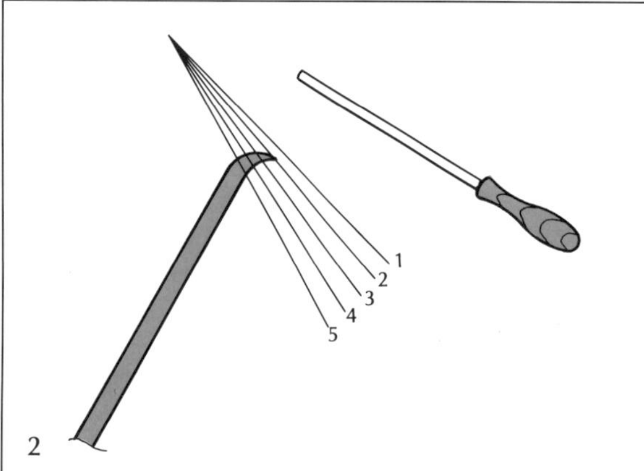

2

To achieve the hook edge, or burr, the burnisher is drawn across the edge of the scraper with a slight downward movement, at the same time moving along its length. On each resharpening, the downward angle is increased.

After the scraper has been sharpened some four or five times the angle of the burr becomes too acute to cut properly. The scraper then has to be reset. This entails removing the burr and making the edge square with the sides. To remove the burr; rub each side of the scraper on the flat surface of the oilstone.

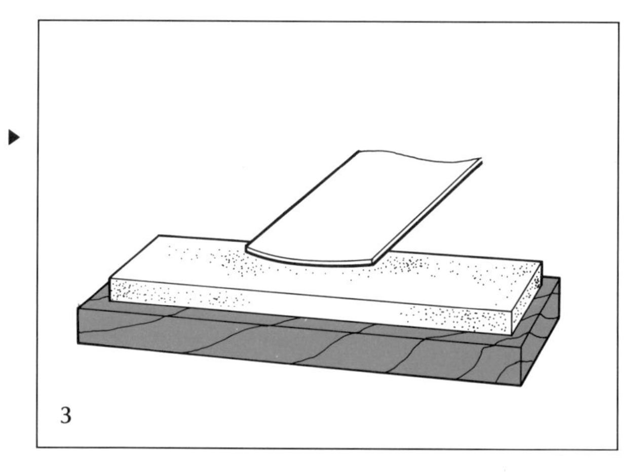
3

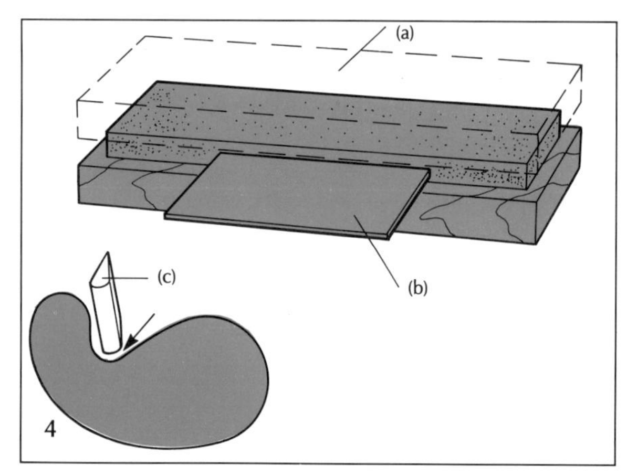

4

To square off the edge, put the lid on the oilstone. By holding down the lid the scraper can be set at right angles (a). Insert the edge of the scraper between the lid and the base (b). Oil should be used on the edge of the stone in the usual manner. Work the scraper back and forth a few times. The goose-neck scraper has to be set using a slipstone in the concave region (c). Finally, hold the scraper in the vice and turn over the fresh burr.

Scrap window glass can be used instead of metal scrapers. Off-cuts can usually be obtained from a glazing firm or from a picture framer. If a piece is too large, place the glass between thick layers of newspaper and tap with the mallet. When using glass, wear safety goggles and work gloves. Usually broken glass has a jagged edge, so it will not produce cuts as smooth as a scraper.

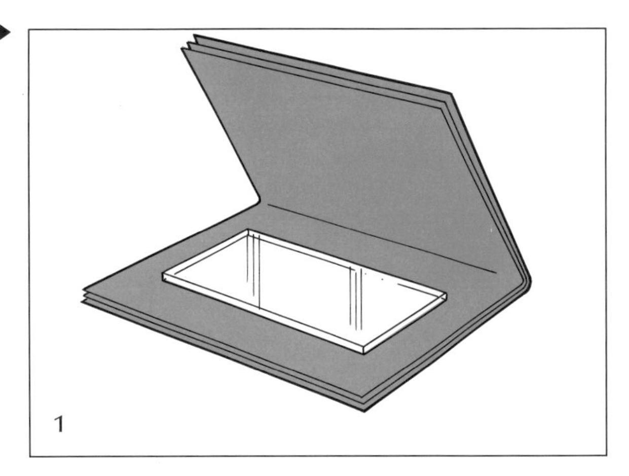
1

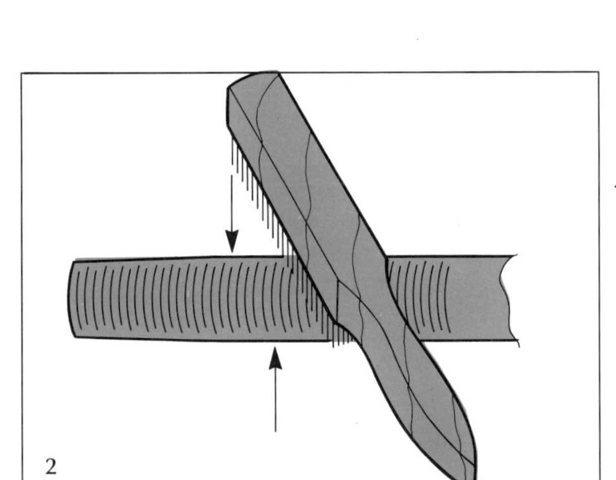
2

Clean out files and rifflers with a brass brush, such as a suede-shoe brush, which will not damage the teeth. Work across the file. Do this regularly to prevent wood dust clogging. A clean riffler will work faster and, if it is the fine-cut type, will produce a smoother surface, which will need less scraping.

Before working on the finishing of the carving attend to the underside of the base. If this is dished in the centre (a) the carving will not rock. Hollow out the centre area. This can be done with the goose-neck scraper. It is necessary to wrap the carving in foam rubber or a damp kitchen sponge to hold it in the vice. This is one of the advantages of the Scopas Chops, which are cushioned to hold finished wood.

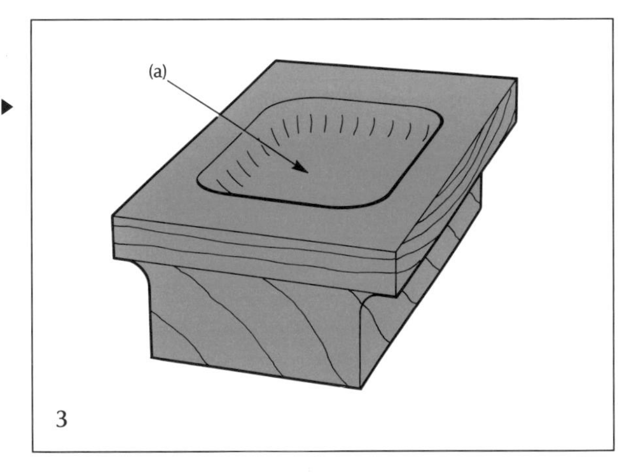

3

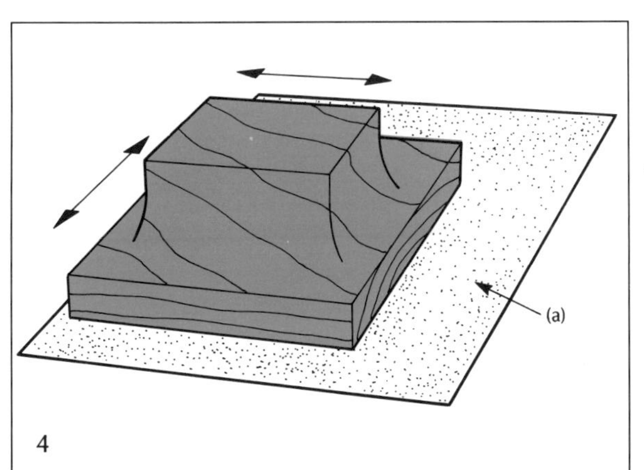

4

The rim that is left on the underside of the base can now be finished off. Stand the carving on a flat sheet of abrasive paper (a) and sand back and forth until the base is level. Make sure the carving is vertical. Finishing off the base underside like this will give a more professional look to your work than if you use felt.

The types of sanding paper most commonly used for finishing woodcarvings are: aluminium oxide, garnet and silicon carbide. All are graded by size of grit. The higher the number the finer the abrasive. For most work, the following will be found useful: 150 grit (coarse), 250 grit (medium), 500 grit (fine), and for delicate work 1000 grit (very fine).

Generally it is best to use either garnet or silicon carbide papers. Both these types have flexible backing sheets. The aluminium oxide type usually has a stiff backing of either paper or woven fabric. This stiffness can be a problem when working hollows. The stiff backing can, though, be useful when shaping.

All abrasive papers work by wearing away the wood. Coarse grades will distress the wood fibres. This can show up on the end-grain surfaces, which will tend to look dull.

Conventional sandpaper is seldom used. It tends to wear very quickly, clogs easily with wood dust and can be uneven in grit size.

Types of Abrasive Paper

Aluminium Oxide Colour usually dark red, it also comes in other colours. Used with power tools such as belt sanders. Very coarse and durable. Both 80 and 100 grit can be used for shaping. The backing – woven or thick paper – does not flex easily.

Garnet Paper Colour orange brown. Works very well; does not clog and is long lasting. Very flexible backing. Available in most grit sizes.

Silicon Carbide Colour light grey. Makes an ideal finishing paper, 500 grit and finer. Very flexible.

Wet/Dry Colour dark grey. Available up to 1000 grit. This grade is useful. Stiff backing.

Wet/dry sanding paper has a stiff backing and offers little real advantage over the garnet and silicon carbide types when dry sanding. However, the finer grades can be useful when applying an oiled finish. Abrasive papers are best bought from established woodworking retailers, who should carry stocks of the types and grades mentioned, and who will usually supply mixed packs by mail order.

All woodcarvers develop their own particular technique for finishing their work, but one thing they will agree on: the better the cutting of the wood, with really sharp gouges, the less time needed in the sanding stage.

Although not an abrasive paper, some mention needs to be made of the use of wire wool. This has more of a burnishing action, and when used in conjunction with a finishing oil produces a very fine surface.

The quality of abrasive papers has advanced a long way since the days when dried shark's skin was used.

A wide range of abrasive papers is available.

Many carvers use sanding blocks. These spread out the pressure and avoid grooves being formed. If sanding is carried out with just finger pressure and the wood is at all soft, or has variable density, a corrugated surface may result. A few larger blocks may be needed. You can buy ready-made cork ones or use scrap wood covered with cork or soft leather.

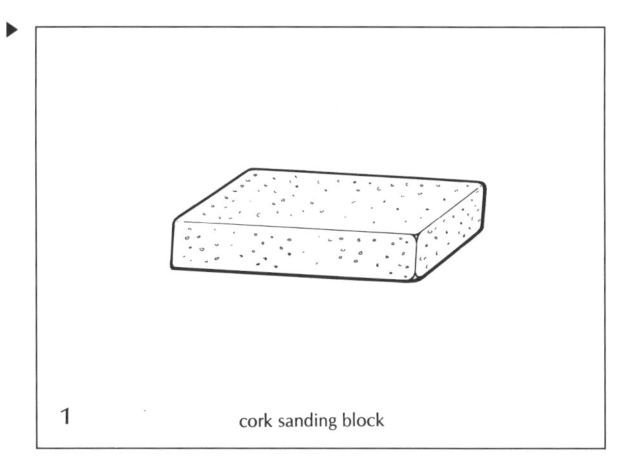

1 cork sanding block

bamboo

leather covering

2

Small pieces of bamboo cane, split and shaped, covered with thin leather to cushion the pressure work well. Also, small lengths of hardwood dowel in varying dimensions are useful.

Almost any piece of scrap wood is suitable. The wider the range of sanding shapes, the better.

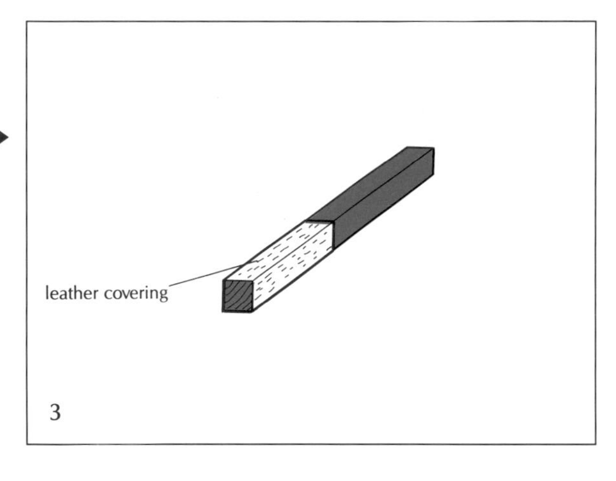

3

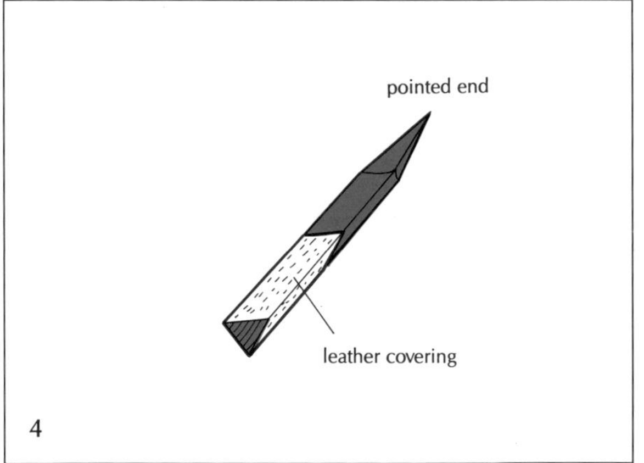

4

Some of the smaller bamboo sticks should have pointed ends. These will help you to work into crevices. Used without sandpaper they will burnish incised lines or undercut areas.

FINISHING – SANDING

Sanding should be commenced only when no further improvement can be made with the cutting tools. A scraper (a) should always be used before sanding. This particularly applies to end-grain areas after using a rasp. Scraping is a cutting action. It will remove defects far more quickly than sanding and will leave a better surface.

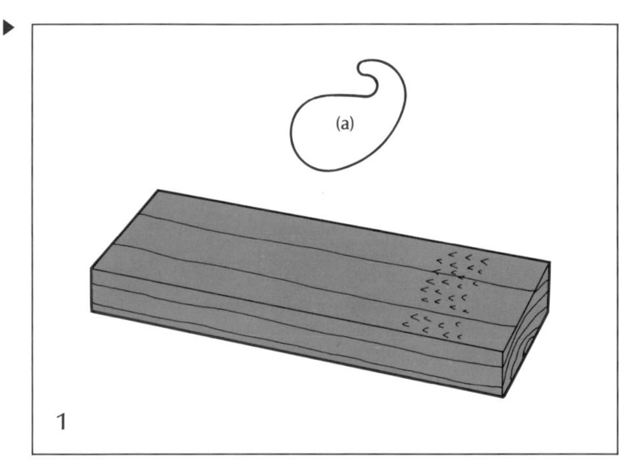

1

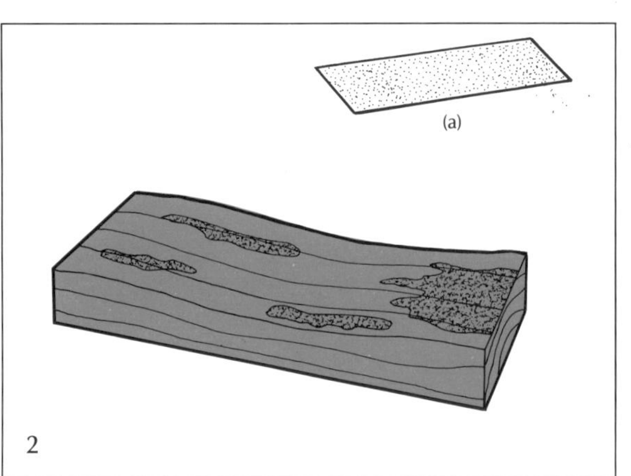

2

Make sure you do not leave scored areas when sanding through the various grades. Any fault should be eliminated at an early stage using 150-grit sandpaper (a) and not left until fine-grade paper is being used. Look critically at the finish being produced. Be prepared to spend time and effort to achieve a good result. There are no short cuts.

If you reckon to take as long over the finishing as you took to do the carving, you will be on the right time scale. Later, as your skill in cutting the wood improves, the finishing time will not be so long, but until then do not rush through the sequences and hope that the wax polish will cover up any faults – it will not.

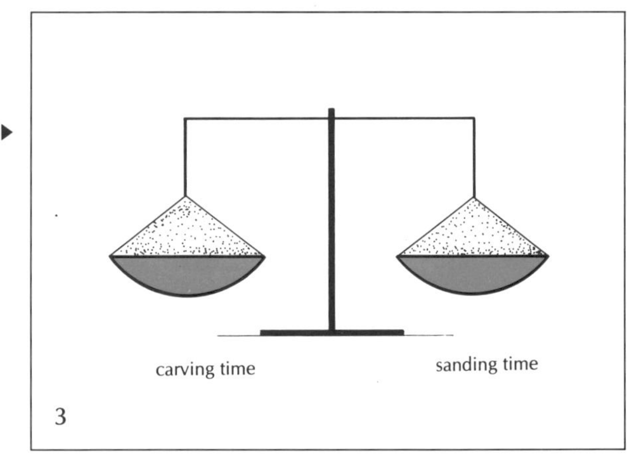

3

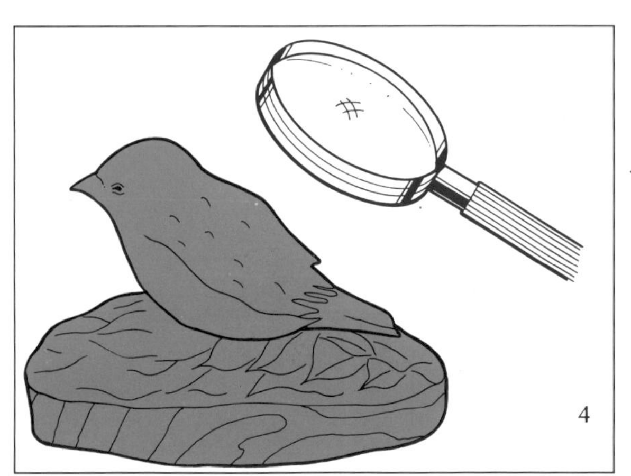

4

Start by using the 150 grade. Work over the whole of the carving, sanding in-line with the grain if possible. Dust off, with a dry, clean brush and inspect the finish in daylight. Remember that fluorescent lighting does not cast a shadow, so flaws may not show. When you are satisfied, work through the finer grades, checking the finish at each stage. The wood may then need sealing, as described in the next section.

Always use the paper in strips, not as folded sheets. Cut with scissors or tear against a metal ruler to avoid an uneven edge which could produce scratch marks. Before new paper is used it is best to flex the backing over the edge of the bench a few times. This will make it more pliant. ▶

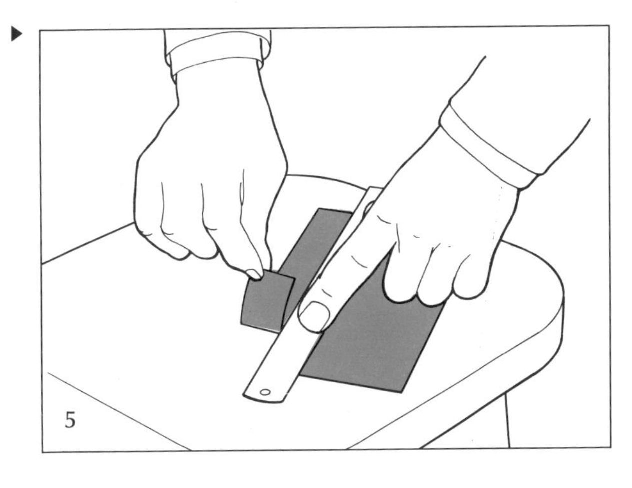

5

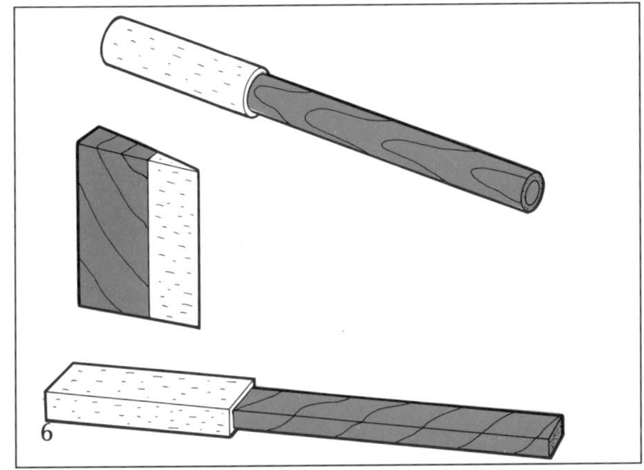

6

◀ Sanding with the paper held in your fingers can create an uneven pressure. It is better to use a sanding block for flat surfaces and small sanding sticks for the curved ones. Make up sticks of various sizes from bamboo cane, split and round, to give a selection of shapes. Cover with strips of suede, or any thin, soft leather, to act as a cushion.

Always sand with the grain of the wood, never across it as this will scratch the surface. Use reasonable pressure, but do not sand too vigorously. Consider the need to wear a dust mask. Some woods are irritant. ▶

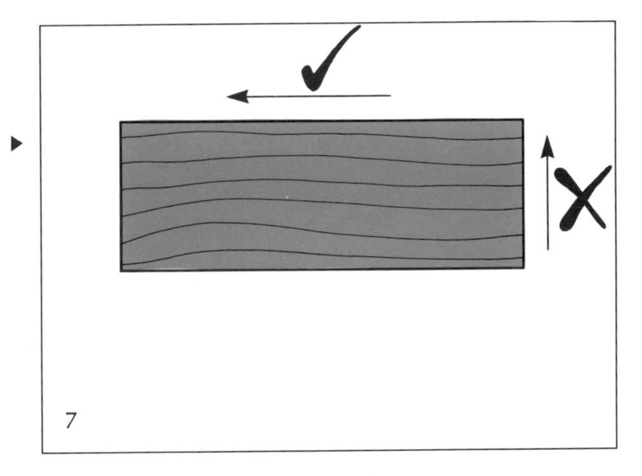

7

8

◀ Note that when the abrasive paper is moved back and forth the wood fibres are lifted on each alternate stroke. Finish sanding with 1in (25mm) strips pulled over the surface in the direction the fibres lie. Use the paper as you would pull tape, lightly holding it to the surface with two fingers.

With the exception of wood that is directly waxed, or when a finishing oil is applied, a sanding sealer is used, both to harden soft fibres and to prevent the wood – end-grain in particular – from being too absorbent. This produces a finer finish.

There are various sealants, but the one which seems to work best on carvings is shellac sanding sealer. This causes very little colour change to the wood. French polish, which uses shellac as a base, can be used as a substitute, but in the regular brown version there may be too much absorption on the end-grain which will produce a patchy effect. Shellac is one of the oldest means of finishing wood.

Applied by brush, shellac can be thinned with methylated spirit (10 per cent by volume is usually enough). It will raise and harden the fibres of the wood. Allow plenty of drying time, then sand back with 500-grit paper.

Under normal conditions two coats of sealer are sufficient, but very soft wood may require extra treatment. The object is to seal the wood by filling the cells and the amount of subsequent sanding is important. If this is too little the shellac will build up as a coating; if sanding back is overdone all the shellac will be removed back to bare wood.

Unfortunately, shellac does not have a long shelf life. It starts to discolour, and after about nine or twelve months it will have a brown tinge. Normally it can only be bought in 1-litre cans. So, if you are not going to do a lot of sanding, you may need an alternative. Try acrylic satin-grade varnish, but water it down well or the coating will be too thick.

Resinous woods, such as pitch pine, will repel shellac and will produce a mottled look. Matt polyurethane varnish can be used instead providing it is well diluted.

Brown woods respond well to sealing with tung oil. The simplest to use is Danish oil, made by Rustins. Do follow their application instructions, since it needs to be used sparingly. A beautiful lustre can be achieved with a combination of oil and 1000-grit wet/dry paper or fine wire wool.

All sealants should be applied in dry dust-free conditions. Pre-cleaning of the wood may be necessary by wiping over with methylated spirit. Remember that you are only concerned with sealing the wood. A high-gloss finish is most definitely not required. This is very important because if too thick a coating of sealant is applied it may have to be cut back with sandpaper. This could negate the sealing effect. Avoid this problem by applying sealants sparingly at all times.

A selection of sealants and other finishing products.

The following guide may prove helpful when deciding the type of finish to use.

Light-Coloured Woods	Advantages	Disadvantages
Shellac Sanding Sealer Can be painted on thinly when diluted with methylated spirit, usually 10 per cent by volume.	Little colour change.	Short shelf life. If stored too long will darken. Normally only available in 1-litre cans.
Acrylic Varnish Use satin grade not gloss. Thin with water, 10 per cent by volume.	Ease of use. Small quantities available. Good shelf life. Little colour change to wood. Can be used to seal end-grain prior to staining.	Slight plastic feel.
French Polish – White Can be used instead of shellac. Dilution rate is the same. Apply by brush.	Available in small quantities.	End-grain may darken due to greater absorption. Short shelf life.
Polyurethane Varnish Use only matt type. Dilute with 10–20 per cent white spirit. Apply by brush, or work into surface with fingers.	Good for sealing resinous wood. In very dilute form, seals end-grain prior to staining.	'Plastic' feel. Will degrade in sunlight. Difficult to remove when hard.

Brown Woods	Advantages	Disadvantages
Danish Oil Apply by brush. Allow to stand for five minutes, then wipe off to thin film. Re-coat after 12–24 hours. Repeat three times with sanding back as necessary.	Very good if applied correctly.	Slight yellow tinge, but not usually noticeable. Must be fully dry before waxing.
Linseed Oil Use boiled variety. Dilute with 20 per cent turpentine. Apply thinly. Do not re-coat until fully dry.	Very durable and traditional. Little advantage over Danish oil.	Appreciable darkening with age. Yellow tinge.
Shellac Sanding Sealer *See* 'light-coloured woods'.		
Polyurethane Varnish *See* 'light-coloured woods'.		
French Polish – Brown Can be applied by brush, or by using a cotton-wool pad in a twist of soft rag. Dilute with methylated spirit if necessary.	Works nearly as well as shellac. Available in small amounts.	End-grain may darken due to greater absorption, especially if applied by brush.

When re-coating after the first application has been sanded back, always apply the sealing medium with the lie of the grain.

In many instances a tooled, or textured, surface is more attractive than a plain one. Reference has been made to this in earlier sections and the beginner will certainly benefit by experimenting with the texture effect produced by the various sweeps of different gouges. Very often a compromise situation is reached whereby some areas of a carving are textured whilst others are left smooth. In this case it may be necessary to blend out the textured cuts by reducing their depth or partially removing them with a scraper and sanding slightly (a).

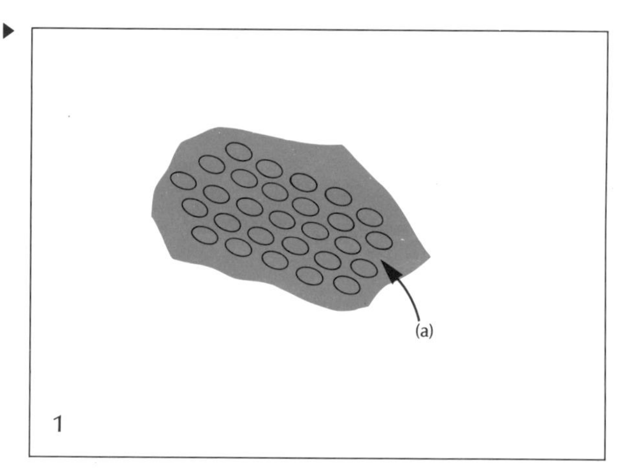

1

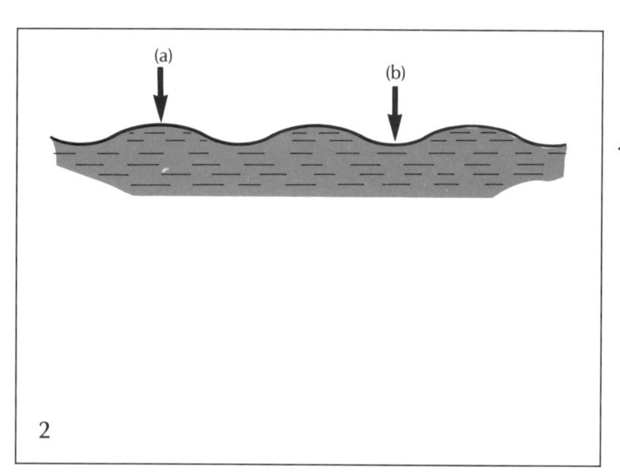

2

Until one has some experience, it is a good idea to take the smoothing and sanding sequences through to the 500-grit stage. Modern abrasive papers do not leave deposits of grit embedded in the wood, as the older types of sandpaper did, and it is quite permissible to use gouges after sanding. A tooled surface will produce high (a) and low (b) areas. The high parts will need a smooth finish. Sand all the carving *before* tooling.

Study the carving and define which parts could be enhanced by a textured finish. Mark in with white chalk. To be effective, the texture needs to be applied in a random fashion (a). If it is done with defined precision it can look contrived (b). This applies particularly to a general tooled finish, which looks better if the cuts are irregular. An exception would be specific scale texturing on a fish.

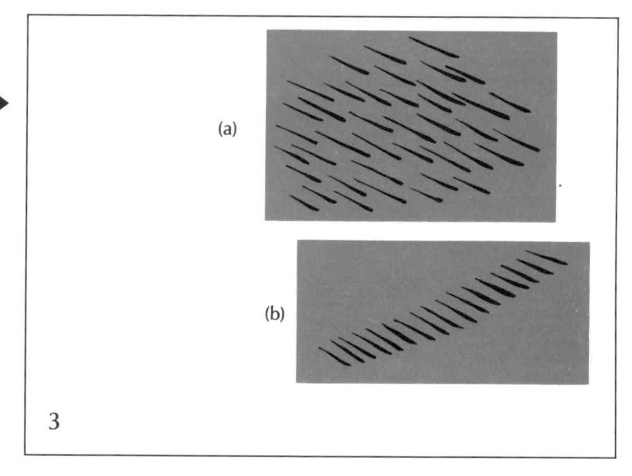

3

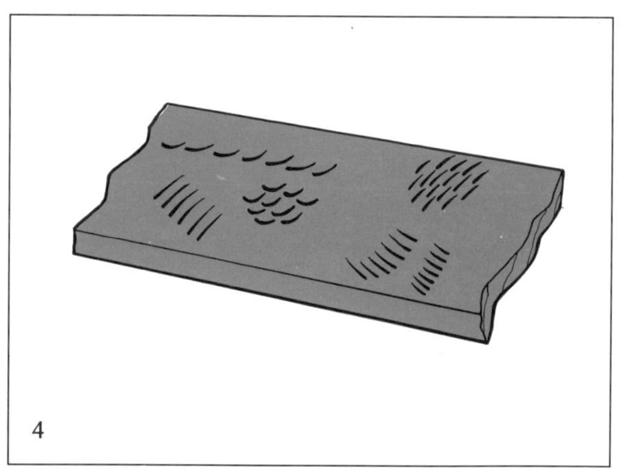

4

It is always a good policy to try out any form of texture on a piece of scrap wood of the same species that you are using for the carving, and then to study the effect under good lighting. Be careful that the texture is not so strong that it detracts from the line or form. This can easily happen in three-dimensional sculpture, where a subtle approach is preferable.

A smooth surface with little grain can be improved by making facet cuts. This applies to both sculpture and relief work. Backgrounds of relief carvings might benefit, for example. Facet cuts are useful when difficult grain, especially end-grain, is encountered. Use a small No. 3 gouge (Swiss cut 2) making sure it has been very well sharpened. Strop frequently, so that each cut is bright and clean. These are called ripple cuts (a).

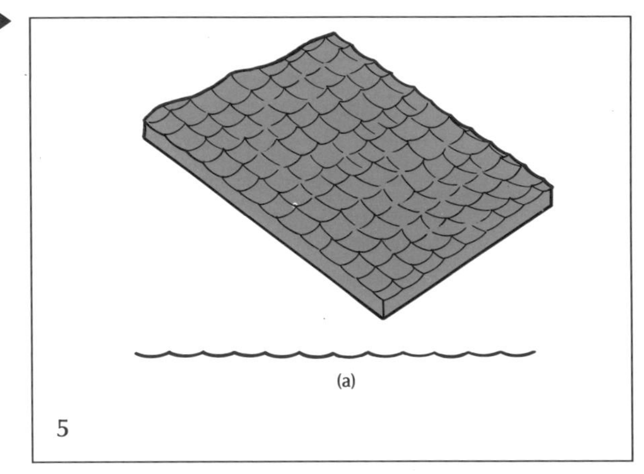

Feather effect can be achieved using a No. 9 gouge (a). Alternate cuts in each row to simulate overlapping. Note that each feather cut is made in intaglio (a small hollow). The gouge must be kept very sharp as each cut needs to dip in and out without tearing the wood. An attractive two-tone effect can be achieved by first staining the wood one shade darker, for example lime stained antique pine, and then texturing.

Scales can be formed with gouges Nos 4–7 depending on shape and size. Note that they need to overlap. Form simple scales with incised cuts by holding the gouge vertically (a). Large scales will need to be shaped and slightly undercut (b).

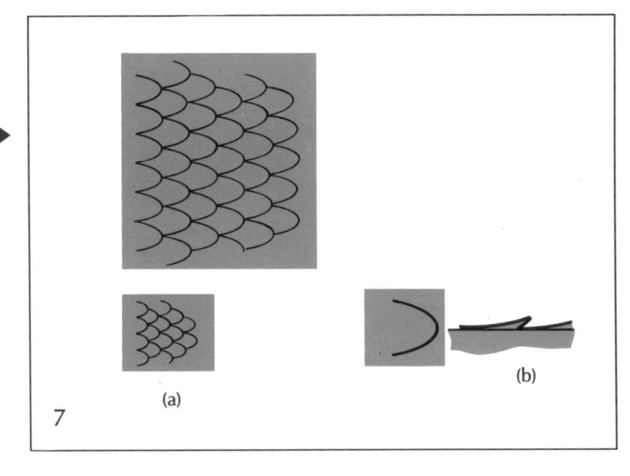

Use a No. 11 gouge to produce the effect of hair (a). Fine detail can be added by making light cuts with a V-tool (b). This is also used to texture fur, or wisps of feathers. The No. 11 gouge is also used for creating the veins of leaves (c).

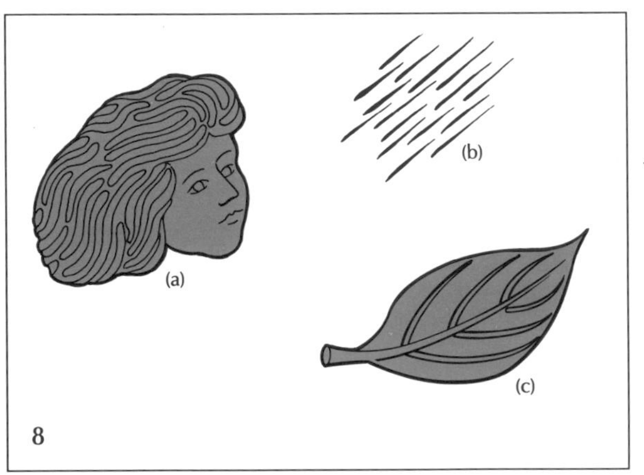

FINISHING – STAINS

Although normally it is best to leave the wood in its natural colour, impressive effects can be achieved by the use of stain. Subtle changes can be made to enhance an overall design. For example, changing the colour of a base, or part of a plinth, can lift the subject. Staining before texture cuts are made will produce a two-tone effect. Always test on scrap wood from the actual carving to prevent a disaster.

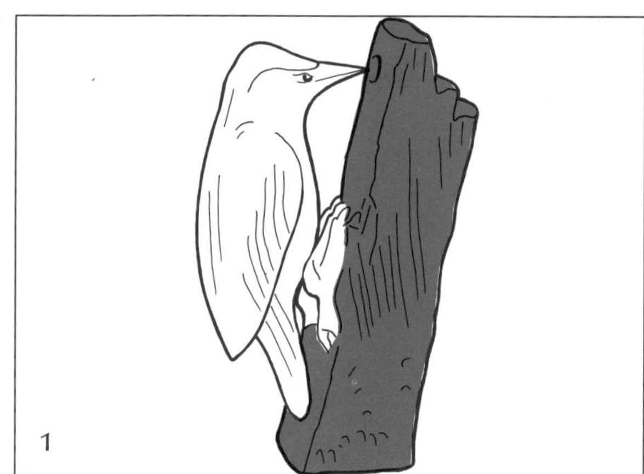

1

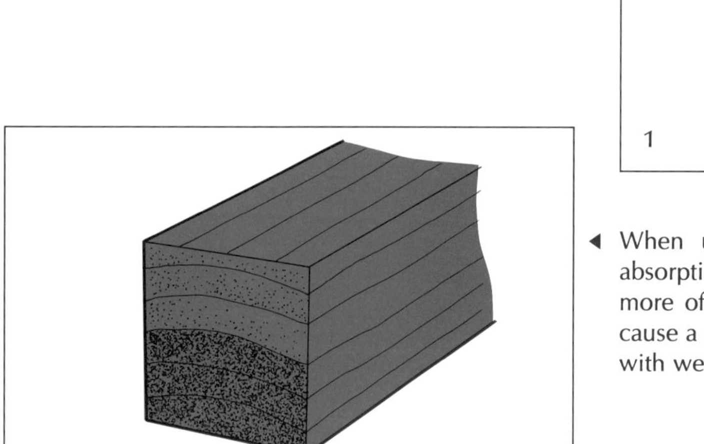

2

When using a stain, one must be aware of the absorption property of the wood. End-grain will take in more of the colour than other surfaces, and this can cause a patchy effect. End-grain may need to be sealed with well-diluted matt varnish.

The amount of stain is difficult to control if applied with a brush (a). Generally it is better to apply stain with a cloth (b). Make up a 'rubber' (c). Use a fluffless cloth and a pad of cotton wool. Apply a few drops of stain to the pad and twist up the cloth. Apply wax to parts you do not wish to stain.

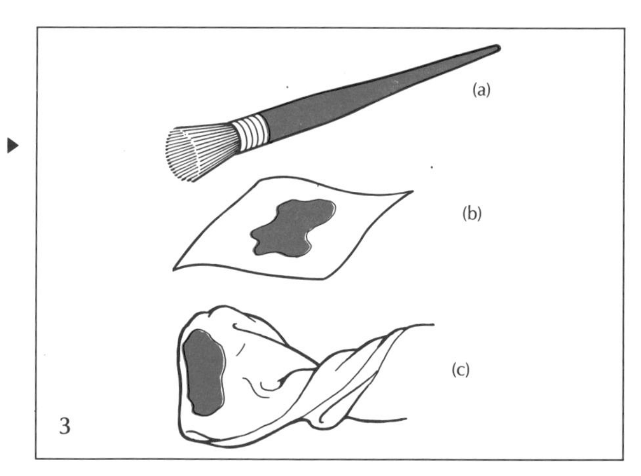

3

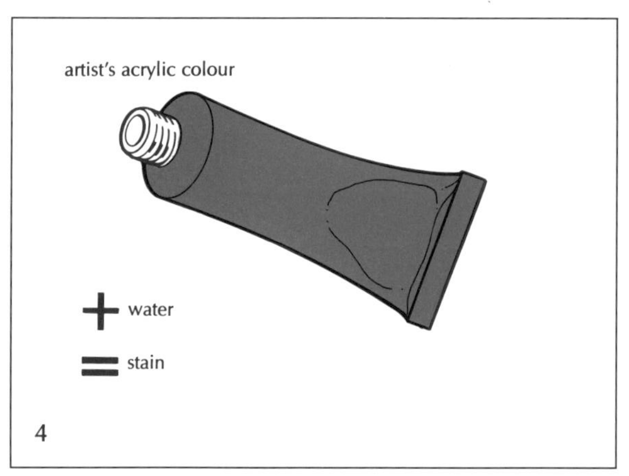

4

Water-based stains have a slower reaction time than the spirit-based types. If you want only a small amount, try using artists' acrylic paint well diluted with water. Always test out on scrap wood of the same species as the carving. For larger areas proprietary water stains are available. Generally these are easy to apply.

Mother pig.

Mother Pig

The wood used for this carving was West African mahogany. The size of the pig required a wood which could be obtained in a thickness of 6in (150mm). The final dimensions were 11 × 6 × 6in (280 × 150 × 150mm).

As mahogany is somewhat uninteresting if left plain, the body was tooled using a small well-sharpened No. 7 gouge, although any number between 5 and 9 would have been suitable, to produce the rough texture of a pig. Lighter cuts with gouge Nos 3–5 were used on the head and ears, which were then rubbed back with 250-grit paper to remove some of the sharpness.

The whole of the carving was then lightly sanded, using 500-grit silicon carbide abrasive paper.

Antique oak stain was applied with a rag. Some of the stain was removed before it dried by wiping with a cloth dipped in white spirit. This produced a shading of the stain over various parts of the pig. For example, the edges of the ears needed to be lighter to increase their reflection property when polished. When it was dry any raised grain was cut back with worn 500-grit paper. Wax polish was then used.

In general, any good-quality furniture wax will be suitable for polishing woodcarvings. The base of a good polish is beeswax. However, on its own, beeswax can produce a tacky surface; a hard wax – usually carnauba – is added to combat this, both waxes being shredded, mixed with turpentine and warmed.

It is a fairly simple matter to make your own polish, but be warned: the ingredients can easily catch fire. The effort involved never seems to me to be worth while, to say nothing of the risk of setting the workshop or kitchen alight. There are some very good proprietary makes available, none of which are particularly expensive.

In most cases it is better to use a refined (white or clear) wax polish, as this will cause little or no colour change to the wood. There will, however, be times when a tinted wax is needed. Always test on scrap wood of the same species before working on the carving. Smooth surfaces can be waxed with a cloth, but coarse-grained wood, or textured areas, are better polished with a brush.

Many woodcarvers favour the use of specially formulated wax polish which can be directly applied to untreated wood. The most popular type is Briwax which is a hard wax polish with a petroleum base instead of turpentine. It is available in both clear and tinted forms. This wax is best applied with a medium-hard brush, such as a toothbrush, and buffed off with a softer one. Deposits of clear wax left in crevices turn white on hardening and are difficult to remove, which is why it is better to use a brush than a cloth. Make sure there is ample ventilation when working with this product as the solvent fumes are toxic.

The other wax which can be used on bare wood, or indeed on a sealed surface, is Renaissance polish. You may have to search around for stockists, or write to the producer, but the effort will be worth while. It is made from highly refined micro-crystalline fossil-origin waxes and is used extensively in conservation work by museums and art galleries. The wax is translucent, permitting repeated applications without obscuring surface detail. It should be applied thinly. The storage time seems to be indefinite and although it may cost more than other types of wax polish it is very economical to use.

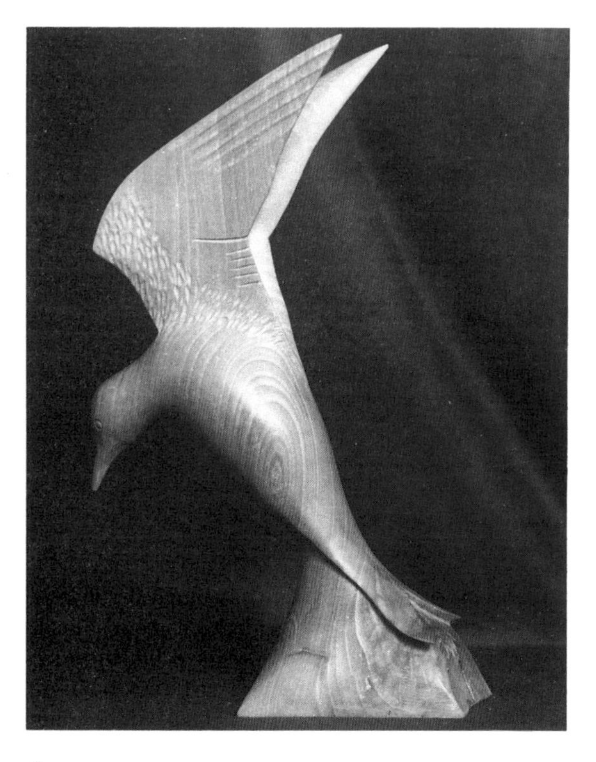

Tern.

Tern

The wood used for this carving was limewood.
Dimensions: 14 × 9 × 4in (360 × 230 × 100mm).

If a sawn block is used for carving wings, then make certain the wood has sufficient grain strength. The cell bonding, if good, will permit delicate parts to be carved with reasonable success. Both lime and sycamore have this characteristic.

In this example, the vulnerable parts are the beak and the wing tips. The beak runs with the grain, but the very tips of the wings lie slightly diagonally to it. However, because the cells (of lime) are well bonded together, it was possible to carve the wings without trouble. Final adjustments were carried out by sanding.

It is also important to choose a wood colour compatible with the subject. Note that lime being bland does not conflict with the line of form. The effect would have been quite different if a strongly marked wood such as cherry had been used.

To retain the light colour only clear wax was used at the finishing stage.

Wood, being an organic substance, is subject to faults in its make-up. These may be internal splits, known as shakes, decayed areas lying below the surface, holes caused by woodworm, or shrinkage cracks. Normally such problems are avoided by using prime quality timber which has been well seasoned. However, it is worth while knowing how to deal with some of the more common faults because, should you choose at any time to try free-form carving using branches, roots or driftwood, you will certainly encounter at least one of these faults.

Life, though, does become easier for the woodcarver who learns to accept that there will be times when there will be minor blemishes, and that these should be accepted philosophically just as we have to accept wrinkles in old age. Wood is a natural substance; not a plastic.

The best filler to use for minor faults is pure beeswax, gently softened with the flame of a candle and pressed well in. Before filling, clean out decayed areas with a wire brush and apply a wood hardener. Cracks and splits may open and close in response to changes in a room's humidity. The advantage of using beeswax to repair splits is that if the wood closes up later, the wax will simply be squeezed out. If a hard filler is used, there is more chance of a secondary split occurring.

Sawdust or sanding dust from the same piece of wood can be mixed with wood adhesive to make a plastic wood. Seal the surface first to prevent glue stain. This works well for the treatment of small areas, but will show up in large ones as it will contrast with the surrounding grain.

Deep cavities can be in-filled with matching wood, but a lot of care is needed to get the colour shade right, or it will show up as much as the fault. If you fill shrinkage cracks with wood, a secondary crack may form when the first crack tries to close. For woodworm holes, use sanding dust and glue after treating with suitable preservative.

Finally, if the wood is really bad you will be better off starting again. There is no joy in battling on with a piece of unsound timber.

Beeswax is the best filler for minor blemishes.

Some power tools can be useful. They are by no means essential, but by saving time and effort they can add to the enjoyment of woodcarving.

Bandsaw.

A bandsaw, fitted with a contour blade will rough shape carving blanks, and with a wider blade will convert planks into blocks. Capacity of cut needs to be 6in (155mm) and the two-wheel types save on blade wear. Bandsaws have a high level of safety, providing maker's instructions are followed.

If you are planning to do much relief carving, a router will prove to be of great use. Not only can background be speedily removed (they should be tooled afterwards), but border edges can be moulded by using specially shaped cutters. Moderately priced models, such as the Bosch or Black and Decker, are quite sufficient.

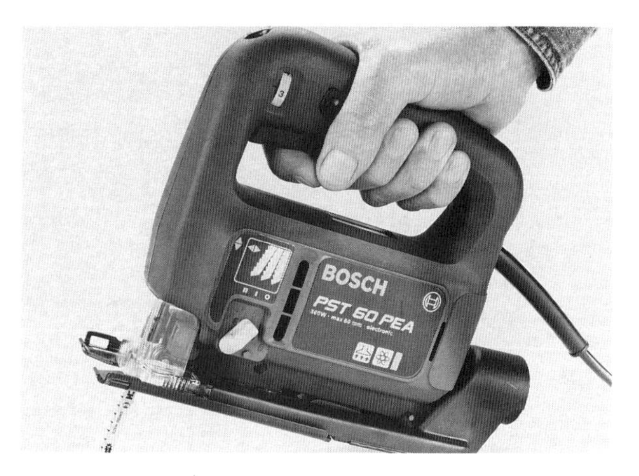

Jigsaw.

A reciprocating jigsaw, having a base which can be angled to 45 degrees, will trim boards to a depth of 2in (50mm). Thicker wood can be cut from both sides. A jigsaw can be used for cutting out voids for pierced carving, or for shaping panels for relief carving. Although it cannot handle the sizes of timber which a good bandsaw will, it is a useful tool.

Router.

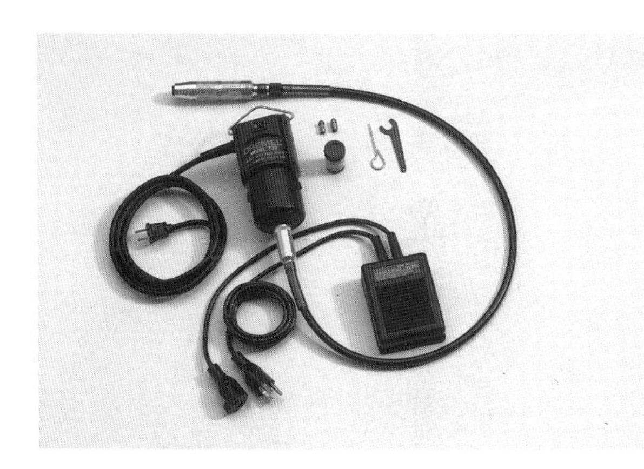

◀ Small cutters and burrs, used with a mini-drill, are very useful for cleaning up parts of a carving difficult to reach with a gouge. The Dremel comes in two versions: as the Moto-Tool, which is a hand-held drill; or as the Moto-Flex, which has an integral flexible shaft fitted with a chuck. An optional miniature router attachment is available for the former.

An orbital sander with a large base plate is generally known as a half-sheet type. Used with the various grades of abrasive paper it will speedily flatten the underside of a three-dimensional sculpture, or the back of a relief carving. Choose one with a dustbag. ▶

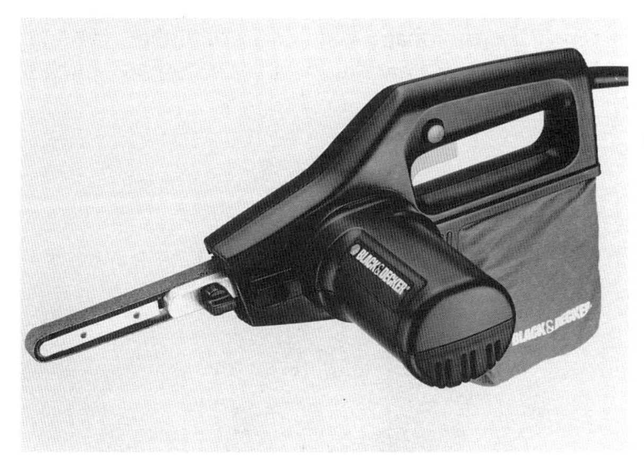

◀ Excessive use of power sanders should be avoided, but when dealing with very twisted grain, such as in free-form carving using roots or branches, there is a definite need for some mechanical aid. The Black and Decker Powerfile works like a small belt sander and is very efficient with either width of belt on flat or curved surfaces. There is an attachment for use in concave/convex situations.

The Bosch Multi-sander, working on the principle of both the disc and orbital sanders, produces a good finish. It would be an ideal choice for dealing with very large carvings. ▶

Safety precautions should *always* include the use of protective glasses and a dust mask.

DO keep your fingers behind the cutting edge at all times. Cut away from yourself, not towards your body. Work with sharp tools – they are safer. A blunt gouge is more likely to skate across the wood and cause an accident. Stop when you start to feel tired. Statistically, more industrial accidents happen late in the day than at any other time.

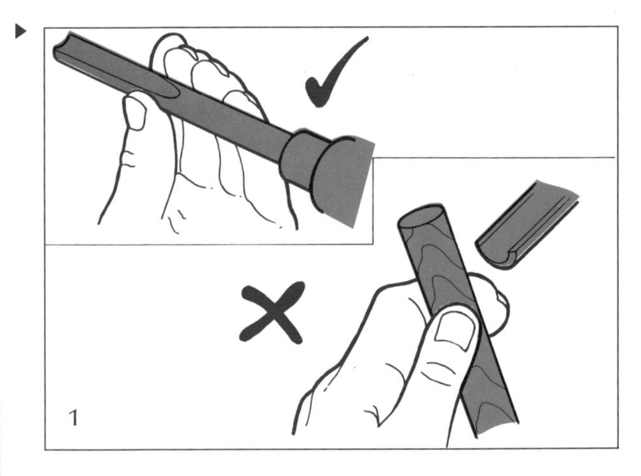

1

2

DO make a habit of wearing safety glasses when using any form of power tool, even if it is just for a few moments. Eye protectors should be worn when scraping with glass, or when carving brittle wood. Always replace them if they become damaged.

DO wear a dust mask when sanding or using power saws. Some woods, particularly tropical species, contain resins which can be very irritating to eyes and nose. One or two woods can produce effects similar to hay fever. Be certain to change the filter pad frequently.

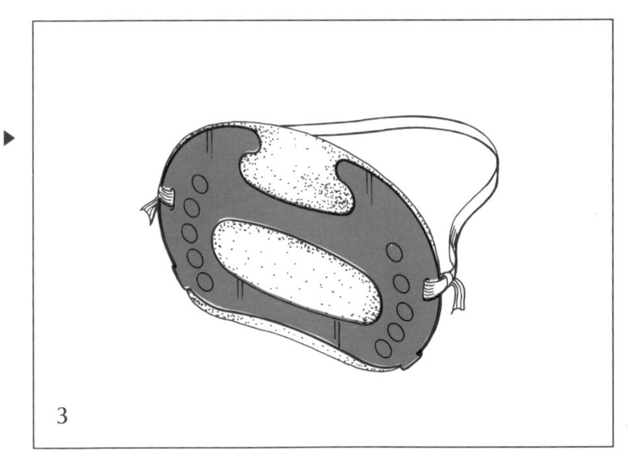

3

DO NOT have more than a few gouges out at any one time. Lay them out for easy identification. It is safer that way and the cutting edges will not be damaged. Being methodical is a sign of craftsmanship.

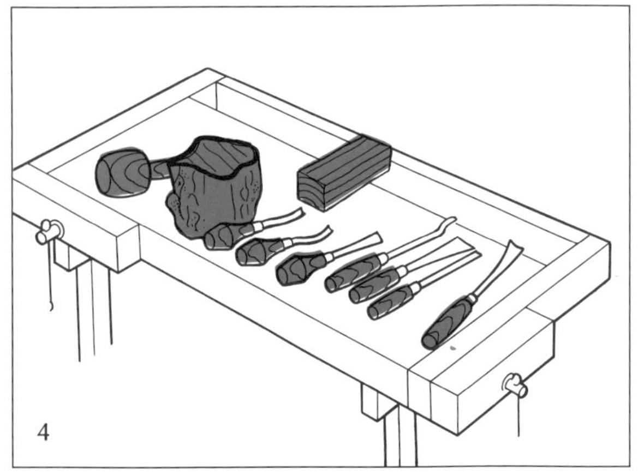

4

DO NOT work in a clutter. Have a good, well-lit working area and keep it tidy. Get into the habit of sweeping up after each session. Sawdust and woodchips on the floor can be slippery. Keep solvents, stains and all other such substances on a high shelf well out of reach of small hands.

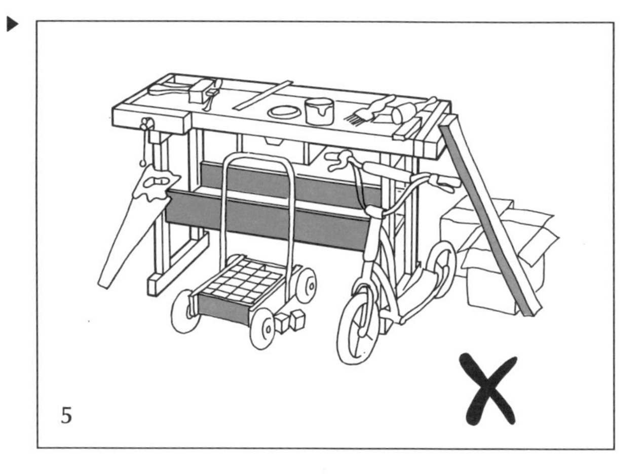

5

6

DO keep a first-aid box in the workshop. It is wise to keep your anti-tetanus inoculation up to date.

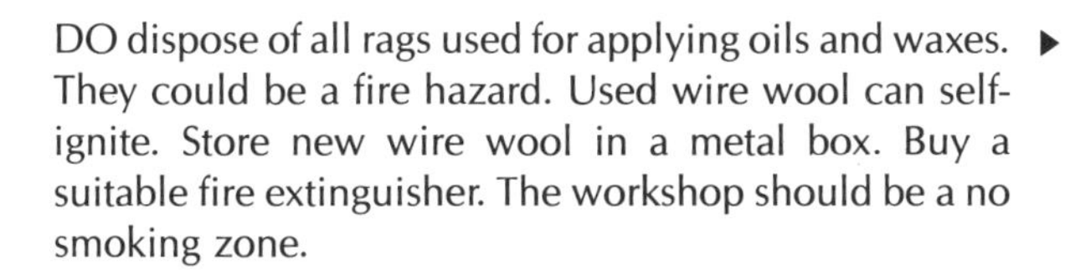

DO dispose of all rags used for applying oils and waxes. They could be a fire hazard. Used wire wool can self-ignite. Store new wire wool in a metal box. Buy a suitable fire extinguisher. The workshop should be a no smoking zone.

7

DO lock the door when you have finished. Not only is your equipment valuable, but a workshop is an inviting place for children.

8

Note: The designs shown on the following pages can be used as a useful means of attempting a first carving. The designs can be photocopied and traced onto the wood as a guide for carving.

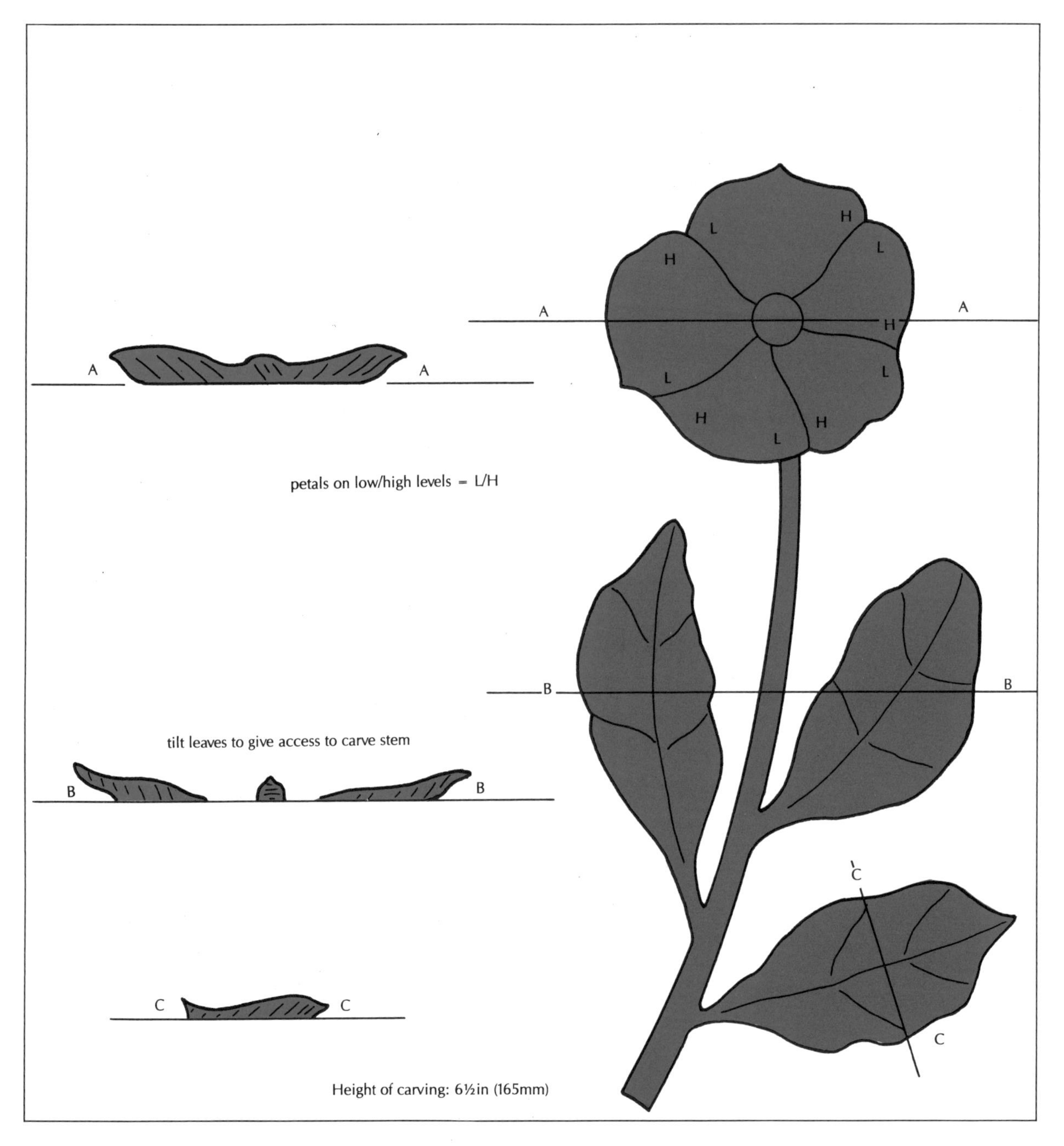

Relief carving of a flower.

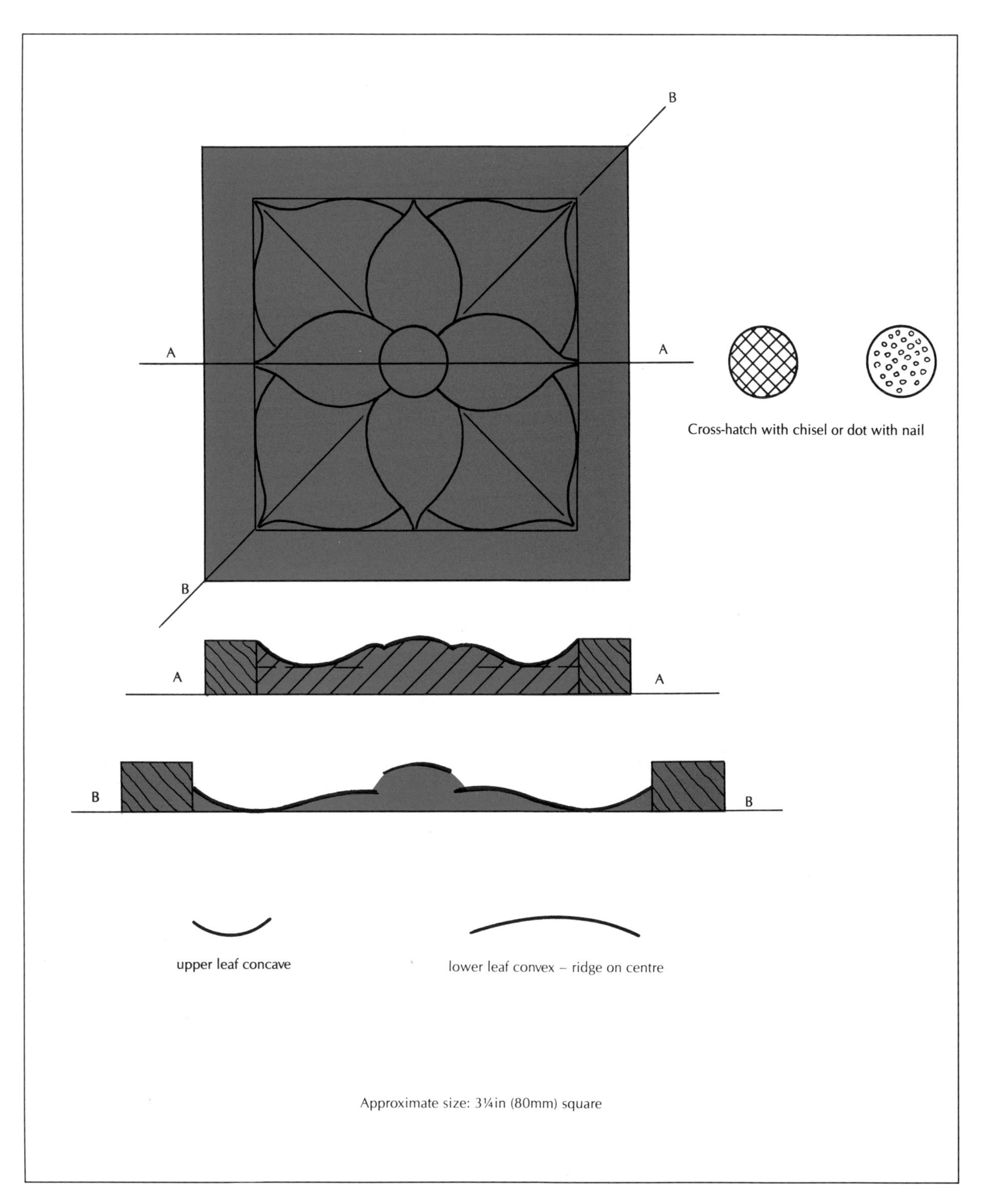

Relief carving of flower petals.

Design for a bird sculpture.

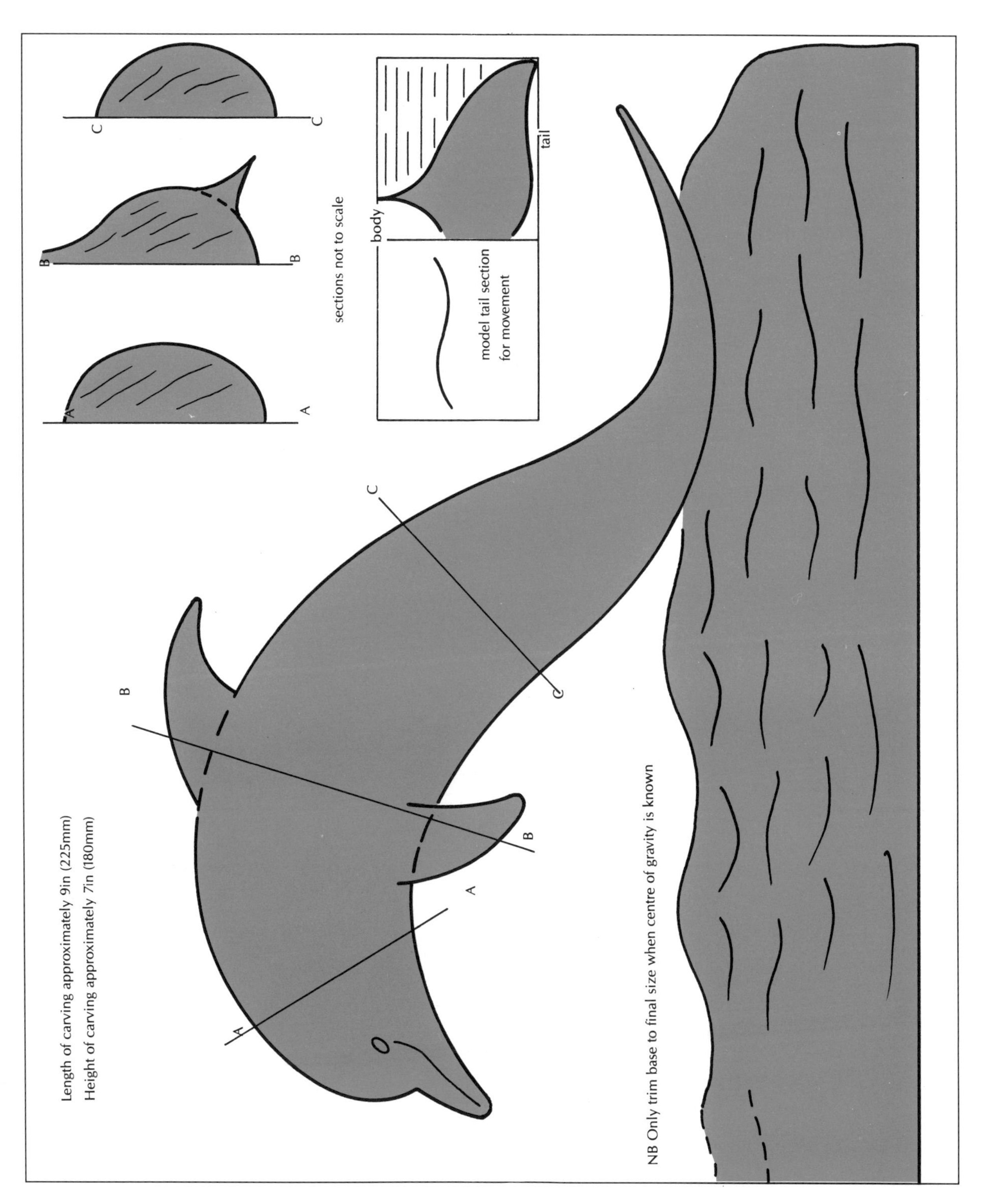

Design for a dolphin sculpture.

Design for a seabird sculpture.

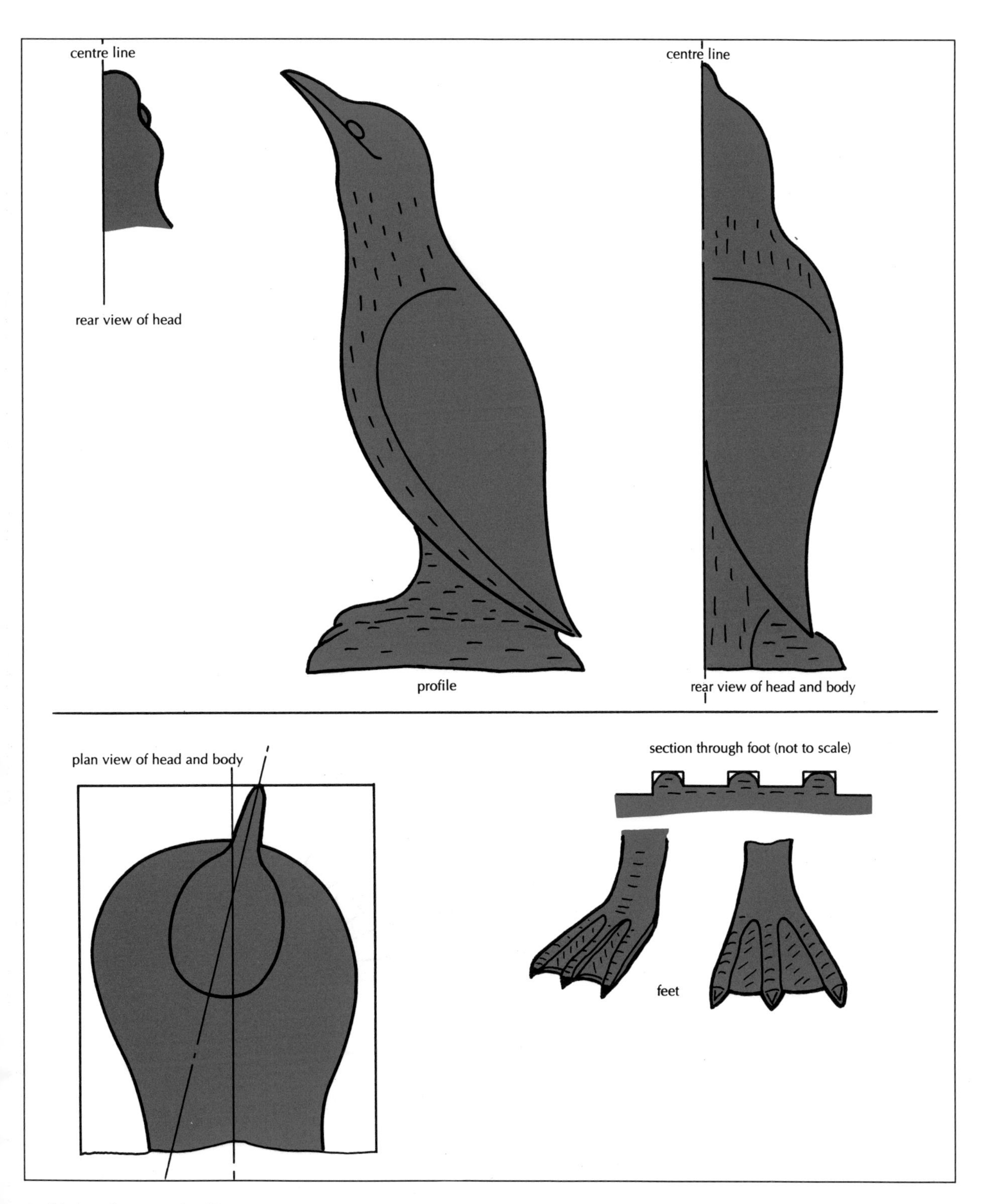

Seabird sculpture – details.

Gouges

Start with:
No. 1 ⅝in (15mm)
No. 3 ⅜in (9mm)
No. 4 ¾in (19mm)
No. 5 ⅝in (15mm)
No. 9 ¼in (6mm)
No. 9 ½in (12mm)
No. 11 1/16in (1.5mm)
No. 39 ¼in (6mm)

Add later:
No. 54 × 3 × ½in (12mm)
No. 3 1/16in (1.5mm)
No. 4 ¼in (6mm)
No. 5 5/16in (7.5mm)
No. 28 ¼in (6mm)
No. 33 3/16in (4.5mm)
No. 47 × 3 × ¼in (6mm)

Note: Numbers apply to the London pattern.

Mallet

Beech and/or Lignum Vitae, 3½in (90mm) in diameter.

Tool Roll

Bench Oilstone

India combination (fine/medium) or Arkansas natural stone.

Slipstones

India or Arkansas. Shapes to suit gouges.

Leather Strop

Strop paste

Scrapers

Goose-neck, curved.

Files

Wood rasp, medium cut. Filemaster, flat and half-round (Sandvik). Surform, round (Stanley). Sandplate, medium/fine (Sandvik).

Rifflers

Medium and fine cut. Shapes: flat, half-round, round. Add other shapes later.

Saws

DIY 8-point, tenon (hardback), coping.

Vice

Carpenter's, or Scopas Chops (Tiranti).

G-cramps

Size to suit bench.

Workbench

Carpenter's, substantial table, Workmate (Black and Decker), butcher's block. Make from reclaimed timber.

Finishing Materials

Abrasive papers 150 grit to 500 or 1000 grit.
Garnet type if possible.
Wire wool (0000 grade).
Shellac sanding sealer.
Acrylic varnish (satin grade).
Danish oil (Rustins).
Good-quality wax.

Alongee Carving gouge having a blade which tapers towards the handle.
Arkansas stone Natural oilstone of US origin.

Back bent spoon-bit Gouge for working in confined areas. Similar to front-bent with spoon reversed.
Bandsaw Power saw having a continuous blade.
Bark Outer protective casing of the tree.
Bench holdfast Used for holding work in the centre of the bench.
Bevel Part of the gouge blade ground to form cutting edge.
Bolster Shoulder of a gouge between blade and handle.
Burnishing Method of polishing by rubbing one piece of wood with another.
Burr Rough edge produced on inside of gouge blade during sharpening.

Carver's mallet Used for striking gouges. It has a round head made from beech or lignum vitae.
Carver's screw Ancient method of holding wood to the bench.
Chisel Tool with a flat cutting edge.
Cleats Small prepared wood blocks for holding work.
Coping saw Handsaw which uses narrow disposable blades.
Cupping Similar to warping.

Dishing Background removed only adjacent to the design in relief carving.

End-grain Surfaces having cell ends.

Facet cuts Small decorative cuts used for surface treatment.
Feather edging Tapered thin edge to improve visual effect yet retaining strength.
Ferrule Ring to reinforce the gouge handle, usually made of brass.
Fishtail Gouge which has the blade wider than the shaft.

G-cramps Screw-threaded device for holding work.
Gouge Basic carver's tool with curved cutting edge.
Grounding tool Flattish front-bent gouge used for background work in relief carving.

Hardwood Trade term for broad-leaf trees.
Heartwood Prime carving wood, which lies between sapwood and pith.
Honing Act of sharpening with oilstone or waterstone.

Incised carving Design cut into wood surface with V-tool or veiner.
India oilstone Manmade oilstone. It is usually coarser than Arkansas stone.
Intaglio carving Negative design as may be found in items such as butter or biscuit moulds.

Japanese waterstone Similar to oilstone but uses water as lubricant.

London Pattern Standard specification used by gouge manufacturers.

Medullary rays Pronounced groups of cells tangentially placed. Can be very pronounced.

Oilstone Sharpening stone which uses oil as lubricant.

Paring Wafer-thin cuts.
Parting tool *See* V-tool.
Pierced carving Design detail combining voids cut through the wood.
Pith Central core of the tree.

Rasp Coarse-cut file for wood.
Riffler Small file.
Ripple cuts More continuous and undulating form of surface cuts, commonly used for background.
Roughing out The process of creating the basic outline shape.

Sap Carbohydrate food of the tree in solution.
Sapwood 'Living' area between bark and heartwood. It is usually unsuitable for carving.
Seasoning Drying time to remove sap and moisture from wood.
Shakes Internal splits in trees caused by wind damage or in felling.
Slipstone Small, shaped oilstone for use on inside edges of gouges. India or Arkansas.
Softwood Trade term for needle-leaf trees.
Spoon-bit Front-bent spoon-shaped gouge for working in confined areas.
Strop Leather strip coated with polishing paste such as rouge powder. Used after honing.
Sweep The amount of curve of the cutting edge.

Tang The pointed part of the shaft to which the gouge handle fits.

Undercut To cut back below the surface of a design leaving the sides set at an angle.

V-tool Carving tool comprising two chisel-like blades set at an angle.
Veiner U-shaped gouge.

Warping Distortion caused as timber dries.
Woodcarver's chops Large-capacity vice.

INDEX